THE HUMAN CIRCLE

THE HUMAN CIRCLE

an existential approach to the new group therapies

Carl Goldberg, Ph.D.
with Merle Cantor Goldberg, M.S.W.

Professional/Technical Series

Nelson-Hall Company 𝑛ℎ **Chicago**

ISBN O–911012–67–2

Library of Congress Catalog Card Number: 73–75523

For information address
Nelson–Hall Company, Publishers,
325 W. Jackson Blvd., Chicago, Ill. 60606

Manufactured in the United States of America

CONTENTS

ACKNOWLEDGMENTS
PREFACE ix
1. WHY NEW GROUP THERAPIES? 11
2. EXISTENTIAL POSTULATES 25
3. EXISTENTIAL-ANALYTIC GROUP PSYCHOTHERAPY 49
4. PRACTICAL AND TECHNICAL CONSIDERATIONS 81
5. PROCESSES AND SPECIAL TECHNIQUES 97
6. LEADERSHIP AND GROUP PERFORMANCE 101
7. THE PROCESS GROUP TECHNIQUE 117
8. THERAPIST–PATIENT RELATIONSHIPS 139
9. THE FOCAL PROBLEM GROUP TECHNIQUE 151
10. GROUP THERAPY WITH DRUG ADDICTS 163
11. NONVERBAL COMMUNICATION 179
12. SOCIETAL CHANGE PROCESS 199
13. TRAINING GROUP PSYCHOTHERAPISTS 209
14. RESEARCH IN GROUP PSYCHOTHERAPY 219
15. CONCLUDING STATEMENTS 231
REFERENCES 235
INDEXES 249

ACKNOWLEDGMENTS

We wish to express our appreciation to Dr. Roger P. Greenberg for
his insightful comments on an early draft of the present book. Appreciation
is also due to our excellent typists, Mrs. Brenda Bergmann Howard and Miss
Sarah Freeman, for struggling with the manuscript from notes to its final form.

PREFACE

The treatment of emotional distress in groups is a novel feature in contemporary American life. Until recently a man was regarded as a prisoner of his life situation. Emotional pain was expected to be borne alone—silently and unflinchingly. Tragedy and misfortune were private matters to be spoken of only within the closed circle of one's family, minister, and intimate friends. In a world in which a display of personal emotion was regarded as offensive, the hallmark of a man's character was the ability to carry on his life without causing distress in other people.

The brilliant notions about psychopathology espoused by Freud, Charcot, Janet, Meyer, and others were in sharp contrast with this stolid world view. The psychoanalytic *Weltanschauung* of these thinkers contested the notion that disturbed feelings should be judged on moral grounds. Because emotional distress responded to treatment, the psychoanalytic practitioner contended that disturbed feelings emanated from an illness or disease. The psychoanalytic practitioner, however, could not entirely extirpate the moralistic stigma associated with emotional disorders and treated his patients in private.

Today emotional distress is not considered to be a condition that is rooted *within* the disturbed person as, for instance, a diseased liver is. Present-day mental health practice has focused increasingly on interpersonal relations rather than on the patient's dreams and unconscious. The practitioner's search is for techniques that will help the patient correct his disturbed behavior in daily interpersonal dealings.

Correspondingly, the individual in American society no longer is seen as a victim of his circumstances. The existential–humanistic movement in the mental health field, guided by such persuasive psychologists as May, Perls, Schutz, and Rogers, has been instrumental in this change of attitude and has urged the individual to accept complete responsibility for shaping the conditions of his existence.

The Freudian *Weltanschauung* held that man is an object in the universe: man is subject to unalterable natural and psychological laws. In sharp contrast, the existential world view has placed man in the center of the universe: Man is as much the lawmaker in the universe as he is the subject of natural and psychological laws. Man is, therefore, capable of choice. However, the existential world view recognizes that the freedom to choose necessitates a struggle with the conditions of one's existence. Choice requires an intimate awareness of one's social and psychological reality. Small groups have been recognized by the social scientist as providing the meeting ground between personality and culture. Thus, small groups are crucial in the individual's ontological struggle to come to grips with his psychic processes and to gain personal competence in dealing with the social institutions that shape his world. For many people in society today, experiences in natural groups have failed to provide a consistent and gratifying concept of self. These people require expert guidance to recognize, grapple with, and finally to master misdirected behavior. Increasingly, these people are being referred by mental health practitioners to designed (therapeutic) groups rather than to individual psychotherapy. (Goldberg, 1972)

Many books have been written about group treatment. None has been sufficiently comprehensive to encompass the current profusion of designed groups. There is a need for a textbook that treats the theory and practice of designed groups in a systematic and enlightened manner. This book is an attempt to accomplish this important and rather difficult task.

Because designed groups are a sociological phenomenon as well as a clinical modality, the theories that are the premise of my work with treatment groups have been heavily influenced by research findings and theory about the group properties and dynamics of non–therapeutic groups as well as those of treatment groups. Knowledge and appreciation of sociological and social psychological concepts are essential to the existential analytic position ascribed to in this volume and are of real value to group psychotherapy. Bringing together these different perspectives for an in-depth exploration of groups renders a more complete understanding of them than is possible from a study of groups based upon a single level of analysis. As a textbook, this volume is a composite of theory, principles, case material, and research findings from diverse sources, systematized in a developmental fashion.

THE SCOPE AND PURPOSE OF THIS BOOK

This book has been written for the inquisitive, concerned layman, the serious student of groups, and the inexperienced practitioner. The

layman today, as perhaps never before in history, is looking for effective ways to influence and modify existing social institutions with a
minimum of strife. He also wants to learn to administer to his own
and to his neighbors' loneliness and despair. Experience in expertly
conducted designed groups may help to enrich his life. Theory is carefully systematized in this book for students, inexperienced practitioners, and practitioners with experience in the more traditional approaches, all of whom are interested in acquainting themselves with
innovative, ancillary, and improved modalities of group treatment
and group work. For all those described above, this book is intended
to explain the theoretical underpinnings of the newer group approaches.

This book is not, however, a methodological text. The aims of a
textbook for students and those of a methodological text for professional practitioners may overlap somewhat but are essentially distinct. The rationale in writing a textbook for students is that the student (with increased study, work experience, and supervision) may
function sometime in the future as a practitioner. In this regard,
writing a student textbook is a more conservative task than that of
writing a methodological text for practicing professionals. Every
methodological text must inevitably raise the question of whether
upon completion of reading the text the reader will be capable of
effectively carrying out the operations essential to the method described in the text. Although many group treatment texts purport
this intent, I question whether any text can be written that will actually teach a reader the skills necessary for expertly leading designed groups. I do not believe that any person can be effectively
trained as a group therapist by academic preparation and reading a
methodological text alone. This important issue will be explored more
fully in Chapter 13 in which the training of the group therapist is
discussed.

A NOTE CONCERNING THE CONCEPTUAL MODEL

My personal philosophy and, therefore, the philosophical stance
that shapes my ameliorative and clinical endeavors are existential–
analytic. In Chapter 2 I discuss the theoretical postulates of this position. However, the reader must be clearly aware that theory does not
always determine technique. Many similar techniques emanate from
rather disparate theoretical positions. Therapists adhering to similar
theoretical positions may operate rather differently. I believe the
competent psychotherapist depends more on his own personal and

clinical experience, the particular type of patient with whom he is working, and the problems at hand than on techniques generally associated with a school of psychotherapy.

It should be clearly evident that some treatment techniques are better suited for certain patients and treatment problems than are others. In addition, to be sensibly employed, each technique requires a conceptual frame of reference guiding its use which best captures the particular sociological and clinical problems involved. This point of view is different from those expressed by most other group therapy textbooks which either stress an adherence to one particular methodology or present an overview of the way therapists of different orientations conduct groups. Because no one treatment technique is equally suitable for all types of patients, a therapist should possess a repertoire of approaches. Techniques can be differentially employed depending upon the psychological demands and limitations of a therapist's patient population, the social conditions in which he is working and his patients are living, and the skills with which he is conversant.

My point of view is not atheoretical; I recognize that in therapy the proper use of theory is indispensable. I also realize, however, that at psychotherapy's present stage of development, group psychotherapy is more an art than a science. The personality of the therapist is as important to his work as his academic and theoretical preparation. Therefore, each ameliorative agent who wishes to employ the techniques described in this book should put much thought into adapting them to best utilize his personal style. The therapist who is skillful with the greatest array of these approaches can probably be the most helpful to a varied population of patients and offer the most complementary range of skills in working with other colleagues.

The practitioner must broaden his therapeutic skills because the individual in society today can no longer afford to closet himself in the social vacuum so frequently created within treatment situations concerned with revisiting intrapsychic ghosts of the past. We live in an age of raging racial and social tensions, indeed, of open combat in the streets of our cities and the corridors of our universities. The old order has collapsed, rendering the traditional societal guidelines for human conduct suspect, if not impotent. New approaches are needed for bringing together dissident factions and healing psychological wounds resulting from deprivation and existential exhaustion. Freud himself recommended that psychoanalysis be only one of many ameliorative methods the psychotherapist is trained in and thought that it should be employed only when other methods fail (Freud, 1904). John Warkentin (1969, p. 163) points out that:

From the Freudian couch to the nude therapies of today (dry or wet) there has never been devised a technique or system that will get people well. There are no tricks in our trade that help us to mature. . . . The various techniques employed by therapists are useful in bringing people into apposition, but no more. Thereafter, the outcome depends on the person's continuing involvement.

Innovation in psychotherapy is of little avail unless blended with understanding, commitment, and concern.

THE SELECTION OF SPECIFIC GROUP TECHNIQUES

This book is a study of several important new group techniques which appear more relevantly to relate therapeutic experience to current social and psychological concerns than do the more traditional psychotherapies. The group approaches discussed in this volume are less concerned with dreams, unconscious material, and intrapersonal processes than they are with the ways in which individuals attempt to make themselves known to others in transactional situations and encounters. This volume, however, does not present an exhaustive survey of the new group therapies, although it discusses in some detail their salient characteristics and contrasts these features with those of the more traditional psychotherapies.

The group approaches discussed in this volume had to be carefully selected. Whereas an editor of a book of readings may include approaches of which he has less than direct and expert knowledge, an author of a textbook cannot sensibly afford to do so. I chose, therefore, to describe in this volume only those group methods with which I have had personal experience as a participant and as a group leader or therapist and which I feel illustrate group properties essential to all group modalities. The techniques described are also consistent with the existential-analytic position postulated in Chapter 2. Attention is given to nonverbal communication, confrontation, group processes, leadership and group performance, the therapist–patient relationship, problem solving in groups, and experiments in societal change. Chapter 1 begins with a look at the social and psychological conditions that have given rise to the new group therapies.

"For this is the journey that men make: To find themselves. If they fail in this it doesn't much matter what else they find. . . ."

J. Michener
The Fires of Spring

WHY NEW GROUP THERAPIES?—1

In my opinion the majority of people who are in need of psychological assistance are not assisted by traditional modalities of treatment. This point of view is supported by recent clinical studies which report that these psychotherapeutic approaches are successful with approximately two–thirds of the patients with whom treatment is attempted.

There appear to me to be four basic reasons for traditional psychotherapy being unsuitable for people who are in need of psychological attention. First, traditional psychotherapy rarely takes less than one year; more often in instances in which treatment is considered successful two to three years are required to obtain a desired outcome. Two or more sessions a week are generally deemed necessary for analytically oriented treatment. Since the majority of analytically trained practitioners are in private practice, analytic as well as other types of long-term treatment are rather expensive.

Second, traditional psychotherapy is primarily concerned with meaning, motivation, and a quest for the identity of the individual in treatment. Admittedly, this may be a profound and meaningful en-

deavor for some patients. But on the other hand, traditional psychotherapy generally does not concern itself with concrete tasks and
straightforward solutions to problems. Traditional psychotherapy is a
process which requires above average intelligence, the ability to
reason abstractly, the ability to verbalize thoughts and feelings, and
a conscious philosophical stance toward life. These considerations
suggest that traditional psychotherapy requires of its patients a good
degree of personal motivation, sufficient personality assets to withstand the stress of daily problems which cannot be resolved until
their meaning is uncovered, as well as superior intellectual and financial resources.

A third reason, then, for traditional psychotherapy not being
appropriate for many people in quest of treatment is that a large pro-
portion of them, certainly those in immediate crisis as well as the
most difficult cases—persons with character disturbances and "deviant" life styles, the severely psychotic, the working class, and the
poorly educated—do not possess the required emotional and intellectual faculties required for traditional psychotherapy. These patients
have been regarded by the mental health professional, in no small
part in the defense of his professional integrity, as resistive and un-
treatable.

Fourth, it is also important to realize that many people today
who appear to possess the required attributes for traditional psychotherapy feel that traditional approaches to personal distress do not
address the problems of alienation and existential concern that characterize the twentieth–century man. Many of these individuals who
have attempted traditional forms of treatment and remedial help
leave these treatments more frustrated and blighted than when they
entered. (Eysenck, 1960; Leavitt, 1967; Schorer, 1968)

In short, it appears both ironic and tragic that the mental health
professions, which are committed to help those who are emotionally
or characterologically disturbed, must often cavalierly attend, if not
outrightly refuse to treat, a large number of patients because their
volitional disorders and other disabilities are resistive and severe. To
be blunt, there are patients who are too emotionally disturbed or else-
wise unavailable to be helped by the techniques present–day mental
health practitioners are prepared to offer patients. This statement
ostensibly seems absurd. However, if the situation as described above
is accurate, this statement is true, nevertheless.

Were the therapeutic situation today simply as described above,
it would be troublesome enough for the concerned practitioner. But
now, through the efforts of professionals and concerned citizens alike,

the human development movement encourages every individual to develop his personal potential to the fullest. Mental health services are wanted for the widest possible group of people. This emphasis on human development and preventive mental health has begun to be a major determinant of the character of psychotherapy. Tens of thousands of people who have been unaware of or otherwise unavailable for help heretofore are petitioning the mental health profession.

This situation has created a need for a large number of practitioners with diversified skills. Presently, there is only a small fraction of the required number of trained group therapists available. This shortage will become greatly exacerbated as mental health endeavors make further inroads into the larger community. Consequently, if psychotherapy is to be more than the conclave of a select few, it must immediately and realistically confront its serious limitations. It must design treatment modalities which have the advantage of greater economy of time and money and are suitable for the specific disabilities of the patients who require such psychological service. This book has been written to address precisely these issues.

GROUP PSYCHOTHERAPY

Group psychotherapy has made a decisive contribution to the study of and the relief from emotional disorders. Several decades of clinical work have convincingly evinced that experiences in well-designed therapeutic groups may make contributions in relieving the patient's problem that are unattainable in individual sessions alone. (Powdermaker & Frank, 1953) In comparison to what many observers regard as the insipid development of individual psychotherapy, the possibility for innovation in group treatment seems unlimited. Historically, dyadic (individual) psychotherapy has been shackled by dedication to the theory and methodology of a few influential thinkers. (Ruitenbeck, 1969) By means of innovative group techniques it may be possible to successfully treat persons with a diversity of emotional disorders who are currently resistive to the strategies of dyadic psychotherapy.

Many psychotherapists believe there is some quality in group sessions found wanting in individual psychotherapy. Casting aside sophisticated notions about differences between dyadic and group therapies in terms of method, problem, and therapist qualities, I find that the most essential and valuable function of therapeutic groups is the opportunity they provide for the patient to be a healer to others. In group therapy we observe

the healing value of the understanding which one patient
gives another——strength of personality and favorable traits
which had not been delineated in extended individual treatment reveal themselves in group situations. (Spotnitz, 1961,
p.19)

A PERSPECTIVE ON THE NEW GROUP MOVEMENT

The reader might appreciate a brief history of the difficulty group
therapy had in becoming an accepted and valued mental health practice. The expectation that seven or eight emotionally distressed persons could convene as a group with a professional person and work
out their difficulties has not always been propitiously viewed.

The employment of a collective setting as an intentionally designed treatment modality, for all practical purposes, did not exist
prior to the late 1930s or early 1940s. The psychotherapeutic philosophy at the time required the therapist to become thoroughly conversant with the patient's life history. Because this kind of material
would have been difficult and impractical to obtain in a group, patients prior to the late 1930s were seen individually for three to six
sessions a week for three or more years.

Most people, up until the 1940s, regarded psychotherapy as an
expensive luxury. Few potential patients could afford to pay the analyst's fee on a regular basis year after year. Recognizing this fact,
Karl Menninger advised the newly-fledged analyst beginning a private practice that a patient should not enter psychoanalysis unless he
has independent means or sufficient funds in reserve. To do otherwise
would result, in time of financial difficulties or loss of employment, in
the patient's analysis having to be interrupted.

As more people realized that personal difficulties did not have to
be stoically endured throughout life, as they became aware of others
who were helped by intensive treatment, there was a large demand
for psychological services. The clinics, hospitals, and social agencies
that offered psychological services to the less affluent realized that
they had an insufficient number of trained psychotherapists to conduct individual sessions. As a result, the physician, traditionally regarded as the healer, was forced to treat his patients in groups as well
as to permit professionals from other disciplines to practice psychotherapy.

Until rather recently, patients were treated in a group rather
than individually only for reasons of convenience and economy. Also
important to the early development of group treatment was the

widely held belief that extensive training and study in psychotherapy were unnecessary for conducting a group.

Individual psychotherapy was initially the private domain of the medically trained professional. Only with reluctance and considerable qualification in terms of fees, the type of patient to be treated, and the provision of medical supervision did psychiatry recognize that the training and education of the clinical psychologist and the psychiatric social worker were relevant to ameliorative endeavors. Less fortunate were other professionals who were barred by the more established professionals from working freely as individual psychotherapists.

Who were the patients initially treated in groups? The impoverished and the less affluent were, of course, treated in groups because they did not have sufficient funds for individual sessions with a private physician. Enjoined for the group treatment modality also were patients who could not be handled in individual sessions because they lacked the proper intellectual and motivational attributes or because their illness had been heretofore resistive to analytic work. On the other hand, patients with hopeful prognosis were generally not seen in groups unless medically trained or medically supervised therapists were unavailable.

Initially, the busy physician did not have time to conduct groups. Subordinate staff were encouraged to conduct group sessions and were expected to talk things over with each of the patients, helping the patient manage his situation until a physician would be available. As several patients in the same group frequently had similar types of complaints, it was assumed that having a staff member speak to patients in a group setting would eliminate repetitious advice.

Allocating patients to groups was seen in the early days of group treatment as a necessary but unfortunate compromise. In groups, patients would receive attention that could be provided in no other way. Group treatment was seen as unfortunate because the inexperienced group leader had to utilize unproven techniques. The psychotherapist who was trained only to treat individuals was as much at loss in a group as were the other staff members who conducted groups. The therapist, no less than his patients, was forced to come to terms with a somewhat puzzling and uncomfortable group situation.

After a while therapists realized that group sessions, when properly conducted, offered the patient more than simply advice and factual information. With the increased recognition of the efficacy of properly conducted group treatment, the need for thorough training in conducting them was promulgated. As in the practice of dyadic psychotherapy, stringent requirements were formulated for conducting groups; again, the involvement of people who were believed not to have had the proper training and education for conduction psychotherapy was restricted.

With the above considerations as a backdrop, let us return to the present group scene. When one compares the utilization of groups today with that of the 1940s or early 1950s, the contrast is striking. Sheldon Cashdan (1970) has indicated:

In the past few years, psychology has witnessed a very curious sociological development—the popular acceptance, and even seeking out, of various types of therapeutic groups.

In our day of rapid communications, fads and social inventions no longer remain private to a region or to a select few. Few of us are likely to be unaware of the enthusiastic announcements that have been made about the new group experiences. (Goldberg, (a), 1970) Currently there is a profusion of innovative varieties of these groups. Advocates of them claim that they have discovered the antidote to such resistive societal maladies as boredom, alienation, and pervasive indifference to mendacity among our chosen leaders. (Parloff, (b) 1970) We have been presented with sundry exciting interpersonal techniques of such significance that the eminent social scientist Carl Rogers (1968) has referred to the new groups as "the most important social invention of the century." Other enthusiasts, such as the humanist psychotherapist Arthur Burton, have seized upon the promise of these dynamic groups with a religious dedication. For those "who can no longer be formally Christian but who want to be fully human" (Burton, 1969), enounter group subscription is invited.

The promise and excitement of the dynamic new groups should not prevent us from examining them critically. A number of observers have pointed out that although many of the techniques employed in the new groups have not been highly publicized or in vogue in the past, they have nonetheless been in practice since the early days of group treatment. S. R. Slavson (1970) and other traditional psychotherapists fervently allege that the techniques utilized in these groups are not really innovative at all, that essentially they have been part of an eclectic psychotherapist's armamentarium for decades. If this is an accurate statement then we need to explore why the new groups have *now* become so popular.

It is now recognized as a historical truism that the climate of the times exerts important pressure in shaping the artifacts of any given era—the sociocultural climate of contemporary America is peculiarly suited to the theory and techniques [of these new groups]. (Smith, 1970)

The individual in American society today has been set emotionally adrift by the traditional anchoring institutions of his social system. In the past the venerable ethical, social, and occupational concepts and beliefs of religious, family, and work guild membership served to define the role and the function of each societal member. The individual who was able to internalize societal concepts derived a sense of identity and value as a member of society.

Today, anchoring societal institutions are no longer able to absorb the emotional and intellectual energies of the denizen. The individual today must define for himself his place in an ever-changing world. Morality is now regarded as situational, tentative, and open to revision. Public and private commitments are no longer absolutely binding as they were within the more ordered and less questioned societal institutions. With the relative absence of societal guidelines, the individual today is forced to question for himself the meaning of life: "Who am I?" "How did I get this way?" "Where shall I go?"

The more the individual must rely upon his own resources for solving personal difficulties, the more he is in touch with feelings of denigration, frustration, and anguish. The individual today feels that he is ailing, possessed by a sickness which is neither physical nor mental, but, rather, a malaise of spirit, a sickness of alienation no less epidemic and socially contagious despite the absence of an organic etiology. The existentialist views this malaise as an existential condition underlying all emotional and social disturbances—be they characterological or due to brief and situational crises. Individuals possessed by existential malaise have attempted traditional forms of treatment and remedial help. They languish in these treatments, more frustrated and disillusioned than when they entered.

Individual psychotherapy, particularly the more psychoanalytic method, is seen as artificial because it has very little semblance to the patient's other experiences in his everyday world. Psychoanalysis is experience not in life but experience in an unreal world. Only in the psychoanalytic therapy session can a patient expect to be enveloped in a fully accepting, tolerant, perpetually analytic vacuum without having to make decisions or censor his intrapsychic ruminations. Individual therapy, many people feel, takes too long, is slow for what currently ails them, and is often unexciting. In traditional psychotherapy, many patients feel that there is not enough give-and-take vis-à-vis patient and therapist to stimulate the patient out of his characterological rut.

Group psychotherapy induces interaction among the patients, making it more difficult to avoid being involved. (Wolf & Schwartz, 1962)

For the disillusioned existentialist, traditional group therapy is more palatable, but nevertheless not fully acceptable because it is contained within a sickness model. Too often it is concerned with reconstructing and working through past situations, and the pursuit of new growth and self-actualization; that is, attention to the healthier parts of the personality is neglected.

Even though the criticisms of traditional psychotherapy cited above are heavily sterotyped and consequently frequently inaccurate, they have induced a considerable number of people who are dissatisfied with their current modes of functioning to seek other forms of care and attention. At the same time, the concept of education has always been viewed favorably in American life. We have been told from our earliest youth that knowledge is power. If one studies diligently or works arduously enough, he can avert difficulties whether they be physical, social, or emotional. The essence of the American dream is that despite one's humble beginnings, through work and effort, and particularly through education and by assuming responsibility, each man can rise to any height he desires.

Each of us cherishes, however unconsciously, a longing for the promise of youth—to realize the exalted heights of personal attainment without feeling dependent upon others. The new group experience, being cast more in the model of education than of treatment, is more palatable to the person eager to emphasize that his problems are not such that he needs others to care for him. Indeed, he attempts to verify this contention by gravitating toward groups that, by their educational orientation and emphasis on choice and responsibility, convey a self-reliant, active, and "healthy" image of the pursuit of self-improvement. The highly popular forms of group experience seem to be an attempt to implement the promise of our unfulfilled youth.

In short, the present new group morphology has arisen from dissatisfaction with prevailing methods of dealing with personal and interpersonal tensions and conflicts. The new groups share the quest with other types of social reform, known as *social movements,* for alleviation of intolerable social conditions. (For a more complete discussion of the personal and social conditions that have given rise to the new group movement see author's *Encounter, Group Sensitivity Training Experience.* New York: Science House, 1970, Chapter 1.)

HOW THE NEW GROUP THERAPIES DIFFER FROM MORE TRADITIONAL PSYCHOTHERAPIES

A comparison of the philosophy and methods of the new groups with those of more traditional dyadic and group psychotherapy will offer some definitive criteria for understanding the discussions of traditional and new group therapies throughout this book. Because a great variety of approaches are described under the rubric of "traditional" and "new group" therapies, a number of generalizations are made which may be more accurate for some traditional and new group therapies than for others.

Three overriding structural features shape traditional psychotherapy. First, the treatment in traditional psychotherapy was long-term. Illness and disease were regarded as having developed over a long period. If treatment were to be successful, it was thought, ameliorative endeavors must be conducted over an extended period.

Second, treatment in traditional psychotherapy was continuous. Absence from treatment, it was believed, would result in relapse. Moreover, the more frequently the patient was treated, the more optimistic was his prognosis. Patients in analysis were seen six times a week, sometimes for more than two hours a session. And even then patients were seen six rather than seven times a week only because the therapist, unlike the patient, required a Sabbath.

Third, in traditional psychotherapy, goals were not specified early. The complaint that brought the patient into therapy was regarded as a symptom. The underlying cause of the symptom required considerable probing and analytic work. Therefore, the final goals of therapy could not sensibly be specified at the onset.

A pessimistic bias also made the setting of goals difficult at the onset. The patient and the therapist were seen as having little or no control over the patient's environment. Most severe emotional disabilities were regarded as largely unamenable; it was believed that the patient had to learn to live with his disabilities. Much of the initial course of treatment was devoted to study and diagnosis of the patient's life history. From the assessment of this material, the therapist tried to help the patient learn to accept himself and others as they were rather than trying to induce radical changes in the patient's life style.

The new group experiences, on the other hand, are short term. Brief, intensive, and complete emotional exploration and involvement are encouraged. The new group leaders seem to be in a hurry—they do not possess the quiet, steadfast patience of the traditional analyst. The new group therapists in this regard seem intrigued by

> one of the unspoken problems of our time [which] is how
> rapidly the human organism can adapt to change. (Rogers,
> 1967)

In contrast with traditional expectations, the goal of the new groups is not to accept oneself and others as they are but, instead, to change oneself and, hopefully, others in very definitive ways. Behavioral change—the more accelerated and dramatic the better—is held up as a premium of treatment. It is currently claimed

> that by developing a high level of intensity and fatigue, group members will achieve a corresponding weakening or dissolution of their usual defensive patterns. (Parloff, (a), 1970)

> The Marathon Group, in this regard, represents a radical alteration in the quality of the psychotherapeutic experience. It assumes that people are capable of coping with undiluted, intense experience and do not require carefully measured exposure to therapy; it has been called a "pressure cooker" because of the tension it builds up. And like a pressure cooker, it also can compress the amount of time required to do its work. (Stoller, 1967)

Unlike the traditional therapist, the new group leader frequently assumes that all patients seek the same goals from treatment and group experience. Where this assumption is held there is an unwillingness on the part of the therapist to probe the deeper underlying recess of the patient's perturbance.

The traditional therapist was more skeptical and patient about trying to reconstruct a personality gnarled and shaped by the trials and tribulations of decades. People, he believed, change when they are ready to change. There appeared to him to be a definitive developmental progression to psychological growth. Each step required a well-timed and relevant response from significant others in the interpersonal field of the individual in the throe of change. The traditional therapist took into account the patient's pattern of growth as well as his style of resistance. He respected both the patient's right to proceed at his own pace or to remain as he was if that were the participant's professed wish. (Goldberg, (a), 1970)

Treatment in the new groups is no longer continuous. Some people who participate in groups nowadays are called "group heads." They follow a strange odyssey. One hears accounts of group hoppers, persons who cruise the sensitivity training oceans sampling groups as if they were remote islands, unrelated to their own world. Whenever their daily existence begins to burden them with unresolved problems, they give themselves a vacation by hopping on to another group. Therefore, even though participants may attend group experiences over a period of years, rarely do they remain in the same group with the same therapist or group leader throughout that period of time. (Goldberg, 1971)

Therapeutic contracts in present-day therapy are generally rather specific from the onset.

> Generally, [group leaders] appear to assume that everyone needs the same type of learning experience—to express greater affect, display more spontaneity, chuck inhibitions, etc. (Yalom, et al., 1970)

Many therapists and group leaders today are also rather vociferous about the kinds of psychosocial experience they have to offer. Around the new group circuit there are therapists referred to as the persons to see if you really want an all-out angry, hostile experience, or a warm intimate experience, or a sexual experience, or whatever else people are in the market for. Whereas traditional therapy, in general, emphasizes relieving repression of anger and sexuality, the new groups emphasize expression of tender feelings (including homosexual tendencies).

In the new group therapies, leaders no longer take professional responsibility for their patients in the way that traditional therapists take medical responsibility or require medical overseeing if they are not physicians. The new group leaders insist that they are not there to cure or take care of the participants; instead, they are together with the participants in order to share a growth experience with them. Denying their healing function in groups, many of the new group leaders from the fields of medicine and psychology have gone so far as to disavow their allegiance to the ethical standards of their professions, entering into relationships with their participants which well may be regarded as professionally unethical according to the Hippocratic oath and the American Psychological Association's code of ethics. It should be stressed, however, that there are also new group leaders who do not take this position.

Another important contrast between past and present therapies is that the traditional group therapist relied heavily upon theory. His conceptual framework was borrowed predominately from work in individual psychotherapy, but it was strictly adhered to, nonetheless, as it was the only anchorage the inexperienced group therapist had in a bewildering, unproven field.

In contrast, many practitioners in the new groups avoid adherence to an explicit and coherent psychological theory. Many leaders are more prone to go with "gut" feelings, letting their "juices flow," heeding feelings rather than assessing the group situation before them from a cognitive frame of reference.

Both the traditionalist and other therapists have, of course, their Mecca. It has been said of the classical analyst that he tended to discredit a colleague's success in psychotherapy if he found that the colleague was forced to abandon the analytic technique in working with his patients. On the other hand, according to the new group movement, if you haven't been to Mecca, that is, Bethel or Esalen, you aren't alive; if you haven't been in a marathon with Fritz Perls or Bill Schutz, you are unable to relate to people or to know yourself. The traditional group method relies on technique, whereas the new group therapies stress personal experience.

This point ties into what was mentioned earlier about the staff member who did not have the skills, education, and training recognized as a prerequisite by the established members of the healing arts. The aspiring psychotherapist has throughout the history of formalized psychotherapy been in search of a technique and treatment rationale which he could call his own. Those who are discriminated against because of meta-personal qualifications, that is, people who lack the required education and training, seize upon techniques in which personal rather than acquired attributes are posited as being crucial in effective performance. The healing arts paraprofessionals have searched for methods which assume that progress is achieved through the change agent's and the patient's being together as existential beings. This rationale contends, moreover, that too much training and education hamper rather than aid the therapist in that a therapist with extensive training becomes technique oriented rather than person centered. The keynote of the new group therapies reflects a quest of the paraprofessional for a personal brand of ameliorative enterprise.

In the new group movement, the relationship vis-à-vis patient and therapist has been radically modified. No longer is the therapist expected to be aloof, detached, objective, and nondisclosing of personal reactions to his patients. Nor is the mandate to avoid relationships with his patients outside of the therapy hour as strictly adhered to as in the past. The new group movement views the detached, withholding therapist model as artificial, lacking in acceptability to all but the most schizoid therapist and schizoid patient, and, as a result, ineffective as an ameliorative endeavor.

The patient and therapist roles, moreover, are no longer clearly defined in the new groups. It is hard to determine at first observation who are the patients and who are the therapists. Further confusing differentiation of roles, a few therapists claim nowadays that they conduct groups in no small measure to resolve their own "hang-ups." Raymond Corsini (1970), a group therapy historian as well as a practitioner, claims that the encounter groups are essentially therapy groups for therapists. They want to get the benefits of group therapy but do not want to admit they are in therapy [or require therapy].

Concurrently these new group leaders assert that it is the group members themselves rather than the therapists who frequently are the most salient therapeutic forces in the group. Moreover, a group leader may conduct a group one week and the next week participate in a group led by one of his group members. And again, a number of psychiatrists, it has been reported, accompany their patients into encounter groups and participate as members of the same group. (Yalom, et al., 1970)

Some historical explanation may be required here. As more and more therapists entered psychotherapy for their own increased growth and maturity rather than primarily to learn the techniques of the trade or to deal with serious contertransference material, they began to realize that the aloofness and lack of warmth of their analysts stood in the way of the growth they wanted for themselves. They transposed themselves into their patients' shoes and were appalled by what they regarded as their own lack of warmth and sensitivity toward their patients.

Group leadership, perhaps as a result of the therapist's role as an active participant in his personal analysis, has become democratic and equalitarian rather than based on authority and expertise as in the past. Where the equalitarian notion is practiced, every group member, be he patient or therapist, is seen as one who heals and as one who is to be healed by others in the group. Equalitarian groups expect the therapist to be open and empathetic rather than to withhold strong affect in order to protect the patient's fragile ego from additional stress.

In traditional psychotherapy, particularly in the more analytic groups, the therapist held that before he could effectively render an interpretation of the patient's behavior and realistically confront him, a warm relationship—a positive transference—had to develop between patient and therapist. In the absence of the patient's positive regard for the therapist, the patient would not be able to tolerate painful aspects of himself which a confrontation with reality would evoke. A patient, in order to face up to the full reality of his situation, it was believed, needed to receive some gratification for dealing with painful material. The new group therapies, on the other hand, confront, even verbally attack, patients before warm, close relationships have developed among patients and between the leader and each of the group members. The new group movement refuses to accept the fragility of the patient and posits, in addition, that it is phony and contrived to extend a warm interest and concern for an "unknown" person. It is only in the heat of battle—the enduring of a painful and risky ordeal together—that people come truly to know one another and develop, as a result, a genuine liking and respect for one another.

In traditional therapy the patient was absolved from having to be responsible for his untoward behavior because it was held that his actions stemmed largely from unconscious urgings. Today, more attention is given to issues of choice and responsibility. An example of this is the ubiquitous practice of insisting that patients say "I" or "me" instead of "it" in referring to their behavior. To make proper choices, the patient requires honest and relevant information about how he is perceived and reacted to by others in the group. In the new groups, *feedback* ("the gift of seeing ourselves as others see us") is accentuated rather than interpretation (trying to understand why the group member is the kind of person he is). Emphasis in the new groups is on how a person is perceived and what he choses to do about how others see him whereas what a person is and why he became that way was underlined in the traditional therapies.

It is currently held that the best way for a person to find out what he is all about is to disclose himself to others. The new groups maintain that there is a consistent pattern between interpersonal and intrapersonal events. The person who is guarded about certain areas of himself with others may be expected to avoid dealing with these issues in private as well.

In the traditional group, the focus of interest was on the historical "there and then." The social philosopher George Santayana warned that he who ignores history is destined to relive it. This dictum was an important premise for the traditional psychotherapist's work. He believed that basic personality patterns were immutably set in the early years of life. To understand present behavior the therapist must trace its origin to relationships with significant persons in the past. By reexperiencing the relationships with a permissive, nonjudgmental parental surrogate, the therapist, the patient could understand and in some instances eradicate his present disturbed thoughts and feelings.

In the new groups, present perceptions and interactive patterns, together with proactive strivings, are deemed more crucial to ameliorative endeavors than is the exploration of childhood experience. It is believed that, at best, the specification of precursory experiences is elusive and speculative. The patient in the present, regardless of his disturbance, is vastly different from that which he was in the past. The new group enthusiasts insist that personality is not fixed early in life but is a continuous process of growth and development through the encounter and conflux of self and others. Vicissitudes in others' behavior and new demands upon self result in personality modification. The expression of immediately experienced feelings and perceptions about the demands upon oneself and the strivings toward others are stressed in the new groups. Participants are encouraged to validate (check out) feelings and perceptions accrued in the group situation rather than to quest after the meaning of the rationalizations that brought them to the group originally.

> Instead of focusing on the diagnostic or causative elements of behavior [the new groups] have been more concerned with the dynamics of interaction. Not about how a person became what he is, but about how does he change from what he is. (Rogers, 1967)

New groups are predicated upon the belief that understanding and skill in human relations can be taught. Hence, relative to traditional psychotherapy, the new groups focus

> more attention on the explicit delineation of characteristic group dynamic patterns such as leadership, competition, subgrouping, [and] scapegoating pressures ... (Garwood, 1967)

A somewhat subtle difference between traditional and present-day therapies is that the new groups insist that it is also possible to feel differently rather than just to think differently. (Weschler & Reisel, 1960) These new groups have attempted to aid the individual to buttress himself against the devastation of alienation and social deprivation. Through participation with peers who share, support, and reinforce the individual's own striving and ambition, a sense of identity is sought.

The traditional therapist was primarily concerned with the discovery and diagnosis of pathology. He operated from a genetic and constitutional bias which held that most emotional disabilities were incurable. The best that could be done to improve the patient's condition was to transform pathology into less disabilitating symptomalogy. Diagnosis and in-depth exploration of the patient's life history were required to assess the parameters within which the patient could successfully function. The new groups have risen in protest against conventional psychiatry which has been content to imitate the principles and practices of general medicine. An increasing array of clinicians have maintained that the manner in which a person is regarded and treated in large measure determines his behavior. If he is forced into a docile, dependent patient role, that is, if he is treated as a victim of social and psychological forces, he can never effectively deal with his situation.

Present-day therapies concentrate on problems in living and tend to de-emphasize pathology in terms of the patient's psychodynamics. Under the influence of community mental health programs, patients are encouraged to maintain themselves in the community even when they exhibit classical psychotic symptoms that in decades past would have meant internment in a psychiatric hospital. The mental health field today places emphasis on growth rather than disease. It is often not the individual who is seen as the "patient," but rather, the situation, the interpersonal relationship, or the social system that is disturbed and needs attention.

The idea has also gathered considerable impetus that every member of society, young or old, affluent or impoverished, disturbed or normally functioning, has both the right and the obligation to become as fully actualized a person as he has potential. In short, psychological attention is no longer extended only to the affluent and the hopeless. Thus, while traditional therapy was class oriented (only the wealthy could afford therapy), the new group therapies emphasize that everyone has the right to fulfill his human potential. With the right to fulfill one's human potential came the right to experience the full range of human emotions.

Thus, today, in all endeavors in life, people are expected to strive for joy and pleasure. The eradication of anxiety, stress, and discomfort is no longer a sufficient goal of psychotherapy. People now crave peak experiences, extreme states of being beyond the pale of the everyday. Some have referred to these peak experiences as a voyage to the center of the self. "Trips from reality" in the form of drugs and aberrant behavior are encouraged because many in the new group movement claim that these "trips" provide new avenues of experience for the individual, not possible in any other way. Some clinicians, such as Ronald Laing, have gone as far as stating that even a psychotic episode may generate a growth experience. Acute, nonparanoid psychotic episodes, it is claimed, are followed by reconstitution and improved psychological integration. (Murphy, 1967)

A number of traditional clinicians have become alarmed at new group leaders who encourage irrationality in their groups. They find it both jolting and ironic to hear participants and colleagues report: "Yes, he is far out"; "Yes, he seems to be quite disturbed himself. But he is so sincere, so honest and open." (Schwartz, 1970) It appears to many traditional therapists that the new group leaders assume that expressing their pathology and urging participants to expose their irrationality is the sine qua non of openness and sincerity.

With the emphasis being on attaining joy in therapy, encouragement is given toward developing gratifying relationships within the group. No longer are group interactions used simply to learn about the patient's interpersonal distortions and transference conflicts. In many of the new groups, relationships with the therapist or group leader, to say nothing of fellow group members, extend beyond the group session. They may run the gamut from telephone calls to sexual encounters.

In utilizing their skills, clinicians are found no longer only at the end of a telephone line and at the foot of the analytic couch. Clinicians nowadays frequently leave their clinics and private consulting rooms to go out into the community to help with pressing social problems. The new groups or, at least, the use of techniques popularized by them are found today in industry, within the educational system, in government, and in the ghetto.

A well-publicized case of new group confrontation took place in Pontiac, Michigan in 1968. At the urging of concerned citizens, the city's school board appropriated $25,000 for establishing black and white encounter groups in the school system. It was hoped that a better appreciation of majority and minority groups would reduce the antagonism and distrust between the races which had reached near-riot proportions in Pontiac. (*Time*, September 19, 1969) The concern of the clinician in endeavors such as that in Pontiac is not to single out and treat the individuals within the system whose personal problems are causing strife for others—as was the approach taken in the past by practitioners who worked with social systems—but to locate and deal with underlying group agendas and social tensions.

Thus, the group is no longer seen as a place where the distressed individual is unilaterally required to come to grips with the demands and expectations of society at large. The group now serves as a situation in which society itself is transformed. The new groups have as their mandate the creation of new and improved social values. The encounter culture, in particular, has launched a campaign to exorcise the superego of modern man. Core values and attitudes which the individual had been led to believe are essential to a regulated society are sometimes skillfully, sometimes unwittingly, reshaped, disregarded, or negated by means of group pressure or identification with the "guilt-liberated" group leader.

In the small group, with both the support and pressure of his peers, the individual is asked to reconceptualize human ideals rather than accept them as givens, as he has done in the past. New group enthusiasts hope that once the individual has acquired new values and improved social skills in the ameliorative group, he will go out and implement changes in the groups in which he holds membership in society at large; in effect, the new groups, through their members, have attempted to change society itself rather than those individuals society has designated as its "problems."

In the traditional group, considerable attention was given to re-entry into society. The traditional groups were designed precisely to help the individual adapt and modify himself to society's demands and expectations. The new groups have the problem of sending a participant back into a community in which support for the participant's life style, acquired in the new group, is absent. The dilemma for the re-entering participant is that to drop his new life style and adapt himself to society's dictates contradicts the new group ethic; but on the other hand, to fight society may result in the same problems that originally drove him into the new group.

In order to modify society, a greater appreciation of the influence of leadership on group performance is required. It is currently held that how patients fare in a group cannot be explained simply by a consideration of the pathology and psychodynamics of the participants in attendance. Examination must be directed to the behavior (role, style, and personality) of the group leader. Today there is greater awareness and attention than ever before of how group leaders subtly influence what happens in their groups. Taking this into account, many new group leaders regard the group members as powerful counteractors to countertransference tendencies by the leader. Traditional psychotherapists appear not to have appreciated this monitoring capacity of group members.

The traditional therapies were anti-somatic and anti-erotic. They stressed rationality and control over impulses. The cultural mores of several decades ago cautioned against touching other people in the group. In contrast, the keynote of the new therapies is their concern with the physical being of the patient. In reaction to the overemphasis on reason in the past, there is today an inordinate concern with sensuality. Fritz Perls, one of the new group movement's deified leaders, suggested that we must go out of our minds to regain our senses. It has also been suggested that the current emphasis on sensuality is predicated on a reconsideration of societal supply and demand.

The core of the old culture is scarcity. Everything in it rests upon the assumption that the world does not contain the wherewithal to satisfy the needs of its human inhabitants . . . [This] leads to a high value being placed on the ability to postpone gratification [since there is not enough to go around] . . . Any act or product that contains too much stimulus value is considered to be "in bad taste" . . . since gratification is viewed as a scarce commodity, arousal is dangerous . . . [For instance] four-letter words are 'in bad taste' because they have high stimulus value . . .

The new culture is based on the assumption that important human needs are easily satisfied and that the resources for doing so are plentiful . . . (Slater, 1970)

The new groups attempt to create modern man in a new image. His stance is immediate, playful, and sensual. His "primary vocation is pleasure, not labor." The new groups have conceptualized their task "as awakening the senses and returning erotic awareness to the total body." They have changed Descartes' dictum—knowledge begins not with "I think therefore I am" but with "I sense therefore I am." (Keen, 1970) In a society with a scarcity of resources, the individual often finds it difficult to satisfy his appetites. In order to survive, he must learn to adapt to society. A common psychological mechanism for this is repression, the most ubiquitous of the neurotic's defenses. In times of affluence fewer environmental pressures to repress lead to a greater incidence of character problems.

In the new therapies, considerable attention has centered on sensory awakening of feelings frozen by "body armor." Traditional psychotherapy sought to interpret the meaning of symbolic behavior in order to reveal to the individual basic drives which impelled his behavior. Only recently have Wilhelm Reich's ideas about character armor become integral in the psychotherapeutic mainstream. Reich's work suggests that the individual adopts bodily postures and physical symptoms as a means of eschewing intense emotion and overwhelming excitation. These defensive patterns, which began preconsciously early in life, have become so automatic in adulthood that the individual is unaware of his characteristic reactions to emotion. He, instead, is only aware of emptiness and apathy. The new therapies have employed sensory awakening techniques with over defended participants in order to rebalance "the nonverbal aspects of the organism with the intellect, focusing attention on simple bodily functions." (Gunther, 1968) In addition to sensory awareness methods, the new groups have become theatrical, using props and gimmicks to circumvent impasses with resistive persons and conservative groups.

The "hot seat," "the vacant chair," role playing, role reversal, analyzing ego states, and games from transactional therapy are part of a rich collection of nonverbal techniques and action exercises that are the standard armamentarium of the new group leaders. These techniques encourage somatic–behavioral changes which foster increased "doing" in contrast to traditional therapy which encouraged cognitive attitudinal changes fostering "understanding."

No longer is the scholarly psychotherapist, versed in pessimistic Teutonic philosophy and psychopathology, deified. The status of intellect in general is declining in society today. (Smith, 1970) We live in an era in which the rationalizations that have brought us, generation after generation, into brutal and irrational combat with dissonant segments within our own and other nations have been called into question. Symptomatic of this, the university professor is no longer society's representative of reason and intellect. Today he has become a radical activist.

The therapist today is less of a healer by technique and more of an identification figure through role modeling. Such leading therapists as Fritz Perls, Bill Schutz, and Albert Ellis are generally perceived by layman and professional alike as "guilt-liberated," exciting life stylers," people who appear to be self-actualized. All three, interestingly enough, were traditionally trained therapists, who broke away from the personless image of the traditional therapist to become attractive as people in their own right. They are the kinds of people many patients seem to wish to emulate. Their attractiveness, it can be argued, is derived less from their success as therapists (which few of us are in a position to evaluate) than from the seductiveness of their personal style of living.

The personal life of the traditional therapist was generally a closed book. It could not, as a result, be employed as a criterion in choosing him as a therapist. In the new groups, experience is romanticized, and mastery and ability are denigrated. He who has lived "fullest" is preferred to he who has toiled most diligently. The new group movement deifies "groovy people." (Culbert, 1968) As a result, expertise as verified by professional degrees, formal training, and proven scholarship is negated. "Who needs a degree?" says one encounter group leader without any formal degrees. "I know I'm a good therapist because I have a 'gut' feeling for people."

In the same way, veterans of group experience feel that as a consequence of their group experience they are, without supervision or formal training, qualified to conduct their own groups. Participants report good group experience with leaders who have no professional training other than that for the theater or nursery school teaching. At the same time, ineffective, poorly conducted groups are reported to be led by fully accredited professionals. (Clark, 1970) Naturally, the setting of standards becomes more and more difficult to achieve. It is a far simpler matter to qualify a group leader in terms of training and education than in regard to the quality of his "gut" feelings.

It is now emphasized that patients improve most with therapists who care about them as people and are able to express their concern in a way that the patient can perceive. (Rogers, 1967) The therapist who knows what is wrong with the patient psychodynamically but is unable to foster a gratifying relationship is regarded as ineffective in improving the patient's condition. Support for these contentions comes from the work of investigators like Margaret Rioch who has demonstrated that psychotherapists with almost no training, provided they have "desirable" personality traits, can facilitate precisely the kinds of growth experience for the patient that the most highly trained psychotherapist strives for. (Shostrom, 1969)

As it has been forwarded that untrained laymen can better empathize with one another than extensively trained therapists, self-help and leaderless groups have gained momentum in recent years.

Research in traditional group therapy had been rather difficult to conduct. Therapists actually have very little data about what happened in these groups other than their own experience, word of mouth, and literary exposition. The techniques were, for the most part, necessarily shrouded in secrecy because of confidentiality requirements and the need to shield from the public an unproven technique.

The only persons in a position to evaluate what transpired in a session were the therapist, his patients, and in the case of a neophyte therapist, his control analyst, or supervisor. None of these could be regarded as an objective observer.

Nowadays, therapists frequently visit one another's groups and participate as group members. Group leaders actually permit, if not encourage, the group members to report what goes on in the group. Video tapes and audio recordings are standard tools of the therapist. These devices are available to any interested party, be he layman or professional. Although this climate contains contaminating factors, it provides greater access to knowledge and understanding of groups than ever before.

The existential-analytic position ascribed to in this book contains features from both traditional and new group therapies. But then, all efficacious types of psychotherapy must. Systems of psychotherapy are designed to grapple with and, hopefully, resolve the psychosocial dilemmas of contemporary man. Therefore, no effective treatment modality can escape the historical issues that shaped its present form nor the current social and psychological forces that it shares in common with other psychotherapies. Every system of psychotherapy does, however, emphasize certain issues more than it does others. My existential-analytic position emphasizes the issues of choice and responsibility involved in being in an encounter with another person for whom the conditions pressing upon him from within and without are in conflict.

TABLE 1

CORE PROPERTIES OF THE NEW GROUP THERAPIES IN CONTRAST WITH TRADITIONAL PSYCHOTHERAPIES

TRADITIONAL PSYCHOTHERAPY	THE NEW GROUP THERAPIES
1. Class oriented (only wealthy can afford).	Everyone has the right to fulfill his human potential.
2. Society has a scarcity of resources; therefore the individual has to learn to adapt to it—repress (neurotic).	Affluence of resources; no need to repress (character problems).
3. Concerned with individual patient.	Concerned with group processes and social systems.
4. Relieves patient of symptoms by converting to a less disabilitating condition.	Make dramatic changes in individual.
5. Therapist's credentials based on his scholarship and academic training.	Group leader acts as role model; is a guru; has attractive life style.
6. Noncontamination of patient–therapist roles.	Role diffusion; blurring of patient–therapist roles.
7. Therapist assumes legal–medical responsibility for his patient.	Group leader assumes personal responsibility for himself only, not for patient.
8. Therapy is expert-led.	Group experience is almost democratic.
9. Encourages interpreting and reliving past experiences and unconscious material.	Confrontation of immediate behavior.
10. Cognitive–attitudinal change = understanding.	Somatic–behavioral change = doing.
11. Analysis of behavior, dreams, etc.	Expansion of conscious (seeking radical departures from past and present behavior).
12. Absence of environmental stimulation.	Stimulation by environmental factors (e.g. drugs).
13. Emphasis on relieving repression of anger and sexuality	Emphasis on expression of tender feelings (including homosexual feelings).
14. Developing a relationship before depth probing.	Confrontation without first developing relationship.
15. Dealing with countertransference through control analysis and outside supervision.	Countertransference handled in group; participants assume responsibility for reality testing.
16. Theoretical.	Experential–exploratory.
17. Long-term.	Short-term.
18. Secretive.	Open for investigation and research.

"The search for interpersonal encounter is a central human quest. Perhaps the most pressing existential crisis of our age is the pervasive sense of aloneness which so many of us feel so much of the time."

G.V. Haigh
"Psychotherapy as Interpersonal Encounter"

EXISTENTIAL POSTULATES—2

Existentialism was the philosophy I studied and believed in as a student in college. As a psychotherapist I am less certain now than I was as a youth about what existentialism means as a formal system of thought. What follows in this chapter, therefore, is how my personal philosophy has influenced my work as a group therapist. The concepts and rationale I propose may have little resemblance to those of other therapists who operate from existential positions.

Some scholars assert that the origins of existential thought are found in the philosophies of the ancient Greeks—Aristotle, Plato, and Heraclitus. Heraclitus pointed out that the process of life was interminable flux, so that a man could never enter the same stream or situation twice: Each time a man enters the stream he is washed by different water and each time he enters he, too, has changed.

I would suggest, however, that the roots of existential thought cannot properly be traced back to any single age or any single philosopher. Existential thought is not a formal system of knowledge nor does it influence a man prior to the first moment of his awareness of himself and the conditions which make him a unique human being, separate from every other person. Regardless of the interpersonal strategies an individual employs in trying to deny the awareness of his existential condition; for example, dependency, symbiosis, or folie á deux, he cannot escape his aloneness from others. A required condition of his aloneness is that he must choose for himself. What he may escape, albeit at a cost to his mastery over his own destiny, is the awareness that he is the author of his life script; for example, it is he who chooses to escape conditions he finds intolerable.

Each of us in our own way tries to escape the awesome responsibility of our creative and destructive powers. Each of us, although some more than others, acts as if we were a mere player entrusted to perform some inscrutable author's dictates, unequipped to rephrase, modify, reinterpret, or modernize a single line or to act impromptu in the exigencies of life.

The present chapter is an attempt to present how I have employed existential thought, as I understand it, to enable people to identify, modify, and more completely take over authorship of their life script. The concepts that will be discussed in this chapter are those essential to an existential-analytic psychotherapy position. These concepts are: aloneness, disclosure, awareness, choice, responsibility, life script, core attitudes, personal strategy, quest for freedom, quest for certainty, satisfaction, security, and psychic economy.

THE HUMAN CONDITION

The condition in which man finds himself is that of aloneness. An individual is conceived by the intentional or unwitting choice of others. Having been born of this choice, the conditions of his being are from moment to moment reshaped or perpetuated through his own actions and reactions. Man finds himself in the position of having to choose for himself. Sartre has referred to this required condition of existence as man being "condemned to freedom."

It is from this ontological prerequisite that man experiences aloneness. Man's choices are his alone to make. No one can choose for him, albeit men may subtly arrange to act for others—as their guardians or their tormentors. In permitting another to act for him, a man chooses to negate some part of his being, to suppress and relegate the expression of that aspect of his being as too meaningless or too troublesome to be recognized. The moment existence becomes conscious of itself, it is forced to bear the awesome responsibility of having to choose itself. Man comes to be that which he seeks to be only through a full acceptance of the responsibility of having to choose for himself.

Man's ontological responsibility although necessitated by alone-ness does not require separation from others. Indeed, separation from human company makes man's ontological responsibility more diffi-cult as a process, unrewarding as an experience, and meaningless as an ethical concern. In this regard, Sartre's ethical imperative states that when I act I do not only act the way I feel is good for myself alone, but I act the way I want all men to act. If one interprets this to mean that all men should act as an example for all other men, then it is evident that a man's separation from his fellows makes the ethical concerns of his life unknowable to others. (I am postulating that one man's life may serve as an ethical experience for others. Unlike Christian teachings that extol Jesus' good life as an example for others to emulate, the teachings of the Zen masters depict a series of experiential paradoxes and existential alternatives to help highlight one's personal experience.)

As a process, man may best choose that which he intends to be by associating with others. Correspondingly, a man permits himself to become that which he does not intend to be through his passive compli-ance with others. When a man withholds himself from others, they, in an attempt to order experience, will define him as they will rather than as he might wish to be known. Man is defined by his actions. He is defined by others when he remains passive and undisclosed. The less defined and disclosed a man chooses to remain, the more others feel compelled to interpret him. Clinicians long have been aware that men attribute their own lurking terrors and tormented motives to those who appear mysterious to them (the projection principle).

The concept under discussion is self-disclosure, or:

'honest, congruent, authentic, and frank expression of one's feelings, reaction and attitude to another person in a conver-sation ... those feelings which have to do with that other person and which are being immediately experienced in the here-and-now interaction with that person.... (T.C. Greening)

Disclosing is vital for a person because in the act of disclosing himself to another he makes his intentions known to himself as well. This was brilliantly pointed out several decades ago by George H. Mead, who described man's need for the mediation of another person's perspective in order to participate consciously in his own choices.

It is also necessary to contrast self-disclosure in a meaningful interpersonal encounter with that of ordinary conversation as it is enacted in day-to-day social situations. To converse does not imply that two persons are engaged in an interpersonal encounter. A conversation is frequently two juxtapositional monologues, each actor responding to his own life script while concomitantly defending himself against the other's assertions.

Early in this century, Hans Vahinger pointed out that men live by a series of fictional ideas which have no counterpart in reality. These fictions such as "all men are equal"; "honesty is the best policy"; "the end justifies the means"; "brave boys don't cry" enable the person to establish fixed rules for each new interpersonal situation without having to take into account the unique demands and expectations implicit in the new situation. Taken together all these fictions constitute an individual's *life script* (or personal strategies). Thus, in most of the social situations in which we find ourselves the French writer La Rochefoucauld's (May, 1969) observations hold true:

The reason so few people are agreeable in conversation is that each is thinking more about what he intends to say than what others are saying—and we never listen when we are eager to speak.

Therefore, although words and phrases are received, the meaningfulness of the thoughts and feelings that have produced these words are lost. The lack of exchanged information about how others think and feel results in feelings of alienation—a separation from full knowledge of ourselves. As we have already said, in relating to others we find ourselves. Alienation is first experienced as incompletion and tension. Prolonged periods of such feelings lead to loneliness, dread, and finally panic and dissolution. Phenomenologically, it has been described as "going out of existence." Man seeks to escape this harrowing and terrifying experience by whatever means he knows. If he believes his cognitive powers have failed him, he may, in resignation and disillusionment, surrender himself to the forces that press up against his existence. Andras Angyal (1965, pp. 5–6), a psychotherapist and social philosopher, has cogently described the existential condition I have been trying to delineate in the following passages:

The organism lives in a world in which things happen according to laws which are heteronomous; i.e., foreign to the organism as such. [The organism] is subjected to the laws of the physical world but it can oppose self-determination to external determination. An animal dropped from a height falls according to the law of gravitation like any other body, simply as a mass and not as an organism. Its fall, however, can be modified by influences originating within the organism—a cat, by means of its righting reflexes, manages to land on its feet whatever its position was at the start of the fall. . . .

Because the organism lives in a world independent of itself, its autonomy is only partial and must be asserted against the heteronomous surroundings.

In the face of any adversity, therefore, the individual may choose to oppose, reshape, or in some way modify the influence of the forces pressing upon him or he may give himself up to the force or will of other objects. By divesting oneself of intentional, assertive behavior in the face of outside forces the choice thereby may be that of renouncing self as an intending being. But still another existential choice is possible. Angyal describes it as being homonomous. The homonomous trend is a process whereby the individual incorporates himself in a supraindividual community. Human existence cannot be regarded entirely as a trend toward self-actualization or a process in which self is relinquished.

Seen from another angle, human life reveals a basic pattern very different from self-assertiveness, from striving for freedom and mastery. The person behaves as if he were seeking a place for himself in a larger unit of which he strives to become a part. [He strives] to surrender and to become an organic part of something that he conceives as greater than himself. ... At the cultural level, the person's conception of the larger unit to which he belongs or to which he strives to belong, varies according to his cultural background and personal orientation. The superordinate whole may be represented for him by a social unit—family, clan, nation—by an ideology, or by a meaningfully ordered universe. (Angyal, 1965, p. 15)

From communion with people having knowledge and resources superior to his own, the individual gains an identity which provides him with refuge from separation and loneliness. Plato described man and woman as cleaved from the same soul eternally seeking a union. In short, the individual desires another to complete himself. It is my belief, notwithstanding, that the individual does not achieve his intent to become complete and self-sufficient by surrendering himself to the force or will of others. When the individual lacks self-assertion against heteronomous forces and gives in to the homonomous trend (preferring death), he is expressing his lack of self-value.

It may be helpful here to give some clinical illustrations of people seen in treatment for whom personal autonomy was subverted by the need to make the homonomous and heteronomous choices Angyal described above.

A thirty-nine year old woman, in her second marriage, was admitted to an intensive treatment ward of a large psychiatric hospital following a suicidal gesture. Her construct of the world was the child's simple dichotomy of "pleasant" and "unpleasant." Her personal strategies centered around avoiding unpleasantness at any cost. She would rather be lied to than told something unpleasant about herself. She tended to act out her intrapsychic conflicts with a burst of emotion. She then would quickly become frightened by her destructive proclivities, withdraw, and become constricted and depressed. She resolved that her displays of emotion would not happen again. She regarded herself, somewhat incongruously, as a "giving" person but also as someone who was rather inadequate in solving her own problems. When difficulties arose, she expected others to take responsibility and make decisions for her. Being dependent upon others, she realized that she could not afford to antagonize them or consciously recognize her hostility toward them. She compulsively tried to keep everything well-regulated so that her hostile feeling could not slip out. The bursts of aggression toward her husband which led to her suicidal gestures resulted from her fear that he had another woman and would leave her. In her mind, this event was a prelude to being abandoned to endless years of loneliness. Mystified and frightened by her own intrapersonal processes, she is a person who required occupation with busy work, to avert self-introspection. Tragically, it would appear that she even preferred death (the homonomous trend) than having to deal with her aloneness.

A seventeen year old youth with above average intelligence, from a white, upper-middle-class home, was admitted to the drug rehabilitation program of a large psychiatric hospital. His parents, well-educated and socially prominent, had placed considerable pressure upon him for scholastic and social achievement that he questioned whether he was able to attain. He felt that he needed some external support to meet these expectations. Unwilling or unable to approach his parents or surrogate figures to serve in this capacity, he had turned to drugs. Turning to drugs was compatible with one of his major characterological defenses, inner negation. He tended to deny to himself that he had any real problems.

Times of greatest anxiety for this adolescent were those occasions when he permitted himself to become dependent upon others; he would view his situation with disgust and attempt to flee it. He regarded himself more as a child than as an adolescent entering adulthood. He felt he lacked self-reliance but was unable to convey this feeling to those whom he wished would help him. As a result, he felt lonely and alienated. He felt he was a burden to his father and was unable to express his guilt-invoked anger toward him. He erected counterdepressive facades to protect himself from awareness of his own vulnerability and the anger he felt toward others for putting himself in this position.

When his father put him into a psychiatric hospital, a place which deeply frightened him, he was careful, nonetheless, to guard against conveying anger about his situation. He told the psychologist working with him that the addicts on his ward are "really nice guys." He suggested that there was much he could learn from them. Unable to express strong feelings and define for himself who he was, he identified with others who had defined themselves as different and separate from the parental figures the patient had so much difficulty separating from. In particular the patient allied himself with the hippies on the ward. According to the patient, a hippie is "a person who is free to show his emotions—a person who doesn't belong to society—doesn't care what society thinks." Implicitly, he was suggesting that he didn't know if he could make it either as an adult or as a male. As a hippie the distinction between male and female, adult and child are not important. The hippie is a Peter Pan, sexless and eternal, a universal protest against being categorized or defined as anything at all —male, female, adult, or child.

The tragedy of the young man described above was that he was unable to encounter and disclose himself to another person and in the process define for himself who he was and how he wished the other to treat him. To the extent he could not engage in an intimate encounter with another, he could not become that which he intended to be; he was unable to become self-actualized. A person does not satisfy his basic yearning for autonomy and self-actualization when he acts or performs, gives, receives, or demands in a unilateral manner. On the other hand, when people tell one another where they stand and what they expect of themselves and others, they exude a sense of their own being. Consequently, those who do not articulate the rules of the relationship they wish to abide by manifest an "embarrassment of being" and are fated to be dictated to by others' rules. When there is reciprocity between people in encounter, the experience enables each to be that which he is. Reciprocity enables each to disclose himself and make known what heretofore has not been recognized and accepted.

The reader may wonder if my statements that self-actualization permits an individual to be that which he is implies a deterministic position in which freedom and choice have been removed. I propose these statements as a clinician and, despite my terminology, not as a philosopher. How can an individual become anything but what he is? The youngster described above had as a child wanted to be a professional baseball player. For this youngster, like many others, the hope of attaining an illustrious athletic career served to compensate for his being regarded by himself (and, in his mind, by others) as inferior in other spheres of his life. He sought a more equal standing with others and hoped that his athletic attainment would reduce his separation from his peers.

His parents forbade his excessive attention to athletics. They expected him to devote his time to academic study and preparation for entrance into his father's Ivy League alma mater. The youngster throughout adolescence sulked around the house. He secretly kept sports scrapbooks and followed baseball on TV in the privacy of his room. He felt incapable, however, of dealing with his parents' condemnation of his wishes. Thus, although the youngster aspired to be a professional athlete, he could not accept his aspirations as a legitimate possibility and develop the skills, attitudes, and technical competence that athletics required. Consequently, his aspirations existed only as a fantasy. (A fantasy is a compromise of some inner need which has not been fully recognized because of the fear of events that would accompany the fulfillment of the desire.)

Only after disclosing his inner strivings about what a professional athletic career meant to him could the youngster appropriately and consciously direct his strivings toward the fulfillment of his desires. In a meaningful discussion with others he might have come to realize that the achievement of an athletic career may not have served his desire for equality with his peers. Success as an athlete often creates a greater separation between the athlete and his peers than existed originally. The fears which prevented his aspirations from being accepted as a legitimate possibility may have had some validity. Unfortunately, this youngster was not in a position to learn from his fears. He was unwilling to experience his feelings deeply.

In the flickering light of half-consciousness, objects bear some passing resemblance to their form in the intense illumination of more complete awareness. Each person makes a choice of how much of himself he is willing to experience deeply. Experiencing the deeper recess of one's self is frequently painful because it reveals unbuttressed the loneliness and dread that result from our ontological responsibility in a world of uncertainty. We may avert these feelings by behaving mechanically. Machinery is only prone to rust, flesh is heir to pain. The defenses we erect provide a respite from pain inasmuch as the probe of our deeper concerns is averted. At every moment the individual's choice is akin to that of Professor M. Von Senden's cataract patients after corrective surgery. Dr. Von Senden was a German optomologist, who reported in a monograph in 1932 the experience of patients who, blind from birth because of cataracts, were given the opportunity of vision being restored by surgical operation. Each patient upon the correction of his vision was overwhelmed and confused by a vastly more variegated world of sensation. Each patient, then, had to make a choice either of trying to make meaning of this welter of new and bombastic experience, or by retreating by putting on dark glasses and returning to the comfortable patterns of blindness.

Some readers may regard my analogy of vision and choice as naïve. To many it seems only too evident that an individual's reactions (choices) are subliminal. Personal experience makes this contention difficult to deny and science has difficulty in verifying it. But be this as it may! An individual frequently may not have much control over the forces that bear upon him or within him, but he certainly has some choice as to how he experiences these forces. My point is that man's basic choice is choosing how he wishes to experience life. Our existential analysis seeks to discover how the individual has chosen to experience the world and the impelling motives behind his choice.

HOW EXISTENTIAL POSTULATES RELATE TO THE WORK OF PSYCHOTHERAPISTS

In order to help the patient, the psychotherapist must select a basis for understanding his behavior. The bases for analysis must consist of concepts which are simply stated, logically and consistently ordered, and which best serve the pragmatic necessity of enabling the patient to appreciate his behavior so that he may influence it. Implicit in every theory of psychotherapy is a theory of human nature and an ontological notion of what a man can become when self-actualized. A practitioner's therapeutic endeavor is therefore an admixture of his scientific knowledge and bias and his personal philosophy.

Whereas behavior accurately may be described on the one hand physiologically, chemically, or physically, and on the other hand historically, culturally, or metaphysically, I have found none of these perspectives to be especially useful in enabling people immediately to modify their interpersonal behavior. To be effective the psychotherapist needs to indicate the goal–directed or functional aim of behavior as a compromise and integration of various wants, emotions, and cognitions which sometimes concordantly, sometimes disharmoniously, operate to influence action. (Kretch, et al., 1962)

In this section I described the behavior of my patients in terms of their attempts to cope with an uncertain world and to create meaning and security amidst bombardment of stimuli and emotional upheavals. These kinds of coping behaviors are referred to as "personal strategies." This unit of analysis has been selected to enable the reader to study the choices and kinds of responsibilities the patient assumes.

WHAT ARE PERSONAL STRATEGIES?

The attitude a person takes toward himself and others can be understood in terms of the choices he makes. People regulate their behavior in terms of the assumptions they make about the contingencies in which they find themselves. These assumptions have varying probabilities of confirmation or rejection. According to assertion-structure theory:

> Life is a constant acturial process: the individual is betting on his assertions (assumptions) and winning (confirmation) or losing (disconfirmation). The neurotic is essentially a person who is constantly betting on a set of assertions that have a high probability of disconfirmation. (Harper, 1959, pp. 120-121)

Why *is* this the case? The world in which we live, devoid of the myriad of theory, explanation, and preconceived notions, is a big, booming, buzzing confusion. Often there is no direct correlation between the objective dimensions of the world and what registers on our sense receptors. In order to engage and master our world or even to survive within the confusion that engulfs us and pervades our thought and feelings, we need to make some semblance of meaning of our sensory and kinesthetic experiences. Without any assurance of a correct interpretation of our experiences we are constantly forced to make inferences about what is going on around us. Inferences that concern our physical and psychological safety are called *core attitudes*. These inferences comprise our attitudes about ourselves and others and steer our interpersonal transactions. Not only do core attitudes influence how we treat others, but as George Kelly suggests, they shape the very manner in which we perceive the universe. We generally respond to the universe in a twofold manner. We behave in a way which is intended to achieve a preferred state of affairs while, at the same time, acting in such a way as to confirm our core attitudes about what we have predicted would happen as a result of our interaction with the environment. Often we achieve the confirmation of our inferences at the expense of what we "consider" to be a desirable state of affairs for ourselves.

The case of Mr. Daedilus illustrates the specific ways a person uses strategies to avoid taking responsibility for the course of his life. Mr. Daedilus's case shows how having a pessimistic attitude toward his ability to affect his fate, Mr. Daedilus created a vicious cycle of unpleasant situations for himself. A person acts as he believes. If he believes that he has some choice about his behavior, he generally acts in ways to maximize his freedom. If, as in the case of Mr. Daedilus, he believes that he has little or no choice about his behavior, he generally acts in ways to minimize choice.

Mr. Daedilus is a thirty-five year old law school graduate. He was seen in dyadic psychotherapy. A therapeutic contract was agreed upon; it stipulated that Mr. Daedilus would be seen for a limited number of sessions, not exceeding ten, to determine whether he wished to pursue psychotherapy and, if he did, whether he and the present therapist could work together. Mr. Daedilus had been in and out of therapy for the past ten years, with at least half a dozen different therapists. He had been hospitalized for a good part of this decade.

From the onset of the present ameliorative work, Mr. Daedilus had been rather depressed. His depression appeared chronic although three situational influences should be noted: (a) Mr. Daedilus suffered insult to his self-esteem from his recent demotion from a commissioned salesman's position to one of straight salary; (b) his history suggested that he suffered considerable tumult due to an annual syndrome of vacillation that he underwent each year trying to decide whether to take the state bar examination, which regenerated intropunitive feelings about his chances of being successful in a law career; (c) he seemed to mourn the loss of the therapist with whom he had worked for over two years.

Mr. Daedilus seemed, for a person of his imputed intelligence and education, to be lacking in communicative skills and insight into his situation. These deficiencies were thinly overlaid by the employment of therapeutic parlance and orientation he had accrued over his ten years of psychotherapy. Mr. Daedilus was unwilling to articulate what he wanted of himself and others; for example, the therapist, the girl he was dating, his supervisors, and co-workers. He expected others to anticipate his needs and act according to his preconceived notions, or core attitudes, about how people should behave, without attempting to make these expectations explicit. When the therapist behaved counter to his expectations, Mr. Daedilus reacted with non-verbal indications of disgust. Inquiry, however, elicited only vague accusations of his being betrayed.

Mr. Daedilus blocked attempts at negotiation of roles and goals by interposing two contradictory motifs into his expectation of himself in therapy. On the one hand, he claimed that he was incapable of progressing in psychotherapy because he needed to work out his difficulties by himself outside therapy. Psychotherapy, he claimed, accentuated his dependency. On the other hand, he behaved as if he were superior to the banal details of having to negotiate for his ends in psychotherapy so that he required the therapist to do the "right thing" for him without bothering him with the details. During the third session, Mr. Daedilus expressed enormous ambivalence about securing a loan to study for the bar examination because of his doubts about being successful as an attorney and his need to prove that he was as good a man as his father and brother. The therapist pointed out Mr. Daedilus's ambivalence and observed that if he presented himself to the loan officer in the same mood of ambivalence in all likelihood he would be turned down for a loan. Implicit was the suggestion that Mr. Daedilus needed to give his petition for a loan more thought. Instead, Mr. Daedilus became angry, accusing the therapist of intimidating him by telling him not to be honest about his feelings. He accused the therapist of being "relentless" and "pushing" him too hard, which was similar to the way he described his previous therapists, his brother, and his father.

The description above illustrates the patient's object relations. He employed a projective mechanism to split his fragile ego into the "bad self" represented by the therapist(s)—the critical, insatiable, demanding father—and himself, the weak, dependent child who is without hope or remedy. Mr. Daedilus seemed unwilling to consider that doubts about his motives lurked within him rather than being an outgrowth of the therapist's wish to destroy him. To acknowledge his critical self would be to face up to his own self-destructive tendencies and deal with them. He chose not to deal with this part of himself and accounted for destructive behavior as emanating from others against him. In short, he refused to acknowledge the critical components of his personality. If he could not admit to possessing critical faculties neither could he use them constructively. To be a lawyer, critical faculties are essential. Thus, because his personal strategies did not permit him to accept negative aspects of his critical faculties, he could not utilize the positive aspects of his faculties either.

Psychotherapy at that time was threatening to the kind of reconstruction Mr. Daedilus was prepared to make. He seemed to be attempting a narrowly circumscribed equilibrium by working on one marginal problem at a time, leaving his deeper concerns aside. His problem in psychotherapy can be likened to a torn cardboard box containing a gift he wished some day to give himself. The box was heavily taped. Mr. Daedilus required the therapist to do patchwork, applying more adhesive tape here and there, assuring him that everything was in control so that the present would not fall out. Mr. Daedilus's compulsive patchwork was unsuccessful for mastering his situation. Several of the panels of the box were open and the gift was in danger of falling out. Mr. Daedilus had the choice of maintaining an illusion that preoccupation with patchwork would accomplish his ends, or being willing to examine the entire package for damages and consider more realistic solutions. Mr. Daedilus's choice was that of deciding whether being healed was worth re-experiencing deep wounds that were thinly closed over by years of supportive psychotherapy.

The kind of personal strategies implicit in Mr. Daedilus's orientation to his difficulties can be explained by two quests that each of us becomes caught up in: a quest for freedom and a quest for certainty. These quests may not be mutually exclusive—most people seek both, except in extreme (pathological) states. A *quest for certainty* is an exerted effort to maintain a fixed, stable organization over one's cognitive belief system. The person who seeks personal freedom is also seeking organization of his cognitive system. However, he seems better able to withstand disorganization or imbalance (anxiety and uncertainty) for a longer period in attempting to gain a new, more complex, and comprehensive cognitive organization. People like Mr. Daedilus are, from this perspective, not equally capable or desirous of risking chafe and insult in the pursuit of more effective personal functioning as are persons who seem to profit from their psychotherapeutic experience.

In confirming our expectation about ourselves we acquire a sense of certainty because the confirmation allows us to believe, however mistakenly, that we are able to take care of ourselves in this precarious world. When perceptual feedback and existing beliefs about ourselves are consistent, they coexist without tension. In such instances there is no internal pressure toward modifying either the reception of the new experience or the existing belief system. On the other hand, experiences which are not syntonic with our existing beliefs are perceived as threats to our ability to survive and the self builds up defenses which deny the awareness of these unwelcome perceptions. In short, there appears to be a natural proclivity toward maintaining a consistency between our beliefs and our experiences.

Information from the environment which is inconsistent with our attitudes is called *cognitively dissonant*. The self has three basic techniques for handling dissonant information: (a) suppressing the existence of the information; (b) distorting or modifying the information in order to render it more consistent with the core attitudes; (c) upon realizing that two or more core attitudes are in sharp disagreement, modifying one or more of these attitudes so that they all are more cognitively consistent.

Mr. Daedilus's selected perceptions, his disturbed and denied meanings of communication, his manipulation of the therapist's words, actions, and intentions can be understood as attempts to maintain a consistent cognitive balance. The more vital the core attitude was in Mr. Daedilus's belief system, the greater was his need to confirm the attitude based on whatever evidence he had at hand, even if it was faulty or contradictory. In other words, the more vital Mr. Daedilus's assumption was in maintaining customary attitudes about himself, the greater was his need to set himself up for conditions that "proved" his position. To insure that these conditions occur, people like Mr. Daedilus generally posit certain assumptions or rules that govern their transactions with others. Mr. Daedilus's life abounded with such rules, for example, "Honesty is the best policy even if I don't get money for law training"; "It is better not to be dependent upon someone even if I need his help," and so forth.

The term "personal strategy" is used to emphasize the rather obvious but frequently ignored fact that an individual has choices about the rules he makes for himself. He chooses the rules because he believes that they have a payoff for him. Personal strategies are inner-directives which each person poses in his transactions with the world of animate and inanimate objects. They are personal because the way they are organized, no less than how they are expressed, and are uniquely characteristic of that individual. That many personal strategies operate from unconscious motives does not alter the fact that these choices are preferable to others and would not be maintained if they were not. Personal strategies grow and develop phylogenetically from the first moments of life. Originally they consist of instinctual and tropismic responses to gross favorable or antagonistic conditions encountered by the organism. Over time they are shaped by societal forces and systems in addition to the raw physical environment as we will see in the case of Poncho described below.

Taken together, personal strategies are the manner in which a person organizes his world and commits himself to that organization. Once he has a reliable method of securing satisfaction, perhaps by making meaning of his experience, he is reluctant to relinquish the strategy and face the threat of no longer attaining satisfaction.

The dynamics of personal strategy are exemplified in the following clinical example. Several years ago I conducted a treatment group that met three times a week for an inpatient psychiatric unit. The group was comprised of newly admitted patients in the throes of acute agitation. One of the patients was a bright, quick-tempered, black male about thirty-five years of age named Poncho. He had been brought to the unit as the result of a suicidal attempt because his wife of eighteen years had left him for another man. Poncho's self-regard had been severely chafed because he regarded this event as an indication that he was not masculine enough to hold his wife. This view of himself was cognitively dissonant with his core attitudes about the kind of person he should be.

Because of this dramatic and jolting event, Poncho could no longer deny, distort, or defend himself against the realization that the woman with whom his self-worth was integrally bound did not regard him as sufficiently masculine. Poncho experienced himself as emotionally unable to revamp his need to be regarded as masculine and his struggle to modify this core attitude resulted in a severe depression which he attempted to fight with alcohol. His core need for masculinity and self-assertion would not be denied. Accordingly, he preferred to resolve his dilemma in a self-assertive act (consistent with his masculine core need), self-destruction, rather than remain passively entrenched in self-pity, misery, and alcohol.

In considering Poncho's situation let us be careful to note the delicate interplay between personal strategies and cultural forces. Poncho had made the implicit assumption that to be masculine is to be sexually virile and, given provocation, physically assaultive. These ideas were supported by the black, inner city community in which Poncho grew up. In his youth, these attitudes, converted into action not infrequently, were his means of survival. Poncho had gone to college for two years and left the black inner city for a well-paying position. His core attitudes, however, remained intact. Whenever his son misbehaved he felt compelled to discipline him by "belting the hell out of him"—doing what he believed to be his parental duty, consistent with his conception of the masculine role. Not surprisingly, he was bewildered by his son's lack of respect for him. He attempted to resolve his conflicts with his wife by impressing his sexual prowess upon her. He was unaware that she, having grown up in a middle-class family, was not satisfied with the housewife role he demanded of her and was frequently asking for other kinds of contact and consideration. When she left him he could only believe, consistent with his implicit assumptions about male–female relationships, that his wife's lover was preferred because the latter was more virile than he was.

An additional concept needs to be discussed in order to delineate the affective component of personal strategies. According to Harry Stack Sullivan's interpersonal theory, satisfaction and security are the two major motivational forces in the individual's repertory. Satisfactions are achieved by a variety of physical and emotional conditions. Continuation of these satisfactions are threatened by the imposition of anxiety and apprehension. These feelings, according to interpersonal theory, are generated by the fear that future conditions may in some unspecifiable way threaten continuation of present satisfactions. In this regard, how frequently do we hear ourselves and others saying "Decisions, decisions—a thousand decisions a day. Who knows if they're the right ones!" The organism attempts to develop security mechanisms to inveigh against this threat.

A categorical means of inducing security is to seek satisfactions that are least likely to fluctuate in terms of demands and expectations of the organism over time. The more time-proven the satisfaction, the more reliable it generally appears. The term employed earlier in the chapter to describe these security mechanisms was *quest for certainty.* Regardless of the appellation, security mechanisms serve the defensive needs of the organism for *psychic economy,* which is a remnant of archaic psychological functioning. Security mechanisms are predicated on the premise that the organism must obtain satisfaction at the lowest cost to his reservoir of available energy. People habitually operate by way of least effort. There is a characteristic tendency in each of us to avoid expending excessive energy in dealing with others. Residual energy had to be available to our primitive ancestors in case of emergency and threat to their survival.

Satisfactions that are habitually and categorically regulated require little or no exploratory or coping energy expenditure because they become straightforward and mechanically regulated operations. Consequently, certain personal strategies are maintained even though they no longer function properly because they nurture the fiction that the individual's present mode of function is adequate, requiring no further expenditure of energy. This may help explain why people try to deny their responsibility for their own actions. If a person claims to have choice over his behavior, energy must be expended in dealing with the manner in which he behaves. If, on the other hand, a person claims no accountability over his actions, his behavior is beyond his purview and he may disregard it since concern and inquiry will not alter the future state of affairs.

Satisfactions that are habitual and therefore require low energy expenditures are favored by the security and defensive mechanisms of the personality. But man is also a self-exploratory organism who seeks new, more intriguing, and complex modes of satisfaction. This self-exploratory or self-actualizing propensity of the personality conflicts with the organism's defensive mechanisms. In a healthy organism the mediating aspects of the personality, the ego functions, are generally capable of reducing this conflict and effecting a compromise. In patients with serious emotional and volitional disturbances the ego's inability to mediate a successful compromise between the organism's defensive needs and its self-actualizing strivings are noted. This conflict influences the disturbance that induces the patient to seek psychological assistance or results in "acting out" behavior.

I have selected the concept of personal strategies as the unit of analysis in my ameliorative work not only because it meets the criteria of economy of explanation and logical and consistent ordering, but because it is in rapport with my philosophy of human nature. The concept of personal strategies is based upon an existential philosophical point of view in which the individual is seen as responsible and accountable for his transactions with others. Accepting behavior as governed by personal strategies, psychotherapy may be conducted in equalitarian transactional terms in which each seeks to explore and come to understand the intentionality of the other. The patient is not relegated to the role of a victim of his inscrutable nature and of circumstance. The individual's behavior is regarded as intending to serve a function which is capable of being discovered and understood. The therapist's function is not to change the patient's behavior but to help him discover his intentionality so that he has more conscious choice about his behavior. Freedom and choice have a psychogenic origin in that an appropriate mode of behavior is feasible only to the extent that it is conceptualized as a possibility; otherwise, it does not exist as a behavioral alternative.

In working with patients one needs to be mindful of the implicit assumptions a patient makes about himself and others. These assumptions are acted upon as if they were valid and proven without being critically tested. Such habits of thought lock the person into a limited repertoire of alternatives which are frequently inappropriate to the demands of the situation in which he finds himself. The nature and quality of his beliefs not only influence the strategies a person enacts but reinforce the continuity of the strategy long after the behavior ceases to be efficacious. Beliefs integral to the maintenance of present behavior require critical evaluation before the individual is prepared to modify his strategies.

A cardinal principle of the existential view of human conduct is that none of us does anything unless he wants to. Whatever course of action we take, we have concomitantly made a choice. A course of action is chosen because we regard that particular choice preferable to other courses of action which we conceptualize as open to us. Many of us believe that we are burdened with insoluble problems because we refuse to believe that we have any choice about improving the courses of action open to us. We prefer to assume that society and other convenient external agents dictate the rules that we *must* live by and the benefits we may receive from interpersonal dealings.

Responsibility, the most crucial personal strategy a person assumes, concerns the accountability he takes for his thoughts, feelings, and actions. The concept of responsibility is important to the therapist not in its moral, ethical, or legal sense but as a personal strategy. The therapist is interested in the individual's functional intent or goal-direction as he takes accountability for his thoughts, feelings, and actions in obtaining satisfaction, seeking the meaning of his experience, and creating security for himself.

There are four types of responsibility from which an individual may choose to take account of his behavior. Two types demonstrate responsible behavior in the legal, moral, and psychological senses, and the other two demonstrate irresponsible behavior.

In the first type of irresponsible behavior, the individual attributes the misfortunes and difficulties he encounters to external causes. The person who employs this form of irresponsible behavior is highly skilled in demonstrating the unreliability of others. He resists improving the conditions he complains about because he bemoans his weakness and the interference and betrayal by others. He uses this rationale to fortify and protect himself against others through manipulation, mendacity, and antisocial mechanisms. The reader will recognize these psychodynamics as those of persons generally referred to as having a character disorder or a deviant life style.

The case of a talented musician in his late twenties illustrates the philosophical stance of a person with irresponsible behavior. This young man with superior intellectual functioning began individual psychotherapy with me after having been in and out of psychiatric hospitals, maximum security installations, and a number of self-help groups for almost a decade. Mr. Loschile had a history of drug abuse, alcholism, suicidal attempts, and assaults on hospital staff and fellow patients. He bemoaned the fact that he could not attain the musical career he yearned for and for which he seemed destined in his youth. His strategies in therapy were toward having the therapist figure out why he was a "misfit", why his plans never worked out. He, on the other hand, strenuously avoided exploring what he could do about his adverse situation in the present. Asked what he wanted from therapy, he recited a long list of platitudes. When told to spend his time outside the session thinking about and formulating his plans by discussing his goals with other patients and staff or even by looking up the information, he fled from therapy, claiming he was being expected to do too much, and never returned. Mr. Loschile blamed his assaultive behavior on his being forced to live with anti-Semitic, illiterate blacks who were envious of his intelligence and talent and, as a result, antagonistic toward him. The attainment of musical success was an interesting kind of personal strategy for Mr. Loschile. It meant to him that others would then have to come up to his requirements and he did not have to accommodate himself to theirs. He refused to acknowledge his own prejudices (his core attitudes about blacks) which influenced his being attacked. For instance, he goaded others into fights but was himself a poor pugilist. He felt that no one had ever suffered as deeply or to the extent that he had. "If they did, they couldn't stand it. They would have committed suicide," he claimed. He felt cursed by an angry god and parents who, in adopting him, were incapable of expressing the love and affection he craved.

His "acting out" generally began with his inability to gain or maintain a goal which he believed would provide him with stability: a job in a jazz combo in a local tavern, "making it" with a student nurse, or avoiding getting caught drunk or high on drugs so that he wouldn't lose his hospital privileges. He would become upset and repeatedly tell himself: "I'm weak. I can't stand anxiety. I feel so anxious I don't know what to do. I can't stand it any longer. It is unfair to expect me to endure it. I can't find tranquility inside me. I need relief from something outside."

He would then forge a physician's name to a prescription sheet and be his own doctor, gaining the immediate and transitory relief which would keep him alive until the next crisis in his life. Because he had a core attitude that no one understood him, he felt justified in his personal strategy of refusing to heed other's counsel and blaming his misfortunes on others.

The second type of irresponsible stance occurs when the individual disassociates what is occurring in the external world, insulating it from his inner life. By choosing not to seek goods and services from others, he abnegates the need to be accountable to society. He has learned to reject other people as either unwilling or incapable of satisfying his needs. Instead of orienting himself toward developing those psychosocial skills that are rewarded by society, he creates his own fantasized relationships which he has in some measure convinced himself satiate his every need. Through hallucination, delusion, and other types of disordered thinking, he creates relationships which he has better success managing and making meaning of than he had with reality-oriented relationships. People in the real world have not reacted appropriately to his needs—objects in his fantasy do a much better job. Typically, the person being described had been required to assume adult responsibilities, albeit if only to care for and feed himself, at a very early age. His inability to be an adequate adult early in life caused him to believe that being an adult was an impossible task for him. His discipline had been inconsistent. He rarely received appreciation for his efforts and, to his everlasting puzzlement, was frequently rewarded for personal attributes and events that he had little or no control over. His resentment toward those who cared for him could never be openly expressed nor was he ever permitted to express strong feelings of any sort. The expression of emotion, he was led to believe, was inappropriate and wicked.

Mrs. Laecuna was referred for psychological evaluation because of marked impairment in her memory functioning and serious alcholism. Psychological evaluation suggested that Mrs. Laecuna had suffered organic impairment due to alcoholism although the impairment was not extensive enough to account for her severe loss of memory. She denied ever having more than two or three beers at a time. For many years she had rarely ventured outside her home and she expressed no interests except in straightening up around the house. Her affect was bland.

That she regarded her husband as ineffectual and abusive seemed evident. Nonetheless, no strong affect or any resentment toward her husband was expressed during the interview. On the other hand, during her periods of "excusable irresponsibility" (drinking bouts), she was reported to have been both physically and verbally abusive toward her spouse. Her long periods of confusion following alcoholic ventures appear to be less involved with neurological mechanisms than with a defense mechanism syntonically supportive of her personal integrity. By disassociating her "improper" behavior through alcoholic bouts she was able to express strong emotion and yet assuage her guilt afterward. We recognize these psychodynamics as those of persons with severe psychopathology.

In the third type of accountability, a person holds himself responsible and blames himself for everything that happens to himself and others. Such a person is imbued with self-incrimination and is ambi-

valent and vacillating. He has considerable difficulty making decisions for himself and prefers, therefore, that others make decisions for
him. He even seems to enjoy being induced to act in self-defeating
ways as if this were a form of revenge on those figures who are too
powerful to confront directly. He hopes to induce guilt in others for
leading him astray. But he seems to be overly altruistic, compelled to
give up his own satisfactions in the interest of others. The person described reveals his lack of personal responsibility by insisting that he
has no choice, that social responsibility must take precedence over his
own interest. If he did otherwise, people would think poorly of him
and this would make life more unbearable than it already is. These
psychodynamics we recognize as those of the oversocialized or neurotic person.

Miss Boring was seen for chronic depression. She had a verbal IQ
of 126 and was irregularly employed as a registered nurse. Miss
Boring found it difficult to refuse the excessive demands placed upon
her. She would work extra shifts although tired and weary, and the
other nurses found her passivity convenient for taking advantage of
her. Miss Boring would conscientiously tell herself that her work was
important, that patients needed her attention. But, on the other
hand, she disregarded the spirit of her endeavor. In a passive–aggressive way she vindictively tried to retaliate for those who made demands upon her by turning in a mediocre performance. Her patients
were, therefore, not getting the proper care and she lost several jobs.
Asked what she wished to derive from psychotherapy, she spoke of
wanting her depression removed.

Further discussion revealed that she assumed that even if her
depression were lifted, life still would be bleak and hopeless. In her
thinking she regarded her disabilities as being inflicted by some external force or due to a characterological lack. Her chronic depression
seemed to have been caused by her resentment about not attaining
the marital–sexual life she felt she deserved. About this matter she
was rather ambivalent. She felt that she had much to offer a loved
one, but no one ever appreciated her. On the other hand, she felt that
she must have done something dastardly to deserve her unhappy fate
and portrayed herself as helpless, incomplete, and needy. Because she
could not understand why she was being punished, she felt she could
in no way modify her situation.

The final category of accountability is that of the person who accepts responsibility for his own thoughts, feeling, and actions. He
does not feel his actions to be determined by what others expect of
him or by other forces beyond his control, but to be of his own

choosing. He is willing to take the consequences of these actions. He is never compelled to act but behaves in ways that are in his own best interest. Accepting responsibility for one's behavior does not mean accepting blame for one's actions. It means both seeking to find out why he often acts in ways which are not in his best interest and then striving to change these tendencies by first coming to understand them. Other people are not expected to change for him. Because he is unhappy, in need, or distressed, it is he who must do something to change this situation. This stance is, of course, only an ideal, in the sense that Maslow's self-actualizing individuals are ideals. We refer to this stance as one of "individual, autonomous responsibility." This position serves as an ego-ideal for the existential-analytic psychotherapist.

The clinician must know into which of the four categories discussed above the patient's personal strategies fall. The patient's willingness and ability to take responsibility for the course of his life and the therapist's willingness to relegate to the patient responsibility for his behavior determine the manner in which therapeutic intervention is attempted. In my view, successful amelioration cannot commence prior to the patient's assuming responsibility for his own existence. A consideration of the category of accountability into which the patient most closely fits to a large degree should determine the treatment best suited for working with his disabilities.

The person who takes no responsibility for his life proceedings, who does not seek help when he encounters difficulty meeting his needs or is unwilling to modify aberrant ways of meeting his needs, generally becomes a nuisance or menace to himself and society. The paranoid schizophrenic who inflicts his vengeance upon those who don't accept his beliefs and the drug addict who steals to support his habit are sooner or later incarcerated. Since they are unable or unwilling to accept responsibility for what happens to them, it is pointless to expect them to correct their situation on their own. In these cases, the most desirable treatment is direct environmental change; the person in treatment has to develop new personal strategies in order to mediate anxiety or has to undergo the stress without relief. Thus, the drug addict who habitually uses drugs when feeling denigrated must find another way to assuage his anxiety or must suffer the discomfort unmitigated while incarcerated in a detoxication program. The environmental change technique is further described in Chapter 10.

Some individuals seek help in indirect ways because they are not altogether agreed within themselves that they need help. They prefer instead that others should change to ameliorate their unhappiness. They vacillate between seeking help and resisting it because they are uncertain about undergoing additional duress. Such individuals go to psychodrama demonstrations, join sensitivity groups, participate in discussion and theatre arts clubs, attend lectures on psychological and philosophical topics because, they claim, they are bored by the routine of their lives. In this category are addicts who join detoxication programs but refuse psychotherapy and persons who push their spouse or child into seeking psychological assistance but deny need of such assistance for themselves.

These people are unwilling to risk giving up their personal strategies without proof and guarantee of functioning better. Because they are unwilling to take responsibility for committing themselves to a risky venture, they are best approached by the trial and suggested change modality described in Chapter 10. Having made some behavioral modification, even on a symptom basis, from the advice and guidance of an expert and subsequently experiencing relief from so doing, they are more willing to undergo exploration of their attitudes and feelings. Psychodramatic techniques described in Chapter 11 and sensitivity training discussed in Chapter 7 are frequently useful modalities for the people described above.

The insight change modality is designed for those persons who traditionally have been the stock-in-trade of the private practitioner. They are people who accept responsibility for their discomfort (even if doing so is frequently a compulsive ploy). To the extent that they are able to internalize themselves as the creator as well as the creature of their difficulties they seek to explore their personal strategies by insight and self-generative modalities. Such persons do well in the existential-analytic group described in Chapter 8.

> "No patient can be expected to drop all his defenses and reveal himself except in the presence of someone whom he believes is for him, and not for a theory, dogma or technique."

S.M. Jourard
The Transparent Self

EXISTENTIAL ANALYTIC GROUP PSYCHOTHERAPY—3

THE ASOCIAL ROLE OF THE PSYCHOTHERAPIST

William Shofield has described psychotherapy as a "purchase of friendship." This suggests that at least some psychotherapists and their patients regard therapy as a social exchange in which the therapist acts as a surrogate for the warm, considerate, accepting friends the patient is unable to obtain outside therapy. Research findings suggest that ingredients such as warmth and acceptance on the part of the therapist may be essential to successful outcomes. However, several qualitative differences exist in the kind of relationship the professionally trained psychotherapist establishes with his patient and the way a considerate person behaves in a social situation. The considerate person participates in a conversation by responding to what the other is manifestly stating, placing the other at ease and encouraging him to express freely his ideas and feelings.

An existential-analytic psychotherapist is not interested in maintaining a social relationship with his patients. Polite social conversation impedes access to significant underlying feelings and processes.

To the casual observer, the psychotherapeutic relationship may appear to be asocial. Frequently the patient speaks without reply from the therapist; at other times the patient will ask a question and the therapist may reply with a question of his own. An observer might wonder if the therapist is trying to startle the patient or perhaps conjure him into disclosure of material the patient had not intended to discuss. I am referring to situations in which the patient speaks on one topic and the therapist suddenly interrupts and indicates to the patient that he is actually speaking covertly about an entirely different issue. The effective psychotherapist responds less to manifest levels of communication than to nonverbal, symbolic, and contradictory messages as well as to what is not said (and which the therapist infers is being avoided) in the patient's communication. An example may be illustrative.

Mr. Thomas, a loquacious but mild federal government worker, was a member of one of my sensitivity training groups held for young adults in a Jewish community center. Mr. Thomas refused to permit anyone (least of all, himself) to express anger at anyone else. He insisted that getting angry was childish. It was important, he indicated, to be in control of one's feelings. His attitude infuriated the other participants. His wife also was furious at him for trying to placate her strong feelings, he reported. The group leader pointed to Mr. Thomas's fingers rhythmically tapping on his chair when the other participants became impatient with him. Only when the meaning of his nonverbal behavior was discussed was Mr. Thomas able to explore the notion that feelings cannot always be controlled.

Existential-analytic psychotherapy is a process within an interpersonal relationship which is intended to allow the patient to become aware of what he strives to be. What he strives to be is often irrationality formulated, unsystematic, and unworkable in regard to the patient's present skills and resources and the information he possesses about himself and his environmental opportunities. The person seeking ameliorative attention is frequently preoccupied with a situationally insoluble goal. This is evident in the case of Mr. Thomas whose goal of being mature meant to him to always be in control. The existentialist's concern with environmental factors should not be interpreted as infringing on the patient's exercise of choice. The environment rarely prevents an individual from being that which he intends to be (notwithstanding current emphasis on social deprivation). An individual lacks the ability to actualize himself to the extent that he is unwilling to accept himself as authentic and worthwhile and therefore as capable of shaping environmental conditions. That which a person intends to be becomes at once accessible to realistic endeavor the moment the person regards his intentions as a legitimate possibility. Stunted ambition, failures in life, dysfunction behavior belie a compromise with oneself as an authentic person. Mr. Thomas had relinquished hope of securing the openness of maturity; he had settled for the mere outward appearance of a mature adult. Mr. Thomas revealed that he felt he was capable of neither attaining nor deserving of the things he sought.

The therapist enables the patient to explore the compromises he makes with himself by getting him to describe his actions in considerable detail, comparing seemingly unconnected events, present and past; in action, choice and value are implicit. If we assume that a behavioral act is chosen, then we must assume that it is preferable to other possible actions. It is chosen because the conditions of the situation dictate certain rules and rewards for that course of action. The therapist seeks to enable the patient to spell out these situational demands to which he has responded over such a long period that they have resulted in entrenched attitudinal stances toward himself and the external world. Mr. Thomas long ago had repressed the need to express himself openly. Only after having spelled out the rules and regulations that shape his behavior can the patient realistically evaluate them. The standards that he lives by may have been acceptable earlier in life (for example, in childhood), but they have not been reviewed, re-evaluated, and appropriately revised.

Self-concealment, defensive censoring, and alert role- and game-playing require much attention, intelligence, and energy. The vigilant maintenance of facades, masks and barriers drains resources which could otherwise be put to work in enjoyable living. This is one of the central points of Jourard's *The Transparent Self* in which he discusses the high cost of guardedness in terms of psychological "dispiritation" and physical illness. (T.C. Greening)

A SYSTEMATIC VIEW OF PSYCHOTHERAPY

Most present-day dynamic therapeutic systems, regardless of whether they stress historical or ahistorical factors, are concerned with conscious or repressed determinants, or with directive leadership or nondirectiveness on the part of the therapist, and are ordered by four basic steps directed toward identifying, contacting, and working through dysfunctional behavior. These steps are:

1. *Description.* The ameliorative process is initially directed toward

enabling the patient to describe what it is that he does that is dysfunctional to him.

2. *Explanation.* The ameliorative process is next directed toward enabling the patient to understand what the behavior that he has described currently is doing for him. Most patients who request
treatment seek to be understood as they are. They come to treatment
not to be made different, not to be compelled or taught how to act differently, but to become more accepting of what they already are. I
will leave the ontological issue aside as to whether successful amelioration involves an unfolding process (the further development of latent personality potentialities) or a change process (the internalization of new role and attitudinal models). As for inducing improved
psychosocial functioning (which I assume is the general goal of psychotherapy), experienced clinicians would point out that an individual does not change dysfunctional aspects of himself until he
comes to accept and understand himself as he is. Otherwise he would
dysfunctionally expend his energy in denying or defending himself
against what he is. (Goldberg, (a), 1970)

The necessity of understanding oneself is illustrated in the case
of Abe, a patient in one of my groups. Abe is a scientist with a brilliant mind and the needs of a child because his needs were not met at
the proper time in his development. He still has a child's curiosity—
the need to know purely and simply, without any commitment to ever
use the knowledge in his own or others' actualization or happiness.
He has been "turned on" by Laura, a young school teacher who is a
patient in his group. She is everything he has ever dreamed of as a
female to romanticize. He is unable to approach her, except intellectually; he asks hundreds of "what if" questions designed to embellish
his fantasy world with her. Abe didn't regard his questions as academic until Laura called him on the emptiness of his academic
queries. She stated that she was ready to go as far as he wanted in a
relationship, but he must take the initiative in order to make the relationship possible. Abe was caught off-guard. He was forced to
grapple with the shallowness of his fantasized images of "the perfect
woman." Laura has desires of her own and she is real! If Abe wants
her he has to come to terms with the realistic demands of a relationship with a woman. He can no longer continue to ask only to understand, he must also learn how to do. Abe needs to accept himself as
being strong as well as intelligent. He had survived a bizarre childhood but now that is past, and he must use his strength to go forward
rather than to guard against the encroachment of the past.

The experienced clinician knows that behavioral pathology may be studied as a series of contradictions. The clinician has been likened to a scientist who studies the subject and his situation under a microscope by alternating the lens to focus macroscopically and microscopically. What psychotherapists try to help the patient reveal for himself is not only what his present patterns of behavior achieve for him, but conversely, his feelings and fantasies about what would happen if he discontinued his present behavioral patterns. In this endeavor the patient and therapist come to a more profound appreciation of the patient's fears and strivings by using a language which is unfettered by ambiguity and which conveys the intricacies of emotions for which the patient heretofore has been unable to find words. Such a venture is best begun by focusing on immediate experiential concerns rather than recasting past events in an archeological search. This process can be described in phenomenological terms as "looking in on a reality that is looking out." The existential-analytic therapist's task is to help the patient disclose the nature of that reality.

"The process of psychotherapy is essentially a process of coming to know one's self as a result of making oneself known to another, the therapist [and other patients when in a group]." (T. C. Greening) This process is delineated in the following material.

3. *Exploration.* Patient and therapist explore other behavioral alternatives which achieve the satisfactions the patient seeks, but at a psychologically smaller cost than the strategies used in the past. Frequently new compromises are found which are more viable than the personal strategies he currently employs. By working through his fears and fantasies about himself and others, the patient discovers more realistic compromises. Only when Abe was willing to share his deeply guarded fantasies about women could he learn that he had more to offer than intellectual acumen.

4. *Action.* During the action stage in psychotherapy, insight is converted into deed. In order to achieve this, emotion must be judiciously evoked. The evocation of deeply experienced feelings helps foster the processes and goals toward which therapy is directed. Feelings are essential to human action because when in contact with our emotions we have an unswaying gauge of what we want of life. Only when Abe became in touch with his feelings was he in a position to choose to go on and have an adult relationship or stay behind as a child and guard against the past. Nonetheless, Abe's awareness of choice is not sufficient, he can only become that which he is through action. To know a person I must appreciate not only what he experiences but, more importantly, what he has done to make his life more congruent with his feelings. Emotion, however, gets in the way of constructive action

when it is overvalued in and of itself. The psychotherapist, therefore, does more than encourage emotion. He helps the patient enjoy the vitality of his emotions in constructive action.

VALUES IN PSYCHOTHERAPY

As psychotherapy sessions progress I become increasingly more appreciative of the values and intentionality of the patient as he makes himself known to me. My attention is with what the other wants and expects of me and himself. In groups, the existential-analytic psychotherapist notes how the patient delineates by word and deed the way the other group members may be of help to him at that point in time. As patients begin to explore what they want of someone else they sometimes painfully must come to grips with what they are currently experiencing. They may seek safety from their current feelings by reverting to what they have cognitively figured out about themselves in the past. Abe could remember every bad thought he ever had about himself. Laura knew why every relationship with a man had failed in the past. It is important therefore, in existential-analytic therapy to:

minimize abstract, theoretical, or fact-oriented discussions
which have little relationship to the on-going relationship.
. . . the delayed reporting of feelings which are not being currently experienced and which are not relevant to the present
process of the relationship. (T.C. Greening)

The primary concern in an existential-analytic group is learning to deal with members' immediate concerns. Participants are encouraged to establish relationships with others in the group, letting the others know what they want from them and how successfully the others handle their needs and expectations.

EXISTENTIAL-ANALYTIC PSYCHOTHERAPY: A STUDY OF ACTION

The patient has the right to seek to be that which he intends. The existential-analytic therapist realizes this while also recognizing that every action has consequences. The therapist can be most valuable to the irresponsible patient by helping him explore the consequences of the course of action he wishes to take so that he does not have to take the beatings he has experienced in the past when he chose to be unprepared. An overly socialized patient who exhibits a "failure of nerve" and whose critical superego has crippled the healthy striving of the ego, is urged to trust his senses, to act more on feeling than by reason. In the enabling process the therapist assumes an array of hats: he is a test of reality—he lets the patient know how he is experienced in an interpersonal encounter; he is a surrogate and representative of society—he takes the stance of significant persons in the patient's life, helping him deal with them; the therapist is also an expert in communication and negotiation—he helps the patient learn skills in understanding his own feelings and those of others, to speak more meaningfully and precisely, and to develop, as Theodor Reik has described it, a "third ear" for what others are communicating.

Nonetheless, the understanding of oneself and others is, in and of itself, an insufficient goal for existential-analytic psychotherapy. The therapist, in helping the patient understand interpersonal rule setting and decision making, must additionally teach the patient how to negotiate for the interpersonal commodities he seeks from others. Existential-analytic psychotherapy has the general goal of enabling the patient to develop interpersonal competence in addition to personal mastery. Realistically, one is impossible without the other.

We are all keenly aware that the therapeutic process is not a smooth, step-by-step progression. There are innumerable road blocks. These impediments to therapeutic progress are referred to as resistance. An example follows.

Sally mentions to the therapist that she hasn't heard from her insurance company which reinburses her for psychotherapy. On this basis she claims that she cannot pay her bill on time. The therapist calmly inquires if she is asking for his permission to call her insurance company. On second thought, he asks if Sally is asking to be excused from her scheduled payment because she has been irresponsible in following up her obligations. The therapist informs Sally that accepting a late payment in this situation would be condoning her irrresponsibility.

THE EXISTENTIAL-ANALYTIC VIEW OF PATIENT RESISTANCE

Central to the issue of values in psychotherapy is the view taken of the patient's refractory attempts to relinquish habitual and self-defeating behavioral patterns. In my view, resistance to therapeutic work is evoked from the patient's need to ward off the therapist's intrusion into his value system. The resistance phenomenon belies a value clash between therapist and patient. Such a clash is an inevitable dynamic of human encounter. It is also the *sine qua non* of ameliorative endeavor without which therapy is a pale imitation of reality. In resistance, the patient indirectly is conveying to the therapist that values important to becoming the person he seeks to be or, at least, to the maintenance of his current equilibrium are being suppressed and threatened by the therapist's obtrusiveness.

A healthy organism resists violation of its integrity. Resistance to intrusion *per se* is a healthy coping mechanism. Defenses, in and of themselves, are not pathological. Psychopathology, in my view, cannot be discerned on the basis of any one behavioral act or tendency. Behavior may be adjudged pathological only when it is overly persevering and constrictly adhered to. For example, enlightened sexologists have long pointed out that no one kind of sexual activity is aberrant in and of itself. It is aberrant when it becomes the only form of activity from which the individual is able to obtain sexual gratification. Correspondingly, disabled patients have restricted their conceptualization of themselves and others to a limited range of means for seeking satisfaction and obtaining security. Unfortunately, the person who finds his way into psychotherapy is generally someone who has experienced himself as unable to confront others directly in order to make his needs and well-being known. Abe, as we have seen, was one such person. Learning how to confront others and cope with their intrusiveness is a vital task of psychotherapy. Hence, the patient who "acts out" or passively–aggressively avoids facing up to the therapist's imposition is, instead, compromising with his own values and his own well-being. "Acting out" suggests that the actor experiences some need which he is unable to express in a manner which will lead to satisfactory resolution.

The occurrence of resistance in psychotherapy indicates that the patient and therapist have reached a crucial juncture in their interpersonal encounter. The therapist must help the patient to experience his difficulty with external intrusion and learn to handle it in a constructive manner. Concurrently, the patient must alert the therapist that he is experiencing a personal difference with him and wishes assistance in dealing with his feelings. Too often in the past the patient has become overwhelmed with his inability to express disagreement with others. As a result, he has chosen to cherish his differences with others as too sacred to question. He therefore in past interpersonal encounters refused to examine his images of himself and others in an open and negotiable manner. We can expect the same reluctance in the relationship with his therapist. The therapist who is able to help the patient tolerate the experience of opposition to others does so by personally demonstrating that the expression of opposition will not cast the patient adrift from human company.

Interpretating the patient's behavior as "resistance," as "nonsense that must be terminated immediately!" casts the patient into the subordinate role of one who must weaken his will and buckle under to those who oppose him. Leslie Farber (1966, pp. 6-7) indicates that Otto Rank, in contrast to his early psychoanalytic colleagues, recognized the struggle of will between patient and analyst as a vital component of psychotherapy.

> The patient responds (according to Rank) to the analyst's will with his own "counter-will." He found it unfortunate that psychoanalysis evaluated this protest morally as "resistance," which had to be dispelled through the examination of the transference, thus failing to utilize "the actual therapeutic value" contained in the expression of "counter-will." The goal of constructive therapy is not the overcoming of resistance but the transformation of the negative will expression (counter-will)—into positive and eventually creative expression.

The existential-analytic therapist supports the patient's prerogative to seek whatever he wishes to be. Even the best intentions, however, will not prevent the therapist's values from shaping his stance toward the patient. The inevitable clash of values has, of course, serious consequences for the therapeutic relationship. The therapist, by dealing immediately and directly with his own reactions to behavior which he himself has strong feelings and convictions about, conveys to the patient that the patient's concerns are not his alone to solve. Problems, tensions, and strains in the therapeutic relationship are issues which can be openly and mutually dealt with. Strains within the relationship involve both patient and therapist, deeply and personally. Such conflicts in therapy are not procedural issues which require simply technical manipulation.

Having encountered a resistance, the therapist and patient together explore ways of discovering the source—be it "in" the therapist or the patient or, more likely, in the conditions of their interrelationship. Sometimes the conflict can be objectified tangibly and then dealt with.

Irving had made considerable progress in a private therapy group after initially being reluctant to commit himself to the group because, as he said, he didn't have enough serious problems to justify twice-a-week group therapy. During the course of therapy some serious doubts about his marriage had arisen. After some struggle to discuss them in the group, he seemed to reach an impasse. Asked to describe his impasse Irving, a bright and articulate person, did so vividly. Asked what he would like to do about his impasse he refused to commit himself. The therapist leaped to his feet, seized a tissue from the table in front of Irving and dropped it in Irving's lap. "This is your impasse," said the therapist, "What are you going to do with it?" Irving chose first to dash it against the wall (the strongest display of feelings he had ever exhibited in the group). He then ripped up the tissue and shared it with each of the group members. Each of us explored with Irving how we wished to deal with that part of his "distress" he had shared with us.

The most important aspect of the experience was the sharing of intimate concern about Irving rather than the specific content of the exchanges. Being involved in a mutual endeavor is more gratifying to a patient than being an object upon whom surgery is performed by means of analysis and interpretation. When a patient's behavior is responded to immediately and is taken as real, rather than as a symbolic facade, the idea of disclosing painful material becomes less threatening to the patient and the groundwork is laid for future gains.

THE THERAPIST AS ROLE MODEL

The claim of the humanistically oriented therapist that he above all must be a "real" person to the patient has reached the point of overstatement and cliché. Can the therapist ever be unreal in therapy —how can he be anyone other than who he is? Even in assuming a role a person chooses to reveal certain aspects of himself. It is inconceivable to regard a therapist as a blank "projective screen." What he chooses to be is predicated upon his own values. In this sense the detached, withholding therapist is real. Unfortunately, he is too prevalent! In assuming an aloof, impersonal role he has chosen to avoid responding to other aspects of himself which cause him anxiety.

It is important to recognize that whatever way a therapist behaves in therapy, his behavior is intended to deal not only with the patient but also with his own anxiety. This kind of behavior is not necessarily counter-indicated. All of us act in ways that are designed to avert our own anxiety. Some of us, for example, become therapists because we need to feel helpful; we may be desperately trying to counter and deny our own dependency needs or be suffering from an array of other anxieties. Thomas Szasz (1965, p. 42) points out:

> ... Freud abandoned the use of mild faradic currents for treating neurotics, not merely because it was not very effective, but because he could not stand the fraud implicit in it. Similarly, he disliked hypnosis, not only because it did not

work well enough, but because he realized that his personality was unsuitable for it; the authoritarian–intrusive role
of the hypnotist was not for him. In developing the psychoanalytic method of treatment, Freud followed his own needs,
not the needs of his patient . . . Harry Stack Sullivan's modification of analytic technique reflects his need for a more
personal relationship with patients than is possible in analysis. Sullivan was a lonelier and more isolated person than
Freud; he used his patients as companions and friends to a
greater extent than did Freud or the early Freudians.

What is important is not that the therapist is trying to avert his
own anxieties but that he realize that it is he who is uneasy and it is
he who strives to become more comfortable. Only insofar as the therapist recognizes his own discomfort is he able to negotiate with the
other in an open manner to make the relationship comfortable for
both parties. If the patient is doing something that disturbs the therapist, he has a right to know about it. Openness and congruence are
essential in therapy, for without them the exercise of choice and responsibility is difficult, if not impossible, to induce. The goal of existential-analytic therapy is a more conscious ability to make choices,
even if, for example, the choice is to terminate therapy. (It is unfortunate that many therapists assume that the goal of psychotherapy is
to perpetuate treatment.) The therapist, through his disclosure and
congruity, serves as a role model for the patient. Openness, however,
creates anxiety for both therapist and patient because of the uncertainty of knowing how to respond to new aspects of one another.
Openness transforms the therapeutic relationship by requiring each
person to take a new stance toward the other.

THE PSYCHOTHERAPIST'S EXISTENTIAL CHOICE

The more unstructured a group is, the more it evokes a projective
screen for activating disturbed and unresolved emotional proclivities
in each of the group members. The traditional psychoanalytic circle,
therefore, creates a "patient" of each member of the group. This is
regarded as good psychoanalytic therapy. It is not good existential-
analytic psychotherapy. The detached therapist fosters a lack of involvement in those he is treating. The existential-analytic therapist,
rather than serving as a mirror or as a figure from some other time
and place, uses his own experiences as an assessment of what is transpiring before him. The existential-analytic therapist relies upon his
direct experience with the patient rather than on textbooks.

An integrative (in contrast to a transitory) experience does not transpire between patient and therapist unless the patient experiences it as "real." It is real to the extent that each person treats the other as he would any other significant person in his life. If the patient is to avert transference distortions, the therapist correspondingly must curb his predilection for regarding the patient in a stereotypic manner. He must free himself from concentrating on the patient aspects of the person, otherwise the healthier aspects of his personality are "frozen." He must respond to the patient's emotional needs, not simply render those needs intelligible by interpretation. If psychotherapy is a process within a relationship, the relationship must be nurtured so that the enabling process can be activated. The mediating gestures and supportive concern of the therapist and group members foster the openness and trust that must precede psychotherapeutic growth.

Elaine, a patient in a private group, had strong counterdependent defenses. She was sensitive and responsive to the needs of the others, but reluctant to share her burdens with them. I found it helpful to say to her in a session in which she wrestled with a decision to make a commitment to a man still responsible to a wife and family: "My feeling is that you and your friend can work out this situation by yourselves. I am more concerned with your reluctance to bring your burden to the group and share it with us."

I believe that the rationale for making mediating interventions deserves more attention in the psychotherapy literature than it has received. High-powered theory for making interpretations already exists in abundance. Too often, interpretation becomes surgery that creates a disabled patient. Mediating responsiveness fosters an autonomous enabling process in the other. In an encounter where the other is treated as an impersonal object, he feels manipulated and exploited, and tension and strain occur.

When the patient senses that the therapist is willing to negotiate how the patient is to be regarded, he is free to reveal himself as he seeks to be known. When both agents can cast aside reactive fears and the excessive need for safety they can accommodate themselves to each other and explore their interpersonal domain, each coming to know himself and the other with increased meaning. This is expressed in Carl Roger's (1961, pp. 345–46) conception of the existential choice:

> In the actual relationship both the client and the therapist
> are frequently faced with the existential choice, "Do I dare to
> communicate the full degree of congruence which I feel? Do I

dare match my experience, and my awareness of that experience, with my communication? Do I dare to communicate myself as I am or must my communication be something less than or different from this?" The sharpness of this issue lies in the often vividly foreseen possibility of threat or rejection. To communicate one's full awareness of the relevant experience is a risk in interpersonal relationships. It seems to me that it is the taking or not taking of this risk which determines whether a given relationship becomes more and more mutually therapeutic or whether it leads in a disintegrative direction.

To put it another way, I cannot choose whether my awareness will be congruent with my experience. This is answered by my need for defense, and of this I am not aware. But there is a continuing existential choice as to whether my communication will be congruent with the awareness I *do* have of what I am experiencing. In this moment-by-moment choice in a relationship may lie the answer as to whether the movement is in one direction or the other in terms of this hypothesized law.

THE THERAPIST'S RELATIONSHIP WITH THE PATIENT

The therapist enables the patient to become what he intends to be by respecting his potential for autonomy and self-development. He does so by not trying to protect the other from making mistakes nor does he mpose his value system upon the other. This sentiment is rooted in both existential and psychoanalytic theory: We can't force the patient to grow, we can only coax him. Only he can prefer it; no one can prefer it for him. (May, 1961)." . . . The patient should be educated to liberate and fulfill his own nature, not to resemble ourselves [the therapist]." (Freud, 1919)

The therapist presents his point of view as his own. He enters into the therapeutic relationship with the intention neither to persuade the other, nor to accept the other's behavior uncritically. He treats the other as he expects to be treated—openly and congruently. He presents himself as an autonomous person and exudes the potence of being autonomous. He proposes by his own behavior that interpersonal exchanges be made on the basis of negotiation rather than by use of threat, manipulation, or authority. He acts responsibly, accepting his behavior as being of his own choosing. He deals openly with the consequences of his choices. The existential-analytic thera-

pist also protects his own integrity and that of the therapeutic relationship. If the patient fails to act responsibly, that is, if he is unwilling to comply with the contract they have both agreed upon and
will not negotiate for another, the therapist severs the relationship
without anger or condemnation. He explains precisely the reasons for
his decision. He points out his responsibility to himself and his work
not to be exploited and manipulated by the other. Szasz (1965, p. 24)
stated the attitude clearly and succinctly: "The analyst tries to help
his client, he does not 'take care of him.' The patient takes care of
himself."

To this we may add H. F. Thomas's (1967) advice: "An important
aspect of therapy is the therapist's refusal to allow the client to use
emotional disturbance as an excuse for not facing responsibility."

In the case of Sally who did not want to pay her bill because she
failed to contact her insurance company the therapist, rather than
treating her as sick and disabled, regarded her as separable from the
therapist and his choices and therefore as responsible for her own decisions. A person's strivings for autonomy, completion, and mastery
over his own growth and development are fulfilled when he takes
responsibility for his own actions. Taking responsibility for oneself is
a prerequisite for accepting one's personal worth and finding the
meaning of one's existence.

FRUSTRATING THE PATIENT'S SYMPTOMS

Patients come to psychotherapy because they are overwhelmed
by anxiety or because they "feel nothing." In either case they are dissatisfied with the course their existence has taken. Nevertheless, at
the same time, they resist treatment. They find the therapeutic situation more benign than their daily world outside, a microcosm of
which they expected to encounter in therapy. By means of a repeti-
tion compulsion (or "life script," in Eric Berne's terminology) these
persons in distress try to mold the amorphous psychotherapy situation into a precise replica of that existential world which has driven
them to seek help. "Strange behavior!" some may say. But one cannot
easily relinquish his disturbed style of living. The daily pains have
become old friends and have accrued considerable secondary gain.
The ability to maintain strategies to handle problems and tension,
although self-defeating in the long run, does offer the patient a degree of certainty and predictability over his existence. The major obstacle to the individual's accepting responsibility for his own actions

is that doing so dissipates much of the security and certainty in his life style. If an individual accepts his actions as attempts to know and master his experiences, he is forced to face limitations in his ability. By identifying or allying himself with a superior being or force, he imagines or experiences himself gaining the protection that his finite being cannot provide him.

The common denominator in all psychiatric symptoms according to Szasz (1965, p. 14) "is the expression of loss of control or freedom." The patient has given up striving for self-actualization and satisfaction in exchange for security. He defines his symptoms as involuntary occurrences.

> Since he is not free to engage in or refrain from the particular act or experience, he usually claims that he ought not be responsible for it and its consequences. (Szasz, 1965, p. 15)

If this is an accurate statement, why then do patients become anxious and seek treatment? Though it may sound strange it is the healthier parts of their personality that "betray" them. Very disturbed people cannot admit that they need treatment or that life is not as gratifying as they would like it to be. Freud recognized this early in his study of psychopathology:

> You will remember that it was a *frustration* that made the patient ill, and that his symptoms serve him as substitute satisfactions. . . . Every improvement in his condition reduces the rate at which he recovers and diminishes the instinctual force impelling him toward recovery. But this instinctual force is indispensable; reduction of it endangers our aim . . . the patient's restoration to health . . . cruel though it may sound, we must see to it that the patient's suffering . . . does not come to an end prematurely. If . . . his suffering becomes mitigated, we must reinstate it elsewhere in the form of some appreciable privation; otherwise, we run the danger of never achieving any improvement except quite insignificant and transitory ones. (Freud, 1919)

Anxiety and discomfort, then, are rather positive and healthy signs in the patient. They serve as a communication from the deeper recess of the self that some important parts of the self are being suppressed and denied. Those parts of the self protest against the neurotic defenses and self-defeating compromises to which the patient clings. It is our task as therapists to help these healthier aspects of the self to emerge and assert themselves.

> The aim of a life can only be to increase the sum of freedom and responsibility to be found in every man . . . It cannot,

under any circumstances, be to reduce or suppress that freedom, even temporarily. (Camus, 1961, p. 240)

We must make clear to the patient that anxiety is not something
to fear and avoid but is an indication, like a toothache or high body
temperature, that something is amiss within the person or in his relation to the external environment that needs to be explored and redi-
rected. The patient's problem is not that he experiences anxiety but
that he fails to heed anxiety as a warning. Anthony Storr (*Book
World, Washington Post*, March 29, 1970) says:

> Without anxiety we . . . could [not] survive, for anxiety ena-
> bles us to anticipate danger and therefore to react appropri-
> ately to it. Anxiety, which functions properly, actually pre-
> vents neurosis; for it enables the individual to take action . . .
> which if he were not so prepared, might be overwhelming.

We therefore must help the patient live with anxiety. More importantly, the patient must learn to use anxiety as an aid in his own
amelioration. Once the person can live with anxiety, his security operations become increasingly less vital and he can devote more attention and energy to achieving satisfaction.

AN EXISTENTIAL ORIENTATION TO GROUPS

My starting point for applying the existential-analytic position to
work in groups may be traced back to the brilliant, visionary, and
existential-oriented thinking of Trigant Burrow. Burrow (1927), a
psychoanalytically trained psychiatrist, recognized early in this century that "the continuity of the group and the isolation of the individual are processes which are of their nature exclusive of one another." To treat the individual patient isolated from the community of
others from whence his neurotic symptoms were derived and from
where he deeply desires to elicit response, seemed artificial and contrary to Burrow in terms of reason and evidence. Burrow's work has
been furthered in theoretical delineation and practical methodology
by such seminal thinkers as W. R. Bion (1961) and Henry Ezriel
(1952) and, most recently, in the concept of the therapeutic community. In this concept of group, each individual entering a designed
group is asked to look at his disorder as part of a neurosis shared
generally by a social community of which his group leader or psychotherapist is also an integral part. Burrow (1927) long ago argued,
without much success with his fellow analysts, that:

> We need to rid ourselves of the idea that the neurotic indi-
> vidual is sick and that we psychopathologists [psychoana-

lysts] are well. We need to accept a more liberal societal viewpoint that permits us to recognize without protest that the individual neurotic is in many respects not more sick than we, ourselves. For we quite lose count of the circumstance that the neurotic in his private substitutions and distortions has merely to ingratiate himself in the collective confederacy of substitutions and distortions which you and I, with no less an eye to our self-protection, have had the cunning to subscribe to under the cover of our arbitrary, pseudogroup symptomatology.

CONCEPTS OF CHANGE IN GROUP PSYCHOTHERAPY

In present day approaches to amelioration there are two widely variant explanations of aberrant behavior. Reconstructive psychotherapy, most closely associated with psychoanalytic theory, posits that emotional disturbance has its root in the individual's early development. Current disturbed behavior is viewed as recasting and projecting primary relationships with significant others onto present object relations. In contrast, the human-potentials advocates maintain that the discovery of archaic roots explains little or nothing about present aberrant behavior. Behavior is best explained, they insist, by examining how the individual's future goals are being expressed in current relationships.

THE CHANGE PROCESS VERSUS THE UNFOLDING PROCESS

All ameliorative endeavors may seem as generally maintaining a position on a locus of change continuum. At one polarity, therapeutic endeavors try to modify the environmental field in order to force the organism, by willful and coercive techniques, to desist from self-defeating behavior. At the other polarity, attention is given to those interpersonal and intrapersonal processes which are conducive to self-generative behavior. (See Table 1). Difference in emphasis may be noted from the attention given to the development of relationship in reconstructive (unfolding process) therapies and the emphasis on abstinence and deprivation in rehabilitation (change process) programs. In reconstructive therapy the patient is seen as essentially fragile and considerable attention is given to developing a supportive, non-threatening relationship in which defenses are confronted gradually. In the rehabilitation programs, as well as in the encounter therapies, interventions are from the outset "brutal," intense, and reality-oriented. The direct-change position is most clearly presented in Chapter 10 and the relationship-unfolding position is best illustrated in Chapter 8.

Variance in treatment philosophies can be the result of semantic differences. For example, what is meant by "change"? Is the normal growth of an individual at age twenty as compared with the same individual at age two, a modification of a basic personality structure or a radical departure in function and structure? Each treatment philosophy also tends to emphasize particular elements in growth and development while devoting less attention to others. Is growth due to the further development of latent personality potentials or to the internalization of new role and attitudinal models? Obviously, both elements are involved but the discerning reader will observe that each treatment approach tends to stress one at the expense of the other. And perhaps as important as the considerations mentioned above, the patient population the treatment is intended for greatly varies. A universal psychological theory has yet to be propounded.

PSYCHOSOCIAL DYNAMICS

In order to understand the development of enabling processes that each therapist tries to effect in his group, some consideration of psychosocial dynamics is required.

The enabling process, with which this book is concerned, is not confined to the arena of therapeutic groups alone. Szasz (1965, p. vii) points out that:

> Psychotherapy is the name we give to a particular kind of personal influence: by means of communication, one person, identified as "the psychotherapist," exerts an ostensibly therapeutic influence on another, identified as "the patient." It is evident, however, that this process is but a special member of a much larger class—indeed, of a class so vast that virtually all human interactions fall within it. Not only in psychotherapy, but also in countless other situations, such as advertising, education, friendship, and marriage, people influence one another.

Theoretically, then, every interpersonal situation in which we enter potentially may enable us to experience, study, and eventually modify our character in relation to those influences and demands which we meet daily in our dealings with others.

TABLE 2

THE PROCESS OF AMELIORATION—CHANGE CONTINUUM

Direct change (External manipulation)	Pressure change (Confrontation)	Authoritative guidance	Trial or suggested change
Detoxification	Synanon-type group	Pastoral counselling	Psychodrama
Incarceration	Self-help group	Traditional education	Behavioral modification
Foster care	Encounter group (Esalan)		Gestalt therapy

continued

Structural integration	Emotional-Cognitive insight	Proactive striving
Psychoanalysis	Process groups	Unfolding (actualizing)
Tavistock group	Small discussion groups	Existential-Humanistic groups

Interpersonal encounters consist both of situations that are essentially spontaneous and natural and of those that are intentionally designed to serve some remedial function. Correspondingly, there are basically two types of groups, natural groups and designed groups. This book explores designed groups in depth, but some knowledge of natural groups is also helpful.

NATURAL GROUPS

A natural group is manifestly a spontaneous grouping of peers who come together to serve some personal or societal function. Functional solidarity, a fundamental principle of both natural and social order, unites solitary elements into categorical or societal aggregates.

> Man, in common with many animals, has to cooperate with others of his own species for survival. He "naturally" does things in groups, activities ranging from actively coping with a hostile animate environment to ... gather[ing] in groups of his fellows to seek solace, obtain information, or take action. (Abrahams, 1947)

Such groups are not organized by outsiders, nor are they seen by their constituents as intended to improve deficiencies in their members.

From an early age most of our existence has revolved around group life. We have eaten our meals, carried out our chores and responsibilities, prepared our studies, stretched out our future plans, engaged in play and experimentation, as well as suffered frustrations and limitations in the midst and as part of a social unit. Initially, our interactions were with family members, later with fellow members in nonkinship groupings. Since so much of our early experience occurs with others, and so many of our needs met by these same others, it is not surprising that each of us is drawn throughout life toward some rather closely knit group that is designed to meet his current pressing needs. In directing itself to these needs, each group develops its own self-regulatory norms and places premiums on certain values. As the group becomes increasingly more structured, group values and the personal needs that the members bring to the group become translated into roles. Roles may be regarded as more or less coherent and unified systems of behavior directed toward goals that both satisfy personal needs and maintain group values. The more functional certain roles are in meeting these needs and values, the more crucial they are to the survival of the group and to the maintenance of its members.

An interesting example of the importance of roles occurred in the

Brooklyn playground I investigated while a graduate student. Anthony, a fringe member of the Staccatos, a neighborhood adolescent gang, was observed during the early part of the summer to bully younger boys, steal lunch bags from the park house and, in general, to be a playground troublemaker. His low member status, despite a homogeneous background with the other members, resulted from limited skills in two of the major activities of the group: basketball and chess. I offered to coach Anthony in basketball and to teach him to play chess. His increased skill in basketball made him more attractive to the group and a more regular group member. Not a very analytic youngster, Anthony didn't take to chess and discontinued learning to play after a few days. An interesting series of events began to occur shortly thereafter. When some of the playground's chessmen were lost during the day's activities, new pieces (but of a different set) were found in the park house to replace them the next morning. Later, Anthony confessed to me that he had taken the chessmen from the local community center to replace the pieces missing from the playground. In this situation we see the differential effects of an emergent group role on Anthony's behavior. Although Anthony's behavior may be viewed as sociopathic, his role in the gang nonetheless was that of a vital social and economic resource. Anthony was the "economic gatekeeper" who regulated the gang's resources to that of other groupings. Although he neither played chess nor enjoyed watching the game, Anthony wanted his gang (with whom he now more fully identified) to enjoy the best possible facilities for their favorite activities.

Anthony's situation indicates that roles which contribute to satisfying group life are not allocated in a vacuum, devoid of the personal histories of the members. They develop day-by-day in the group's struggle to find for the member "a place in the world"; to gain for him affection and approval and the other qualities of living that the members value. To the degree that earlier groups have not fully met an individual's needs, he seeks new groups with hope of redressing the deficiency.

One of the most important personal needs the group addresses is the conceptualization of one's function in the world. In this sense, roles are developed and employed by the group to help define for the individual three basic existential concerns:

"What is life?"

"What is man?"

"Who am I?"

Groups may not answer these deep philosophical questions directly. Nonetheless, since roles within a social system are socially developed and socially sanctioned, they contribute toward a definition of what is good and what is desirable, and tend to set limits on the means of expressing these values. In short, groups establish the parameters in which their members are expected to deal effectively with their fellows. The role structure of groups, as Robert Bales has indicated, can be understood essentially as a system of solutions for the functional problems of interaction which becomes institutionalized in order to reduce the tensions growing out of the unpredictability of the actions of others.

Frankie was an important in-group member of the Staccatos early in the summer of 1962. He left the neighborhood for three weeks during the summer to take a job upstate. When he returned to the neighborhood and playground, he appeared less involved and more passive than he had earlier in the summer. He previously had no trouble "getting up" a game of basketball. If there were other Staccatos in the park they readily joined him at the basketball court as soon as he was spotted. On his return to the playground, this had abruptly changed.

During the weeks Frankie was absent from the neighborhood, there had been a serious threat to the group from another neighborhood gang. Roles, responsibilities, and lines of communication had shifted. What Frankie remembered as his neighborhood peer group was now a gang. In a sense, one could say that the Staccatos now spoke a new language. Since Frankie had not communicated with the group during this period, he could not be expected to understand the language. Until he could relate himself to the new language, he would not be able to regain his former group status. In sum, roles are shaped by group values; they are an expression of expected standards of conduct and needs of the group members. Members who cannot adapt themselves to these roles tend to be ostracized.

Thus, in the process of translating values into roles, personal interests and incentives are often sacrificed in favor of group needs. Individuals enter groups because groups can accomplish things that individuals alone cannot. To the extent that roles fail to permit group members socially sanctioned access to personally desired goals they are considered inadequate. In terms of the individual's psychosocial development, roles are inadequate when they are allocated in such a way that the unique limitations and abilities of the group members are not taken into consideration. When roles fail to regard the uniqueness of the role incumbent, they fail to conceptualize for the group member "who he is." Such roles are not internalized in the group member's self system, and they are not experienced as being useful in his becoming the person he would like to be because they fail to apply to him. Prolonged maintenance of inadequate roles leads to dysfunction and eventual disintegration of the group, and may deleteriously affect the psychological integrity of its members.

If a group is to survive, it must be in dynamic equilibrium in order to adjust the needs of the members to the demands and opportunities of the social system. These group dynamics hold true for the small, closely-knit family unit as well as for larger and more loosely connected informal friendship and vocational associations. This necessity for equilibrium held true for the Staccatos.

The Staccato gang was forced to foster among its members a commitment to one another over and beyond obligations to any other organization or person. The demand for cohesion is exemplified in the risky business of pursuing a game of basketball. Without the organizational cohesion of the gang, necessitating congregation of all the gang members on the basketball court at one time, the Staccatos seldom would have had the opportunity to use the basketball court. The park was regularly frequented by a group of Cocaies. The Cocaies were adults (a group of young men in their twenties who were habituated to cocaine drugs) while the Staccatos were yet adolescents. A youngster alone had no chance of defending himself against these men. When the men were under the influence of drugs, they frequently exhibited violent and psychotic behavior. Two or three boys shooting baskets would be exposed to irrational attack. On the other hand, when a large group of the members were assembled in one place, the Cocaies were less likely to interfere with their activity.

Experience in natural groups may be beneficial for the members or it may have dire consequences for an individual's psychosocial development as some of the examples from the adolescent gang suggest. Sociologists and anthropologists point to the character-building aspects of natural groups and suggest that social scientists should study the beneficial effects of natural groups instead of designing "artificial" groups. Clinicians and psychotherapists, on the other hand, generally emphasize the malevolent features of natural groupings, pointing out that every interpersonal situation also contains forces which potentially lead toward disturbed, irrational, and maladjusted thoughts, feelings, and actions toward ourselves and others. They maintain, moreover, that planned personal change is impractical in natural groups due to their complexity and the social scientist's lack of control over group process.

Natural groups that adequately meet the psychosocial needs of the individual are, of course, preferable to designed groups. Designed groups are formed only when important psychosocial nurture and interpersonal skills cannot readily be obtained by the individual in natural group life. Hopefully, the intelligent group leader will employ this book to improve the performance of his natural group without turning it into a contrived and "therapeutic" group. In society at large, rather than converting natural groups into therapeutic ones, we need more deeply to appreciate the affect the norms, values, and processes of natural groups have upon our well-being. When we come to this appreciation, perhaps we will lend support to the enabling process in natural groups, while at the same time exposing and ridding ourselves of the pathological and dysfunctional forces that we, as members of society, heretofore have contributed. Until then, designed groups will be necessary and will have an important place in society.

DESIGNED GROUPS

Designed groups are devised to supplement the needs that the individual's natural groups have failed adequately to address. The designed group is planned precisely to resist rules and directives that have frustrated the individual's attempts at a consistent and gratifying conceptualization of self. Designed groups enable the group members consciously to appreciate the interrelation of whatever intrapsychic discomfort is being experienced in a group interaction (uncertainty, frustration, anger, alienation) and the roles, defenses, attitudes, and sentiments group members evince in reaction to these feelings. Designed groups are intended for the individual who needs expert guidance in coming to recognize, grappling with, and finally mastering misdirected urges and behavioral tendencies in himself. They are also intended to help him develop skills for reconsidering and modifying conflictual value systems and directives in the groupings in which he has membership. Efficacious group treatment provides the individual with both personal mastery and interpersonal competence.

In general, designed groups are devised for individuals with the following deficiencies or difficulties accrued in relation to natural groups:

1. *The marginal person.* The marginal individual, because of personal (psychological, social, political, economic, or other) characteristics, has been unacceptable to the natural groups to which he has had access and as a result has been deprived of important psychosocial experience. So-called "psychotic" individuals fall predominantly in

this category but also may be a part of the other categories described below. The focal problem group described in Chapter 9 is designed for the marginal person.

2. *The deviant person.* The deviant individual has, as a member of an antisocial natural group, developed a value system and strategies for gaining his satisfactions in ways which are discordant with society at large. The confrontation group discussed in Chapter 10 has proven most successful for this population.

3. *The isolated person.* The isolated individual may have suffered not so much from insufficient personal resources as from retarded psychosocial growth. Because of a dearth of natural group stimulation at various junctures in his life, he has been prevented from maintaining continuous psychosocial growth. Psychodrama and sensitivity training groups (See Chapters 7 and 11) are frequently useful for this person.

4. *The oversocialized ("neurotic") person.* The oversocialized person generally has been exposed to natural and self-help groups which lacked sufficient resources to challenge and modify self-defeating behavioral patterns he developed in his primary (family) group experience. The existential-analytic group explored in Chapter 8 is recommended for the oversocialized person, among others.

5. *The dominant person.* The dominant individual, through employment of power, exploitation, and manipulation, has in the past subverted "healthy" psychosocial patterns from developing in the natural groups in which he had membership. Because these groups have not successfully handled him, he continues to attempt to secure his gratifications in ways discordant with others. This person may do best in either existential-analytic or in confrontation groups.

6. *The unmobilized person.* In this category belong groupings, not individuals. The unmobilized are not so much lacking in psychosocial experience as in a particular kind of psychosocial experience. They are deficient in organizational skills necessary to meet their community needs. These unmobilized persons are generally not marginal or isolated. Frequently they have experienced gratifying primary and peer group associations. On the other hand, they are often members of unstable and chaotic larger groups, such as work unions or neighborhood associations. The larger groups in which they hold membership lack clear goal direction and skillful leadership and, as a result, have not achieved viable community goods and services which have been afforded to similar large groups with more articulate and skillful leadership. Intervention in such groups is regarded not as therapeutic but as didactic and exemplary through modeling by an

expert skilled in group and organizational dynamics. Persons in this group may profit from the leadership and group dynamics skills explored in Chapter 6.

COMPARISON BETWEEN NATURAL AND DESIGNED GROUPS

A designed group generally is organized by an outside expert to address personal and social needs that have not been met in individuals' natural group associations. There are also a variety of self-help groups. The reader interested in the distinction between expert-conducted and self-help designed groups is referred to Nathan Hurvitz (1968).

The purpose of the designed group is to give attention to and explore problems and conflicts which are preventing its members from effectively functioning as individuals and as members of natural groups through observation of how they behave as members of the designed group. Natural groups, to the contrary, generally come together to carry out a concrete task. Infrequently, do natural groups of any type concern themselves with how individuals in the group function as group members. Nonetheless, both natural groups and designed groups have a task.

Natural group tasks, as I have said, are generally concrete. The task of a social group may be as fleeting as spending a few hours of abandon and delight watching a stag movie and talking with old fraternity friends in a smoker. Some group tasks are socially transcendental such as a church or parent group organizing a war protest or lines to strengthen the moral character of the community. In yet another kind of natural group, the discussion group, enduring personal enrichment is gained intellectually but other areas of the participant's personality, his affective and task-oriented capabilities, are largely ignored.

I have, of course, presented but a few instances of natural groups and their task orientation. In contrast to the concrete goals of natural groups which use limited aspects of the personality, the designed group aims for permanent and thorough modification of the whole person of the group member. Because of this large and, perhaps, grandiose goal, the task of designed groups frequently seems ephemeral and obscure.

Members in designed groups seek means of meeting societal demands and personal incentives at a smaller cost to their personal integrity, happiness, and productivity. A goal of the designed group, then, is inculcation of new personal strategies and attitudes which will make the group members' behavior in the community more effective. Personal disagreements and inter-status conflicts interfere with the attainment of a successful group product or a pleasant group climate in a natural task or social group. Conflict, on the other hand, is grist for the mill for the designed group. Consequently, what is experienced as detrimental and antagonistic in natural groups is essential for the work of a designed group. Without the opportunity to confront and deal with conflict, the members of a designed group cannot be expected to increase their skills in handling similar problems and situations in the community.

Designed groups are generally effective in influencing modification in very basic interpersonal behavior because the agendaless, simple structure of these groups force the group members to come to grips with their deep-seated reasons for coming together. This consideration is neither intentionally nor effectively dealt with in natural groups because natural groups are concerned with accomplishing concrete tasks, not with trying to understand why these tasks are considered important.

With the above discussion in mind it is important here to present several issues which an existential-analytic position suggests that group psychotherapy theroists have tended to ignore.

THE PROCESS OF SELF-HELP

One of the most important components of mental health has often been neglected in other group therapy texts. Above all else, we must help the patient help himself by encouraging his contribution to the amelioration and well-being of others. It is my firm conviction that the most ameliorative aspect of any therapeutic endeavor is not the insight accrued about one's situation or the empathy and support received from others. The experience of seeking to be helpful to others and finding one's efforts appreciated is more basically therapeutic for those whom we call emotionally disturbed but who are actually emotionally impoverished. In this regard, the concept of "preventive" mental health is misdirected; we want not to prevent something so much as to encourage something.

Mental disturbance is a deprivation and impediment in growth rather than an actual entity. The so-called emotionally disturbed person has been deprived of meaningful and significant relationships with others in the home and in the community. Each of these relationships serves as a life line which sustains and maintains the individual, keeping him alive and healthy. The fact that the community has given up hope for these citizens and has withdrawn their life lines has exacerbated their disturbance. Sociologists tend to believe that behavioral pathology in a community is directly related to the absence of responsibility citizens take for the actions, outcomes, and influences perpetrated in their community. Being of assistance to others is emotionally sustentative to those who are labeled "emotionally disturbed" as well as to those who are functioning adequately. Whereas we need to be emotionally stoked, we, in turn, need to stoke others.

One community mental health program provides the opportunity for its clients to compensate the center and the community by services-in-kind for others. For example, school teachers who receive marital counseling from the center compensate the community by tutoring students who are having problems in school at low or no cost instead of paying a fee to the center. Housewives with less formal education attend the children of other mothers who are being seen at the center, contribute to car pools, and perform other services. In this program are clients who do not earn sufficient income to pay fees and might otherwise feel guilty and self-denigrative for getting something for nothing and those who would benefit more from giving of themselves than from paying a fee. When a person is enabled to perform needed social and emotional functions for others and is recognized for doing so, he again becomes an accepted community member. (Goldberg, 1972)

ROLES PATIENTS TAKE

Sociologists and social psychologists have devoted considerable study to role behavior in groups. Group therapists have largely ignored these findings. Roles in natural and designed groups may differ but the study of roles, nonetheless, is essential to understanding events in treatment groups. My observation is that those who attend therapeutic groups assume primarily one of three roles. The role of patient is most common to a treatment group. A "patient" is a person who, because he regards himself as sick or disabled, is unable to be of help to himself and others. A second role common to therapeutic groups is that of student, or learner. A "student" doesn't regard himself as having emotional problems. He convenes with the group in order to learn what happens in therapy and to accelerate what he regards as his normal psychosocial development. He is generally too intent on observing interesting events in the group to be of much help to others. Finally, there is in all therapy groups the healer (or assistant therapist). The "assistant therapist" tries to compete with or win favor from the therapist by demonstrating his ability to be helpful to other group members.

Each of these three roles is essential to healthy psychological functioning at appropriate times. Without the emotional recognition of our dysfunctional aspects, we cannot ameliorate problem areas. Without utilizing the cognitive skills of the student, we cannot generalize from one life situation to the next or learn from the experiences of others. Finally, without the experience of being of assistance to others and being recognized and appreciated for these efforts, our interpersonal relations remain sterile and ungratifying. Persons who join designed groups are experiencing difficulty in their everyday functioning, not because they have assumed one of the three roles but because they perseveringly maintain one role in exclusion of others. Growth is facilitated in groups when these roles are welded together in a realistic manner by group members. (Goldberg, 1972)

An example of a patient who maintained a "patient" role in a group was Sally, married, in her early forties, whose husband was contemplating divorce proceedings. Sally ostensibly had come to therapy (she asked for counseling) to regain her confidence about herself. She felt that it was essential to develop some self-confidence now that she would be living on her own, having to make her own decisions. She claimed that she never had much confidence in herself, abdicating to a strong father and a self-righteous husband. She generally permitted her husband to regulate their social relationships. She missed having close friends; the friends she had were turned off by her dependency on them and her need to be constantly reassured that they liked her rather than just put up with her.

In large part, Sally's predilection in seeking therapy was to escape blame for the failure of her marriage. She conveniently informed her therapy group that her parents had a marriage very much like her own. She rhetorically questioned the possibility of recasting dysfunctional family patterns. In therapy, she fantasized that she would regain her father, who this time around would be supportive, interested in her, and reassure her that she was a worthwhile person.

Sally, according to her husband (both spouses were seen in the initial interview), had made several suicidal attempts with large doses of sedatives, accompanied by drinking. Sally tended to deny this —she had considerable difficulty taking responsibility for her own actions. Utilizing the "oversocialized" type of accountability described earlier, Sally manipulated her desperation to match how others in the situation expected her to behave. She was, for instance, a very different person when interviewed with her husband, who regarded her as a witless nuisance, than she was in an individual interview with the more supportive therapist. This change in behavior suggested that Sally would be strongly influenced by the normative strictures of the group. Sally was likely to act "sick"—feel desperate and overwhelmed—when there were no clear directives from others as to how they expected her to behave; she wanted the others to set clear limits on her behavior. To help her deal with her dependency, she needed to be put in touch with the basic choices she was exercising in the situation.

An example of a person who maintained a "student" role in treatment was Murray. Murray was about thirty when seen in treatment, married and working as a school psychologist. Murray found groups valuable in that he could identify with the therapist. He, more than anyone else in the group, assessed the therapist's style, technique, and manner. Generally, he was supportive unless he felt that the therapist had made a technical error, such as failing to intervene or misreading what a group member had said or meant. Because the therapist encouraged feedback about how he came across to the patients, Murray was able to make some impact on an "authority," something he could never do with his parents.

Murray was comfortable in the group because, as a perceptive person with clinical training, he had the tools to understand what was transpiring. On the other hand, Murray had trouble dealing with the other members' impatience with his neutrality and academic orientation to the group. They asserted that he was biding time in the group while getting a degree, picking up whatever clinical techniques he could from the therapist. Murray claimed to be concerned about his flat affect and neutrality which, he stated, were inconsistent with what he was experiencing. He insisted that he was being misunderstood. Murray had a slippery quality and could neatly sidetrack the group from staying with their confrontations. Until Murray accepted accountability for how he came across to others, he would remain neutral and misunderstood.

Elaine was a patient who essentially maintained an "assistant therapist" or "healer" role in a group. She was in her mid-twenties and separated from her husband. Symptomatically, no one in the group but the therapist for the first three months of therapy knew that she was separated from her husband and was involved with someone else. Although Elaine claimed she was in despair, she tried to maintain an image of being capable and in control of the situation. She said that she stood at a crossroad in her life and asked the group if she were sufficiently adequate to face up to making decisions. The members of the group were puzzled by Elaine's request. They perceived her as warm, responsive, and caring, and wondered why she was in treatment. This confused Elaine, who saw herself as neither warm nor capable. She was perplexed at the group's failing to see the "bitch" in her. Under Elaine's cool intellect and studied sensitivity resided an alluring warmth. The others in the group were aware of this quality. Elaine could not relinquish her need to be in control of herself because she experienced herself as incapable of giving as much as she craved in return. To guard against her insistent needs, she found it safer to give than receive.

"Too much science will kill therapy; too little science will reduce it to the status of faith-healing. The therapist must steer an uneasy course between the two, trusting to his scientific training and experience to keep him off the rocks."

S. H. Foulkes & E. Anthony
Group Psychotherapy

PRACTICAL AND TECHNICAL CONSIDERATIONS—4

The psychotherapist needs to feel that in some real sense he is a necessary and responsive agent of healing for those who petition him with their burdens of distress and uncertainty. Long years of experience and proven expertise generally do not blunt this deeply felt need.

The inexperienced therapist watches the clash and interchange of divergent and conflicting forces within a therapeutic session and marvels at the compatible and facilitating energies and behavioral modalities which are their synthesis. Struggling with uncertainty as to whether he possesses the attributes to induce these enabling processes he, of necessity, queries how these processes come about.

The experienced therapist, on the other hand, is often so busy facilitating the therapeutic process that he does not always have the opportunity to figure out why what happened in a particular session happened as it did. But as an inquiring and critical person, he, too, questions the marvelously complex and obscure process which is his daily professional endeavor. Successful as he may be relative to his colleagues, he is forced, nonetheless, to acknowledge resistive and befuddling failures in particular cases and, to a degree, with every patient.

In order to transmit to younger colleagues the essence of the procedure he has developed through the years, as well as to become more effective in what he does, he draws generalizations from his large stock of "successes" and "failures." In this way he tries to sort out the specific processes and procedures that have contributed to particular therapeutic outcomes. He can never be certain that his generalizations are substantial and valid. In canvassing his therapeutic endeavor he is forced to admit that clinical procedures that lead to successful outcomes with some patients are the same procedures and conditions which seem to stultify and antagonize effective work with other patients. At this juncture the clinician may abandon objective assessment of his therapeutic procedures as fruitless labor replete with epiphenomenological implications and revert instead to introspection in search of subjective truth.

Aside from a growing number of mechanistically oriented behaviorists and an exacting core of hard-nosed empiricists, clinicians generally posit that there is something about the existential "being together" between patient and therapist which is necessary but generally not sufficient for the patient to come to grips with himself and achieve increased psychological maturity. Advocates of the human potentials movement, however, seem to think that a therapist's "gut" feeling for people, an ability to get into the other person's skin and to empathize with him, together with the employment of interesting interpersonal games are sufficient to influence successful amelioration. The hyperbolic statements the human potentials advocates have made to this effect have yet to be convincingly demonstrated. The value of a relationship was intelligently queried by a recent social work graduate: "For two years all we talked about was how to form a relationship with a patient. What I want to know is what do you do with a relationship once you've got it?" Her concern, like mine, is that the particulars of the successful "being together" of patient and therapist are as elusive and undefined as the method of locating effective treatment procedures by objective assessment. The reader may affirm this by trying to discover the important processes from the double-talking, self-fulfilling, and inadequate accounts of the therapist's being together with his patient rendered by even those psychotherapists and social philosophers who are generally considered most articulate.

The stance taken in this book is that a balanced emphasis need be accorded to both the transactional relationship between patient and therapist and to systematic theory, clinical skills, and procedures. The latter are necessary for rendering an interpersonal relationship a therapeutic and enabling one beyond its inherent influential, educative, and affect stimulating qualities. From this perspective S. H. Foulkes and E. J. Anthony (1957, p. 148) have stated:

Too much science will kill therapy; too little science will reduce it to the status of faith-healing. The therapist must steer an uneasy course between the two, trusting to his scientific training and experience to keep him off the rocks. He must put himself in a position to exploit the conditions fully, both for therapy and research, and must deem it unsatisfactory or unethical to practice one in the absence of the other.

Research data seem in agreement that therapy is apt to be most successful when a warm, giving, optimistic therapist feels comfortable and experiences an empathetic bond between himself and his patient. (Mahrer, 1970) Therapists are not capable of relating equally well with each patient who enters their consulting room. Therapists empathize best (and probably are most effectively) with patients who have similar personalities and conflict areas. On the other hand, the therapist who has been unable to resolve his own personal difficulties in certain areas will have distorted interpersonal perception in these areas. As a result, his effectiveness will be reduced in areas which he shares with his patient and with which he has not himself successfully dealt. (Dymond, 1950; Jourard, 1959; Strunk, 1957)

Each patient is helped by particular procedures and therapeutic conditions, depending upon the state of his psychological maturity and the nature of his previous psychosocial experiences. Correspondingly, a therapist feels most comfortable and works most effectively with a technique which is congruent with the compromises and resolutions to the crisis in his own development. A therapist, therefore, cannot prepare beforehand to be a specific kind of ameliorative agent because it fulfills a conversant and sensible treatment philosophy. He can only be that which he is (himself). Having revealed himself as a being involved with the patient, he is able to find out who the patient is. From this knowledge he is better able to modify his therapeutic behavior in some desired direction. The therapist cannot decide ahead of time how to behave in therapy, insofar as he can not predict how the patient will behave. The therapist can only meet the contingencies of his relationship with the patient as this relationship develops.

The process of therapeutic endeavor is, of course, complex. In addition to the therapist's subjectively being with the patient, he must also take care of a number of specific procedural tasks. The therapist seeks to explore the identity of the unique person before him who metaphorically is in a collision course with his own history and in opposition to the conditions of his being. To know a man one must know from whence he came. The therapist first must take an adequate history in order to appreciate where the patient is in his psychological development. The therapist is interested in his previous experience in treatment and educative endeavors and in what skills he has that will facilitate therapeutic work and improved modes of functioning. This information gives the practitioner some appreciation of the kinds of interventions and learning modalities that have succeeded and those that have failed. Consideration is given to the specific goals, both long range and immediate, that the patient is seeking help with, as well as to what the therapist infers are the real reasons for the patient's entering therapy. The conflict between the patient's environment and his history may be an impediment to goal-directed behavior. The therapist must evaluate the personal and environmental resources necessary for implementing the patient's goals. In working with a patient whose marriage is an issue of discontent, for instance, it is necessary to ascertain whether or not both spouses are willing to undergo treatment, and if so, if they are willing to be seen together.

In working with an adolescent from a pathogenic home situation, it is essential to know whether the family will retain legal as well as psychological custody of the youngster, whether returning the child to the home is in his best interests, and, if not, the resources in the community which are available in assisting the youngster. In evaluating treatment goals, the patient's psychodynamics are matched to the environmental opportunities. In the above case of the child in treatment, the therapist needs to ascertain whether the child's age, psychological maturity, vocational skills, and so forth, are sufficient for functioning in a less sheltered environment or whether a protective environment is required. The therapist must also assess when, or if, other family members should be interviewed.

Once these and a myriad of additional factors are properly evaluated, the therapist has the task of recommending a *treatment plan* to the patient. The implications of this plan are worked out through a *therapeutic contract*. The therapeutic contract is essential to successful psychotherapy and therefore must not be overlooked. If the contract is unclear or unacceptable to either party the ensuing psychotherapy will be fraught with uncertainty, resentment, and anxiety and may be doomed to failure from that moment on. A therapeutic contract is characterized by two major features:

Administrative. The administrative concerns are related to time, day, and length of the therapy session. In some cases, the number of sessions of treatment is specified. Requirements of payment and attendance are also noted. Such issues as whether attendance is required for all scheduled sessions and whether the patient is charged for missing a session are clarified. Also discussed are how sessions are rescheduled, how vacations are taken, and how phone calls or emergencies and upsets outside of sessions will be handled.

Psychological. The psychological aspects of the therapeutic contract concern the roles and responsibilities patient and therapist agree to assume in their endeavor together. The details of this feature of the therapeutic contract will be discussed in terms of particular designed groups in the chapters to follow.

CRITERIA FOR SELECTING PATIENTS FOR THERAPY GROUPS

Unlike the therapist who is involved in individual psychotherapy exclusively, the group therapist is faced with the task of combining patients in a group that will emerge as a therapeutic ensemble. The criteria discussed below are intended for pulling together the best possible group of mixed patients. Creating an ideal group is not the purpose; the groups discussed in this volume are intended, for the most part, for clients who have not been helped by other ameliorative endeavors. My criteria serve as an approximate base line for convening patients for the groups discussed in this book. Whereas the possession of these qualities should not be construed as an absolute assessment of suitability for group therapy, the qualities listed are relevant to the patient's ability to make use of therapy in a heterogeneous group. Patients who do not fit these requirements are best served in a homogeneous group with members having a narrow range of problem areas.

1. *The person who takes responsibility for his own thoughts, feelings, and actions.* The things that happen to a person do not occur capriciously. They occur because they serve some desired function for the individual. Patients who seem to profit most from group experience are those who accept the responsibility for their own actions, who seek to find out why they often act in dysfunctional ways and how they may change these tendencies. They come to the group not to persuade others to accept their attitudes and beliefs about themselves but for a candid exchange with others. This requirement for candor discourages, if not eliminates, the culturally deviant and psychopathic character who should be seen in a homogeneous group.

2. *People who experience anxiety consciously and are therefore aware of their distress.* People who are comfortable with their present modes of functioning feel no compulsion to modify their behavior. In their own minds they have reason to maintain their present behavioral patterns. Only people who are uncomfortable with their present functioning seek relief. This requirement would eliminate the chronic monopolist who attempts to dominate the group in averting anxiety and resisting behavioral change. Like Hugh Mullan and Max Rosenbaum, however, I have found that a *provocateur* can stimulate interaction in a group of stolid patients. He may be included, providing that he is not so overbearing that he becomes more of a nuisance than a group catalyst.

3. *Persons who are verbal.* Group therapy is enacted through the use of verbal communication. This restriction eliminates from a mixed group not only seriously withdrawn and recalcitrant persons but also those individuals undersocialized in verbal skills or who employ communicative patterns greatly in variance with those of the other group participants. Unless a person's verbalizations can be understood, one cannot assess what is going on in him. However, in a mixed group such individuals often find situations approximating those outside therapy with which the person needs to come to grips. The verbally restricted person finds the world outside made up of individuals from all walks of life and with a great variety of personal characteristics, not just those with similar difficulties as he has. Patients with verbal difficulties, however, profit more in homogeneous groups or groups which stress nonverbal techniques (see Chapter 11).

4. *People who are concerned about other people's approbation and disapprobation.* Unless the patient is concerned about his persona, the way he presents himself to others in the group, he finds no need to place himself under their influence and open himself to them. To those individuals who have given up hope of gaining others' approval and who wish instead to avoid their disapproval, a group is a place where they have nothing to gain and everything to lose. This fact would eliminate the seriously guilt-ridden person who should initially be seen in individual sessions to build self-esteem and confidence. Once having developed some self-esteem he may be suitable for a group.

5. *The person must be able to tolerate tensions engendered by his own hostile expressions and those of other persons toward him.* (Bach, 1954) When he experiences a situation warranting it, the patient must be able to evoke anger without fear of loss of control. This would

eliminate the seriously self-denigrated for whom a supportive individual-patient relationship is a better choice of treatment and the impulse-ridden character for whom a structured, clear limit-setting program is the preferred treatment (see Chapter 10).

6. *The person must be in contact with the environment.* If the person is unable to relate with some fair degree of fidelity to what is taking place in his external world, then possessing the qualities mentioned above are of little use. Flight mechanisms are defensive strategies to avert a threat with which the individual feels he cannot contend. A person's need for flight is predictable. If, for instance, he has given up hope for securing approval from others and is concerned only about avoiding disapproval, he is more likely to employ flight mechanisms than is the person who is actively seeking approval.

In summary, patients who do best in mixed therapy groups possess the following personal attributes: insight and analytic reasoning skills, accountability for their own behavior, and ego strength sufficient to form a relationship with several other persons in which he must tolerate critical scrutiny of himself and be willing to disclose his painful, threatening, and also tender and compassionate concerns to others. Patients who seem to profit most from group therapy have these characteristics in sufficient degree. Nonetheless, in composing a designed group the therapist generally wants to bring together group members with a variety of symptoms (see pp. 125-26 for rationale). Having a variety of backgrounds, personality styles, and presenting complaints tends to activate and maximize differences among the patients in terms of their personal goals, attitudes, sentiments, and defensive strategisms. Thus, whereas the educational and vocational backgrounds of the group members should be reasonably syntonic so that the participants speak a common language, interpersonal differences among members provide the clash and interchange from which dynamic, enabling groups take shape.

A word about those who should be excluded from group treatment: The group therapy literature suggests that there are eight patient categories which should be excluded from treatment in groups. It is my belief that no patient should be excluded without the therapist evaluating the patient's situation in relation to the goals of the group, the group's composition, and the therapist's level of anxiety about working with such a patient in a group. Moreover, many patients fit into a group rather well after first having had individual sessions. Each case must be evaluated individually. However, most often when the following clinical categories are seen in groups, these groups should be homogeneous: brain damaged, paranoid, extremely narcissistic, hypochondriacal, suicidal, drug and alcohol addicted, acutely psychotic, and deviant character disordered.

PATIENT ORIENTATION TO GROUP THERAPY

There is some evidence that it is preferable for the group leader to be explicit about what the participants are expected to be doing in the group. Florence Powdermaker and Jerome Frank, Irving Yalom et al, and Charles Truax found that therapists who informed their group patients what was expected of them lost appreciably fewer patients than those who left the patients to their own devices in commencing a therapeutic group. Perhaps in all forms of designed groups, the leader and participants need to be prepared for a mutually agreed upon endeavor. The discussion of orientation to group therapy will be confined to the most prevalent designed group, the therapeutic group of hospitalized psychiatric patients.

Patients usually resist group psychotherapy initially regardless of their psychological sophistication. We live in a society where, to an alarming degree, privacy and individual attention are becoming obsolete. For many of us individualized aspects of living that historically have been regarded as our "natural right" are today luxuries and dreams of yesteryear. Small wonder then that for many patients individual sessions with a prestigious professional are preferred and group treatment is viewed distastefully and with suspicion. The patient regards group treatment, in which he has to compete with others for the therapist's attention, as inferior to dyadic sessions. Often he may be right, but frequently he attributes an omnipotent magic to the dyadic session in which he has the exclusive attention and support of the "powerful" therapist, which precludes the real need to deal and compete with others to satisfy his wants. For many patients, group therapy is the treatment of choice. They need to share their distress with others and directly petition others' assistance. Moreover, the experience of being of assistance to others and being appreciated in a group setting is, for many patients, the most important factor in their treatment. (This is my personal observation and it requires further confirmation.)

Resistance to being a member of a group treatment endeavor must be dealt with. It is often best handled by adequately preparing patients for a group. The therapist should begin by assessing the patient's difficulties and his motivation for ameliorative endeavor by means of a focused personal interview. Having a clear conception of

the patient's psychological maturity and his goals, the therapist eluci-
dates, in terms the patient can comprehend, those features of group
treatment which are particularly effective in fostering the goals the
patient claims for himself. The therapist, of course, makes no prom-
ises but suggests how the objectives of the group are syntonic with
the patient's goals.

The contribution of group therapy to the patient's progress has
been succinctly summarized by the American Mental Health Foundation:

> In a group the members work through the problems in a
> true-to-life situation of constant personal interaction. They
> soon become aware of similar emotional difficulties in others.
> By understanding the feelings of his fellow members, the
> individual gains quicker insight into his own emotional prob-
> lems and difficulties. His psychotherapeutic progress is con-
> tinually stimulated by observing, experiencing, and sharing
> in the achievements made by the other group members. (De
> Schill, 1964)

In terminating his interview with the group therapy candidate,
the therapist secures from the patient a commitment to the group.
First and foremost, he must attend all sessions—other hospital activities are secondary. The therapist must stand ready to support his
group members on this issue, except in exceptional circumstances.
The patient is in the hospital for therapy; custodial and administrative considerations are secondary. As a group member, the patient is
expected to abide by certain group norms such as confidentiality of
material discussed. Commitment to group norms is only alluded to in
the interview. Normative latitudes are more effectively negotiated at
such time as members express concern over threats to their own ego
integrity or the work of the group.

For patients who have had relatively little or no exposure to psychological work, the therapist may wish to provide an orientation to
what is expected of them at the beginning of the first session. In a
reconstructive insight-oriented group the therapist may state something to the effect: "The purpose of this group is for each of us to learn
about our own behavior in interpersonal situations. This will not be a
question and answer period where you ask me questions and I, the
therapist, am supposed to provide answers. We will speak in turn and
direct our remarks to the group. I will intervene from time to time to
interpret the emotions of the group as a whole as well as to interpret
the feelings and attitudes of individual members and to help clarify
members' comments. At the end of the session we will summarize

what went on in the session." (The summary may be in terms of the roles enacted in the group or in whatever theoretical framework the therapist feels most comfortable.)

Orientation to therapy should not be rendered as a prepared script. The above orientation is intended only as a general frame of reference. It is not possible to provide here an orientation for all designed groups. The intent of the group leader may vary from improving the communication system of a large management firm (see Chapter 6) to modifying the suicidally inclined behavior of the drug addict (see Chapter 10). In each instance the focus of the group leader will vary.

FOCUS OF THE GROUP LEADER'S ATTENTION IN A GROUP

In-depth investigation of a group may be seen as falling within three general approaches. The group leader may focus on the entire group as an entity rather than as a collection of divergent members. In doing so he tries to ascertain what general mood, emotional need, or apprehension is being experienced in common by each of the participants as members of the group. This viewpoint is referred to as the *integralist* position.

> They believe that the study of the group as an entity reveals the functioning of the individual member in his full complexity, since all group activity reflects overt or covert aspects of the behavior of the individuals composing it. The group as a unit engages in activities which provide the individual with experiences and responses which are different in degree and perhaps in kind from those found in the dyad. The integralist believes that a major aspect of the patient's problem is his inability to be an effective member of a task-oriented group. (Parloff, 1967)

The group leader may instead concentrate on a subgroup within the larger body of the group. He may wish to give special attention to the interaction among a few persons in the group, for example, the three group members who have the highest regard for one another. This is the *transactional* approach.

The therapist may simply disregard the group as a configural reality and instead concern himself with each member of the group as an individual in a situation where other social objects are present. This perspective is called *intrapersonal*.

The therapist need not maintain any of these perspectives exclusively. His focus may shift during the course of the group's development or even several times within a single session. He may test his observations by attempting to conceptualize the phenomenological data before him according to the three different levels of analysis. (Goldberg, 1970 (b), pp. 177–80)

Nevertheless, it is characteristic of group therapists that they generally concentrate on a single level of analysis and do not use a balance of the three approaches proposed here. This being the case, the major advantages of each of these approaches are delineated below.

Attention to the group as an entity permits access to the patients' shared hopes and fears. Each individual enters the group with his own idiosyncratic rumination of problems, issues, and concerns. Certain common motives are activated in each of the patients as a result of his endeavor to relate to other group members in such a manner that they will recognize his needs and enable him to achieve personal goals. The integralist position permits investigation of the roles and personal forces that prevent the articulation of personal incentives, no less than the forces which foster them. Such a survey permits us to study how to recognize, appreciate, and employ these forces in a constructive manner.

In essence, the integralist position states that groups are not perpetuated by manifest objectives alone, nor understood by the summation of individual psychodynamics. Latent purposes in group activity often stand in direct opposition to the articulated group and personal goals. (Parloff, 1967) Without considering these common underlying group tensions we are unable to grasp the socio-emotional dynamics that make men want to satisfy their wants together rather than through solitary activity.

A transactional or interpersonal focus permits an observation that perhaps most commonly and characteristically mirrors our daily world. We live in families generally comprised of several persons. But we rarely come together as an entire family. We work for organizations whose employees often number in the thousands. Large staff meetings, nonetheless, are infrequent. We ride in buses, trains, and airplanes with scores of others, but we seldom interact with more than a few at any one time. Most of our daily interactions, therefore, are with one or two other people. Transactional analysis consequently imparts information about a salient, natural interpersonal grouping.

Intrapersonal attention is predicated on the observation that our bodies bound us one from another. Intrapersonalists assume that the best way to understand the individual is to be concerned with what transpires within the skin and body shell. Ascertaining his goals, ambitions, fears, and fantasies, the intrapersonalists hope to explain why the individual behaves as he does with others. Intrapersonalists make the assumption that social objects have little or no authentic meaning. Other individuals serve as transference objects onto which the person projects his experiences with significant others in his life.

GROUP SIZE AND ITS EFFECT ON GROUP DYNAMICS

The sociological literature has traditionally had a small section devoted to the effect of group size on group process and performance. Edwin Thomas and Clinton Fink (1963) on the basis of thirty-one empirical studies of small groups, concluded that

group size has significant effects on aspects of individual and group performance, on the nature of the interaction and distribution of participation of group members, on group organization, on conformity and consensus and on member satisfaction.

The effect of group size is of some concern to the practitioner of a designed group who on occasion may find as few as one or two participants appearing for a session. Initially, the question of concern to the practitioner is: how many participants are necessary to constitute a group? One participant obviously does not comprise a group, although one participant interacting with one or more group leaders comprises an interpersonal situation and, consequently, a field where social influence can be effected.

Are two people a group? Two persons constitute an interpersonal situation. The sociological tradition as far back as Emile Durkheim does not recognize an interpersonal situation as a group situation unless a superstructure is imposed. A group situation prevails only when the interactive field is influenced by a previously established set of rules, roles, and sanctions. When group members interact with disregard to the group's established way of conducting business, these persons are no longer functioning as members of the group and their status may be called into question by the other members. In the same way, three or more persons collectively do not constitute a group unless they have regulated expectations about what is required of them, or until such a time as these attitudes are developed. Development of these social attitudes generally requires direct personal experience with fellow group members.

What importance do these considerations have for group therapy? If two patients are not a group, then the presence of the therapist may make them a group. There will be greater pressure to draw the therapist into the group when fewer than three patients are present than when the group is larger. Two participants who are unable to establish a regulated interactional system by themselves will apply more or less subtle pressure on the therapist to become a group participant who they hope can provide help in regulating their relationship to one another. The therapist in this situation may be perceived by the two group members as a parental figure who is judging their sibling-like interchanges. If a therapist finds himself in a group situation with only two patients, it is suggested that he intentionally employ the family model as his prototype. Depending upon the ages, social maturity, sex, and other characteristics, he may conceptualize group interactions to capture the mother–daughter, mother–son, father–son, father–daughter, and husband–wife interactions that the dyadic configuration activates in each of the patient's behavior. The therapist, in interpreting the interactional pattern of the dyad, impresses upon them how each is behaving with the other as if the other were the mother, father, brother, sister, or spouse. It is important also for the therapist to ascertain in what way he is relating to this interactional pattern.

What if three patients appear for a session? Three persons constitute a group providing that they have had prior interpersonal dealings sufficient for developing regulated expectations in regard to their interaction. However, a three person group is a rather unstable grouping. Only two persons can relate directly to each other at any one moment. One person, therefore, is excluded. Each patient harbors fears of his being excluded from the interaction. This activates primitive fears of abandonment which, in turn, precipitate dominating and alliance-seeking reactions. In this provocative setting group process moves at a rapid pace. The therapist usually will not be called upon to stimulate group process. His primary role in a triadic patient configuration is equally to disarm as well as reveal the volatile climate in the group. He should convey to the group members, by pointing out what is occurring inside and among them, how fears of loss of protection and feelings of insignificance lead to strong anger and aggressive behavior.

The optimal size of a group is one in which there is a sufficient number of participants so that each participant feels that he does not have to speak more than he wishes to prevent dead silences or to keep the group going. Correspondingly a group should not be so large that members have to wait their turn in order to speak and when they do, the issue is no longer of concern to the other participants. Four or five patients form a viable sized group that generally gets to know one another rather quickly. When the size of the group fluctuates, the therapist and group members have an opportunity to appreciate the interrelation of group size and group and psychodynamic processes.

THE FAMILY AS A BASIC UNIT IN GROUP PSYCHOTHERAPY

Basic to group therapy is the concept of the designed group as a new family—a family in which earlier and distressing life experiences can be examined, modified, and more satisfactorily re-experienced. Unresolved issues, antagonizing further psychological growth, are the residue of early family relationships. In the new family, it is hoped that these issues will be explored and dealt with, removing impediments to maturity. In the family the patient has been broken and in the "family" he will be healed. This is a modification of the motto of L. C. Marsh, a group therapy pioneer, who reportedly claimed, "The crowd has broken them and the crowd shall heal them."

J. W. Klapman, in an early group therapy textbook (1946, p. 63), pointed out:

In the group there is a reliving of the family drama, but now the patient finds himself sitting on terms of equality with the therapist (parent-substitute-central person). Here is a permissive atmosphere [where] the patient's hostilities are accepted and not reacted to with counter aggression. . . . For the first time in his life he will receive a measure of understanding and acceptance from a just parent whom he will share equally with his siblings.

In the new family the old upsetting feelings about one's self and others emerge to the surface and can be usefully dealt with because they need no longer fester and be retained. The emotional ground upon which the old primary group pitched battles and conflicts were lost can be recovered and reconstructed.

In the designed family, pathological forces are identified and worked upon. The designed family's greatest asset (as well as its greatest liability) is that the very kinds of dysfunctional behavior patients acquired in the original family are restimulated. Those same behaviors that have prevented the individual from getting what he wanted from others outside the group initially prevent him from getting what he needs from members in the designed group.

At first glance it would seem that congregation of these individuals in groups of this kind would result in a worsening of their disturbed state. One would think that they would tend to "pick" on each other even more than otherwise through the familiar mechanism, and that they would tend to raise their barriers even higher than with "normal" people. (Abrahams, 1961)

Group psychotherapy poses a dilemma for the therapist: In order to discover what the patient's problem is the same feelings and attitudes that have prevented him from functioning adequately in the past need be restimulated in the designed group. But, restimulation of self-defeating feelings and attitudes prevents the group members from being helpful to themselves and to the others. The more disturbed the group members are, the less helpful they feel they can be to others. But no behavior, no matter how aberrant, irrational, and useless it may appear to the outsider, is without utility to the individual who employs it. The aberrant behaviors the patient brings to the designed group are the means of survival he has acquired in his original family and other natural groups. Without them he feels unprotected and helpless. Indeed, his defenses are vital to him because he feels that they rather than he, who designed the defenses (and can, therefore, design improved means of relating to his difficulties), are his strength. Because he may regard his defenses as his only strength, he is unwilling to relinquish them without a struggle.

Possession of defenses are indications of strength. The therapist must be skillful not only in teasing out pathological tendencies in the group members but in recognizing and fostering the healthy tendencies and inherent strengths in each group member so that each may offer to the other sufficient inducement to risk himself (risk relinquishing habitual ways of handling his difficulties) in the presence of the other. The therapist who treats the group members as a collection of disabilities, who cannot permit them to struggle with and develop the skills necessary for growth because he needs to perceive himself as the only healthy member in the family, rekindles the original pathogenic feelings of the patient's primary groups. Such a therapist negates the family's most valuable resource—its ability to heal through the warmth, encouragement, empathy, and support of its members.

In summary, a group therapist cannot expect to work in a group as he does in a dyadic relationship. He needs training and experience in groups to supplement his knowledge of psychodynamics. Not only must he be able to understand the individuals in the group but he must be able to appreciate and work appropriately with the members as a group. Those therapists who are most concerned with group forces do not generally regard themselves as the primary therapeutic agents in the group. They believe that it is preferable to operate as indirect, albeit crucial, perpetuators and facilitators of supportive group forces, encouraging and teaching by role-modeling, the group members to take over the therapeutic, healing functions in the group.

"Through opportunities for spontaneous, unguarded openness, expressiveness, and self-disclosure, and
through the feedback reactions of
other people, we may discover aspects of ourselves which would have
forever remained hidden from our
best efforts at introspection."

T.C. Greening
"The Transparent Self"

PROCESSES AND SPECIAL TECHNIQUES—5

The message of this volume is that each practitioner must take
into consideration his own skills and personal defenses and those of
the persons with whom he works in selecting an appropriate technique. The ameliorative process has several phases of development;
Chapter 10 discusses the major modalities for ameliorative change.
Each phase of psychosocial development and its accompanying
growth objective require different kinds of enabling techniques.
Chapters 3 and 4 discussed the psychodynamics of the kinds of persons for whom designed groups are conducted and the criteria for selecting members for each of these group experiences.

The six chapters to follow explore important group processes integral to all group experiences—be they therapeutic groups or not.
These group processes are discussed in terms of their role in specialized groups, for example, sensitivity training groups, process groups,
existential-analytic groups, problem-solving groups, drug addiction
groups, and communal groups. Each of the techniques chosen for in-
clusion in this volume represents a new group approach and clearly
illustrates the group phenomenon under discussion. There is no topic

more salient to the study and edification of groups than that of the effect of leadership on group performance. Chapter 6 presents three distinct approaches to group performance which taken together offer a multidimensional perspective from which to view dynamic group life. Each of these three levels of analysis (the study of leadership traits, group dynamics, and social system theory) has a long and venerable history in social science. Each alone, however, has been criticized for offering only partial understanding of group life and group performance. I hope amalgamation of these three approaches will correct this narrow vision. Chapter 6 outlines a conceptual model which can accurately predict group process problems which all groups and organizations encounter in attempting to implement their goals. The conceptual model is illustrated in the study of a sensitivity training group.

Chapter 7 explores the process group, one of the most controversial of the sensitivity training–encounter group approaches. The process group studies group behavior in the here and now. The role of the group leader is that of a consultant rather than that of a group leader, therapist, or trainer. His task is to help the participants understand their behavior as members of a group rather than in terms of their psychodynamics. The manifest content of the group discussion may embrace any topic, but regardless of the manifest content, there always rapidly develops an underlying group tension or emotion of which the participants are unaware but which significantly influences their behavior. It is the job of the consultant to indicate these tensions and delineate their meaning to the work of the group.

Chapter 8 describes the intensive reconstructive group modality referred to as existential-analytic group therapy. The concepts of choice, responsibility, and the patient's selection of defenses have already been explored in some detail. The philosophical rationale and principles of an existential group, as I conduct it, is contrasted with those of the traditional reconstructive group psychotherapy. Chapter 8 presents actual transcripts of existential-analytic groups with explanatory notes.

Chapter 9 is concerned with problem-solving in a group setting. The focal problem model is an approach which has been used in conjunction with reconstructive group therapy and sensitivity training as well as a separate modality. The focal problem approach is also taught to trainees who have little or no background in group psychotherapy. It is used for working with rather diverse and resistive patient populations who are not profiting from reconstructive therapy. The group leader in a focal problem group deals primarily with symptoms (ineffective problem solving skills) rather than under-lying character traits which are dealt with in reconstructive therapy. The typical group has definite and specifiable goals and focus. The duration of the group is generally short-term.

Chapter 10 describes a resocialization technique originally devel-oped in Synanon for working with hard-core drug addiction problems. This technique, referred to as confrontation group therapy, has been modified for treatment of other types of "acting out" character dis-turbances, including those of the "deviant" life styles. Confrontation group therapy is not concerned with the addict's obsessive-compulsive rumination about drug usage, but what he is experiencing as he is being confronted in a group. It is these feelings that govern his dys-functional life style rather than the rationalized reasons he prefers to offer.

When the patients were addicts (they are not currently so if a drug-free program is maintained), their entire existence was involved with the drug habituation. In the treatment situation the therapist is concerned with the addict as a person. If he can successfully convey the idea that he is concerned with problems in living which the addict has in addition to his addiction, then he can explore a more fruitful avenue of investigation—not why the addict uses drugs but what life would be to him without drugs.

Chapter 11 is concerned with nonverbal communication and ac-tion group techniques. Many of these techniques are derived from psychodrama which was originally developed by J. L. Moreno in oppo-sition to the deterministic, nonactivistic philosophy of Freudian psy-choanalysis. Chapter 11 discusses how nonverbal and action tech-niques may be utilized with resistant patient populations for whom traditional treatment has proven unsuccessful.

Chapter 12 explores the proliferating movement toward com-munal living. The serious crisis the natural family system now faces is discussed as well as the alternatives offered by the communal system. The communal community, as I view it, is largely an attempt to utilize defined group techniques to modify life styles and social sys-tems. The commune is clearly an important part of the new group movement.

> "And as a single leaf turns not yellow
> but with the silent knowledge of the
> whole tree, so the wrong-doer cannot
> do wrong without the hidden will of
> you all."

Kahlil Gibran
The Prophet

LEADERSHIP AND GROUP PERFORMANCE—6

Choosing to work with a group rather than with individuals separately raises other more complex and specialized issues than that of simply conducting treatment. One of these is the issue of leadership. Beyond whatever skills and experience he possesses in working therapeutically with individual patients, the therapist is required by the nature of the dynamics in a group situation to assume some leadership role in the group. The role he adopts absorbs his own personal attributes and experience in groups as well as his theoretical conceptions of treatment. Leadership roles in designed groups vary widely. The consultant in a Tavistock study group and the psychotherapist in a Slavson-type activity group for children assume a permissive, non-directive attitude to events in the group. The behavioral therapist in a desensitization group and the rational–emotive psychotherapist are extremely directive, authoritative, and specifically content-oriented. Whatever the therapist's approach to treatment is, he must assume some leadership function for the patients. Why? Because of his training, experience, and personal treatment the therapist is assumed to have a clearer notion than his patients how to accomplish the ameliorative aims for which the patients entered treatment.

Knowledge and expertise in dyadic treatment, however, will not insure gains in a therapeutic group unless the therapist takes heed of and effectively utilizes the processes and dynamics operating in that group. Understanding what occurs in groups requires more sophistication than a summation of information about the individuals who comprise the group. Group dynamics operate in addition to individual psychodynamics, heavily shaping transactions in the group. But the group therapist cannot be content in only observing and appreciating group and interpersonal processes. He must foster facilitating processes and a conducive work climate in the group.

The quality of a group's performance is highly related to the efficacy of its leadership. No leader, be he a plant manager seeking release of the constructive energies of his workers or a clinician seeking identification by his group patients with therapeutic work attitudes, can be effective if he is not cognizant of the effect his behavior has upon the thoughts, feelings, and actions of his followers. No leader can monitor his behavior to maximize the group's objectives without taking into consideration the transactional system between leader and led.

The purpose of this chapter is to relate concepts of leadership to group dynamics and social system theory. The presupposition informing my conceptualization of leadership and group performance is that members of a group perform the tasks for which they have convened best when they have a reliable model for anticipating the issues and concerns with which they must successfully deal in order to achieve their aims.

This chapter is organized as follows: First, what is meant by the term "leadership" is considered. Second, a conceptual model which relates group functioning and performance to the qualities of leadership is formulated. Finally, these principles are illustrated by describing the group functioning of a typical training or sensitivity group.

A PROSPECTUS FOR THE STUDY OF LEADERSHIP

Of all the topics investigated by those interested in social dynamics, the nature of leadership and its interrelation with group performance have been probed most persistently over the longest period of time. (Cartwright & Zander, 1960) Leadership has its roots in man's earliest attempts at collective effort and social control; the qualities that comprise leadership have been a concern of the man in the street as well as the historian, the political scientist, and the social philosopher. Every individual at one time or another in his life aspires to some form of leadership. This aspiration is understandable since leadership is generally regarded as the pinnacle of social and political strivings. At its base lies the individual's deep emotional yearning for recognition, acceptance, and esteem from other people.

Leadership means many different things: to one person, a leader is someone who holds public office; to others, a leader is a person of distinction in the artistic, scientific, athletic, or business worlds; to a third, a leader is simply a phenomenon to be understood in terms of the person's unique capacities and talents; to still another, a leader is someone who influences other people. (Sherif, M. & C.W., 1948) Leadership can be seen to have its prototype in a dyad in the smallest social units. For instance, leadership can be discerned in the relationship of a businessman to his partner and in the interrelationship of one family member to another. Leadership, however, more ubiquitously manifests itself in large collectivities—by corporation executives, monarchs, and ministers of nations, as well as spokesmen for professional, political, and social reference groups that cross the boundaries of nations and continents.

Leadership relates, without exception, to every conceivable social and collective issue. It has been imputed as the cause of every unsuccessful social and political endeavor no less than the source of every successful one. Regardless of the form it takes, leadership phenomenon is a power and force that intrudes deeply upon our daily existence. As such, it is a phenomenon that we must clearly understand in order to develop our own leadership qualities and to appreciate the development of these qualities in the collectivities to which we belong.

A proper study of effective leadership, reason dictates, requires knowledge of the personal qualifications necessary for leadership. What do we know about the personal characteristics of leaders? Until the last decade or so, the vast literature on bureaucratic and military leadership concerned itself primarily with leadership traits—the personal characteristics of leaders, which included intelligence, daring, resourcefulness, autonomy, empathy, and so forth. (Sprott, 1958) Unfortunately, exhaustive efforts to summarize traits found to be characteristic of various leaders in similar and differing situations revealed very little overlap and no discernible and consistent pattern of personality types. (Sherif et al., 1948)

> As is so often true, the accumulation of facts has revealed that simple formulations are inadequate. The belief that a high level of group effectiveness can be achieved simply by

the provision of "good" leaders though still prevalent among many people concerned with the management of groups appears naïve in the light of research findings. (Cartwright et al., 1960)

It is insufficient, therefore, to study the phenomenon of leadership by investigating the qualities of the individual alone. Muzafer and Carolyn Sherif (1948) have stated the issue succinctly:

If the aim of leadership study is to understand actual leaders in social life, the term "leadership" must refer to those realities which make its investigation important ... Leadership can occur only in relation to other people. No one can be a leader all by himself ... Leadership [consequently] implies rather definite kinds of relationships to other people.

What are the relationships and activities that define leadership? According to the group dynamics school, leadership consists of

those acts which help the group achieve its preferred outcome ... Such actions by group members as those which aid in setting group goals, moving the group toward its goals, improving the quality of the interactions among the members, building the cohesiveness of the group, or making resources available to the group. (Cartwright et al., 1960)

To be meaningful, the concept of leadership must refer to an object, a subject, and a direction. Leadership denotes one or more persons who represent or embody the attitudes, values, and norms of a particular collectivity or group. The group's representative, or leader, is heavily contributory in moving in a specific direction toward particular goals (or, in the case of expressive leadership, away from particular threats to the survival of the group and toward a comfortable climate for the members). Leadership is a way of relating oneself to others—it is assumed by those who take account of others in ways that facilitate group life and group cohesiveness. (Jennings, 1943) In terms of direction:

No matter what kind of group is involved, ... there is no place for a leader unless there is an objective [to be sought], a goal to which to lead [the group members]. (Hartley, L.L. & R.E., 1955, p. 603)

The nature of the group as an entity also requires consideration. The need for relativistic consideration of leadership becomes understandable upon realizing that different groups seek different goals, which require different talents for their implementation. Were two groups to seek similar goals, the ways in which these groups would support cajolery, urging, manipulation, or other means to get group objectives accomplished would depend upon the particular meshing and juxtaposition of the leader and members' personality, intelligence, social background, aspirations, attitudes, defenses, and so forth. Not only the task to be performed but also the nature of the group to be led specify the qualifications of the leader. (Hartley et al., 1955)

The foregoing describes the current approach which regards leadership as situational. Leaders are dependent upon the specific exigencies facing the group and the nature of the group's resources to meet these exigencies.

"A leader in one group is not necessarily a leader in another. Nor is a leader related to every member of a group in the same way." (Jennings, 1943)

Once having said this, it is important to indicate that the situational approach to leadership presents a serious obstacle to the student of groups. If viewing leadership as situational is valid, then every situation is idiosyncratic and unique. The findings of groups in one setting cannot be generalized to those in another setting, situation, or period; and the study of leadership is no longer conducive to scientific investigation. (Sherif et al., 1948) The careful student of leadership is not satisfied with this state of affairs. He may well ask if there are not certain functions that leadership must meet in all groups in order for the group to survive and achieve its objectives. This question is considered in the following sections.

SOCIAL SYSTEM THEORY

In spite of the long standing and wide interest in the study of leadership, the accumulation of leadership theory is yet unsystematically ordered. Therefore, at this juncture a systematic and comprehensive scheme is presented for purveying the functions of leadership in terms of the maintenance and goal attainment of the group. Later this scheme will serve as a frame of reference in delineating the process of the sensitivity training group.

The conceptual system proposed is expressed in terms of social system theory which is concerned with the social behavior of persons bound together for reasons relating to common needs and interests. Social system analysis is a study of the positions (roles and status) that persons within a social system take vis-à-vis one another in order to achieve common objectives.

A canvass of the literature on the influence of the social system theory in diverse social situations reveals that social scientists have posited a small set of organizing principles that characterize all durable human groups. (The material on the Functional Imperatives of Social System Theory to follow is based on pp. 379–87 of H. W. Polsky, D. S. Claster, & C. Goldberg, *Social System Perspectives in Residential Institutions*, East Lansing, Michigan State University Press, 1970. See also Polsky, Claster, & Goldberg in *Dynamics of Residential Treatment*, University of North Carolina Press, Chapel Hill, 1968.) In more complex configurations, to be sure, these principles undergo considerable elaboration. Social system analysis is greatly useful precisely because it cuts across groups with diverse configurations in revealing fundamental system dynamics. Some very helpful distinctions in social system process have been made by George Homans and by Robert Bales. The analysis of a social system reveals two fundamentally distinct problems:

1. What are the kinds of procedures a group undergoes in attaining its goals within a social environment? Homans calls the social environment the "external system" and the activities necessary to carry out the goals are termed "instrumental" by Bales. In terms of small group functioning, examples of instrumental behavior would be: initiating an activity, keeping group members' attention on the goal, clarifying an issue, developing an agenda, evaluating the quality of work, and so forth. (Cartwright et al., 1960)

2. What are the operations for maintaining satisfying and efficient cooperation among the members of a group which enable it to carry out its goals? For Homans, development of group solidarity and cooperation is part of the group's "internal system," and Bales refers to the activities necessary to bring them about as "expressive." Examples of group maintenance behavior are: keeping interpersonal relations pleasant, arbitrating disputes, providing encouragement, giving the minority a chance to be heard, and so forth. (Cartwright et al., 1960)

In other words, every durable functioning social system has a concrete job to get done; at the same time, it promotes among its members loyalty to each other and the goals of the group. This distinction between task performance and system-maintenance underlines every social system.

Further analysis of social systems indicates that human groups are not maintained instinctively or automatically. Interacting human beings behave so that differential consequences, the result of individual incentives, are constantly emerging. "Functional imperatives" (Talcott Parson's term) tend to harmonize the differential consequences for attaining collective goals and mediate the differential kinds of gratification individuals receive from group membership. If any group tasks or functions fail to be executed at some minimal level, the entire system is upset and in danger of collapse. The functional imperatives consist of the following spheres:

1. *Adaptation.* Adaptation is the process whereby a group mobilizes to meet the requirements and expectations of the external system. As "no man is an island, entire of itself," similarly no group or social system is so self-sufficient that its needs and purposes are not in some part directed toward the larger community or surrounding social system. Adaptation is frequently unpleasant in that the group must impose demands upon its members which restrict their latitude of acceptable behavior, making certain behaviors which are habitual or pleasant to individual members unacceptable to the group as a whole. For instance, some group members repeatedly point out to other members that certain things are expected of them, that the group has come together to get a job done, not just to have a good time. These adaptational leaders object to excessive levity and procrastination in their groups.

In sum, the adaptational task is that of properly perceiving and carrying out rules and regulations (expectations) of the larger society. In order to do so, a certain amount of cooperation or enforced order must be imposed upon the group. The fulfillment of the adaptational requirement often leads to frictions and dissatisfactions in the group members' relations to one another.

2. *Goal Attainment.* Like adaptation, goal attainment is an external system imperative. It refers to articulating and carrying out the purposes and autonomous goals of the group. Although each of the functional imperatives must be maintained if the system is to survive, goal attainment may be regarded as the fundamental aim of a social system. Whether fully aware of the fact or not, individuals enter into groups because groups can attain goals satisfying to their members which the members cannot obtain separately. The group's goal orientation and accomplishments are not only the major payoff for group membership, but actually its raison d'être. The group's ability to foster goals and carry them to fruition in ways that individuals cannot alone attracts and holds group membership.

In informal groups, where common motives conducive to interaction lead to the group's formation, neophytes enlist and veterans depart as the group's objectives shift from one interest to another. In bureaucratic organizations, on the other hand, officers and leaders generally are appointed politically or in other ways unrelated to the norms, values, and goals of the rank and file whom they are called upon to mobilize. When the needs of the membership are frustrated, obvious difficulties are bound to arise.

Integration is an expressive function, a prerequisite of the group's internal system.

3. *Integration.* Integration is a feature of the internal system of the group whereby the group develops a satisfying social and emotional climate among its members. A spirited rapport, a feeling of well-being in a group of persons who hold similar interests and accept one another as important, is essential to group interaction if the members are to apply themselves to the group's tasks. Integration, like goal attainment, is both an attraction and a payoff of group membership. The level of group integration serves as a barometer of the functional quality of the other system spheres. Where the other functions are adequately met and the aims of the group carried out, group cohesiveness appears to be "instinctively" engendered. Under normal conditions, however, strains do occur in the social system and are reflected by the level of group integration. Such strains must be smoothed out if the system is to continue functioning. The group member who is characteristically able to get the other members to laugh at themselves during a period of strain and tension and thereby encourages concerted group effort serves as a leader in this sphere.

The group continues to function as long as it has the ability to reduce the tensions and strains incurred in executing goals as well as those stemming from individual personality problems.

4. *Pattern Maintenance and Latency.* Pattern maintenance is the interlude between meeting societal expectations and attaining group goals. It consists of "bucking up" the group members so that they carry out the activities connected with goal attainment and adaptation. Latency is involved with the individual members' personality problems; its management is an attempt to prevent personality problems from disrupting the effective functioning of the group. Social system analysis alerts us that whereas each group member is group-oriented, he is also an individual with a personal history who acts, at least in part, inconsistently with other group members. Consequently, at one level a social system is a consolidation of norm-directed individuals, and at another, a matrix of conflicting intrapsychic processes. The latency sphere links together these two levels. Group functioning is generally facilitated by successful reduction of psychic and status conflicts of members.

Individuals characterized by considerable psychic conflict are severely impeded in employing adequate social skills. They tend to project their inner conflicts onto other individuals and in so doing attribute their own motives as the intentions of others. Projective behavior by an individual emanates from the belief that others pose threats to the individual's instinctual demands. Such a belief leads to a highly stereotyped defensive attitude which is maladjusted to changing external conditions.

Such an individual is unable to view the situation from the perspective other than his own. It is difficult for him to comprehend the implications of his own social behavior and its consequences for others. The inability to take symbolic roles prevents him from adequately predicting the responses of other people. He finds it difficult to anticipate [or appreciate] how others respond to him because he cannot take into consideration their attitudes and viewpoints. (Parker, 1957)

The less able he is in predicting others' behavior, the less successful he will be as a group member because successful group functioning requires a high degree of implicit understanding of other's expectations of oneself. Intrapsychic conflicts among members, then, lead to a breakdown in the group's ability to communicate and to accommodate to one another. However, the group member who is sensitive to others' feelings and finds ways to get them to express their feelings and opinions in the group serves as a leader in the pattern maintenance sphere.

The major functions of group leaders correspond to the functional imperatives of every social system. At various times, the leader must play the role of custodian (adaptation sphere) to see that group members apply themselves to the tasks at hand; counselor and advisor (goal attainment sphere) acting as an idea getter or pace setter in developing and implementing group goals; friend (integration sphere) putting the members at their ease, making the tasks at hand less onerous; and nurturer (latency sphere) encouraging and administering to personal conflicts of individual members so that these conflicts do not interfere with effective group functioning. The role structure of groups is essentially a system of solutions which become institutionalized in order to reduce tensions growing out of uncertainty and unpredictableness in the actions of others. (Bales, 1950)

Leadership can thus be viewed as the articulation of certain salient group roles to other roles in a social system. Making these system roles fit together harmoniously is extremely complicated. Leadership roles are frequently ridden with potential conflict. For example, an appointed officer in a bureaucratic organization finds it extremely difficult to conduct himself casually as a peer with those he is expected to lead and, at the same time, command enough authority to keep the rank and file with their noses to the grindstone as they carry out agency policy which is not overly acceptable to them.

Leadership is inadequate and dysfunctional when it either frustrates the socio-emotional needs of the group members or fails to mobilize the workers' energy and cooperation in meeting the objectives of the system. The leader, in large measure, mediates the allocation of roles which successfully combines the personal skills and incentives of the members and the tasks required by the system. Prolonged maintenance of inadequate roles leads to dysfunction and disintegration of the social system. If a system is to survive, leadership must facilitate a dynamic equilibrium which adjusts the needs of the members to the requirements of the external system.

LEADERSHIP AND GROUP PERFORMANCE IN A SENSITIVITY TRAINING GROUP

The presentation of group functioning as it is generally enacted in a sensitivity training group will illustrate the principles that have been discussed. The prototypal training group to be discussed is one that failed both to formulate specific group goals and evolve effective leadership.

The system to which the group is subordinate is a factor in determining the outcome of the initial struggle for leadership. When participants in a training group are attempting to develop leadership, one of the few anchorages available is the formally delegated leader. The group consultant (or trainer), because of the status associated with his professional position, is examined for cues about required group conduct. Participants entering a training group commonly expect that the consultant will heavily influence, if not determine by fiat, the goals and activities that take place under his auspices. The group members, having carried over norms and expectations from their experience in other groups, generally expect the consultant to tell them what the purpose of the group experience is and how they are required to behave.

The consultant, following the didactic philosophy of sensitivity training discussed in Chapter 7, refuses to fulfill the group members' preconceived expectations about his leadership. The loss of the formal leader as an expert and as a dependable anchorage is invariably upsetting to the participants. They abruptly shift from emotional excitement to depression, seem unable to mobilize their own resources for leadership, and almost shamefully plead with the consultant to take charge. Without an expert to guide them, the participants seem reluctant to take up essential adaptational tasks and the group is cast hopelessly adrift. For example, standards for group procedure and the establishment of norms must be attended.

Norms are rules of behavior, proper ways of acting, which
have been accepted as legitimate by members of a group.
Norms specify the kinds of behavior to which members are
expected to conform. (Hare, 1962)

Norms shape the group climate in which goals are articulated, fashioned, and implemented. Without supportive norms, personal incentives of the participants are not translated, through confrontation, reconciliation, and, finally, compromise into group objectives.

The failure of a formal leader to carry out the required leadership functions, together with neglect of establishing norms and rules for procedure will initially incapacitate the group from utilizing the latent social–emotive sentiments and task–skill resources of its membership. Reliance on an "ineffective" formal leader is, of course, not interminable. The training group consultant who refuses to enact the role the group expects of him and leaves them to their own devices will inevitably earn the participants' hostility and rejection for "not doing what is clearly his job." The adaptational function is generally the group's first challenge. The group members are required to decide which tasks and functions they need to attend to in order to achieve the objective for which they have convened. To effectively set goals and objectives, some knowledge of how groups operate and get things accomplished, generally gained from previous group experience, is essential.

Once it is apparent that the formal leader will not carry out his expected role and functions, emergent attempts at leadership are encouraged from within the group. When the leader fails to live up to group expectations, despite whatever his past accomplishments might be, he is replaced. This is no less true in a training group than it is for bureaucratic organizations and informal friendship cliques. Members of newly formed sensitivity training groups who strive for leadership, I have found, are people who carried out leadership roles in other groups—hardly an astounding finding, of course. A person's "reputation outside the group tends to support his standing within the group." (Whyte, 1943)

Frequently we find that in the early stages of the group the participants look to leaders who tend to be autocratic. I mean by "autocratic" that these aspiring leaders generally attempt to dominate the discussion and arrive at group solutions with little or no attention to the feelings and points of view of group members holding divergent opinions. These leaders talk more frequently and ask for less orientation than do other group members. While giving more orientation to the group as a whole than to the rank and file member, these leaders also largely ignore feedback from any but influential group members. Autocratic leaders tend to be more highly motivated than other group members while, at the same time, less concerned about taking exception with the opinions of their fellow group members. During periods of uncertainty, strong, unswaying leaders provide anchorages for the group in consolidating its resources and directing its energies toward unified group action. Group members in trying times

do not object to "strong" leadership, provided that they know
that they can participate and take the initiative if they wish.
(Bonner, 1959, p. 193)

Generally, these strong aspiring persons fail to sustain their leadership because in their attempts at gaining control of the group they direct too much antagonism toward the other group members and are supplanted. Replacing them are instrumentally-oriented persons who have open communication systems with the rank and file. Studies of small groups have shown that rather than relating less to other group members, these

leaders tend to give more information, ask for more information, and make more frequent interpretations about the situation than do the rest of the members. (Cartwright et al., 1960)

The inter-status conflicts generated among the group members in their leadership struggles (a latency problem) reawakens untoward and unresolved personality difficulties in each of the participants. To stabilize the group, expressive leadership must concern itself with the socio-emotive needs of the group members as individuals. The expressive leader fosters in the group a mood which is conducive to cooperative work in a supra-individual endeavor. The mood established is also one in which conflicts and tensions engendered in status rivalry, threatening the members' personal need for security, affection, and recognition, are reduced.

Fred Fiedler's work suggests a direct relationship between individuation of group members and high group productivity. Leaders of highly productive groups evaluated the members of a group as individuals to a greater extent than leaders of less productive groups who tended to evaluate the group members as part of a nondifferentiated entity.

A salient characteristic of the expressive leader is a sense of timing. For example, clowning by a member of a T-group may be ex-

actly what is needed in a tense moment to relieve strain but at another time such levity may block locomotion toward a goal. (Cartwright et al., 1960)

Groups in which leadership has difficulty emerging are also
generally delayed in formulating group objectives (the goal attainment function). In large measure, group goals are impeded because so
much time is spent in leadership struggles, which require attention
in soothing over socio-emotional chafe (the pattern maintenance task)
emerging from the struggle. The more time spent on latency management, the less time is available for planning goals. But latency management cannot be aborted without a cost to the overall effectiveness
of the group. Expressive problems must be resolved before a group
can successfully handle instrumental goal orientation and promote
cooperative interaction among members. (Heincke & Bales, 1953) On
the other hand, experience has also shown that a group cannot be
effective by devoting exclusive attention to its external system. Too
much initial emphasis on "task orientation leads to insufficient attention to group maintenance." (Cartwright et al., 1960)

Most of the antagonism and negative orientation in sensitivity
groups are generally resolved in the first two-thirds of the laboratory.
The climate in the sessions are smoother and more positive during
the last third of the sessions. Goal orientation develops more
smoothly as the group resolves its internal system impediments, provided that adaptation by this time has been adequately attended.
Clear norms and rules of procedure must be formulated before activity toward goals can commence. These normative standards derive
chiefly from the objectives which the group has set for itself. Not
having formulated norms, the group cannot establish definitions of
how to conduct a group session nor specify what is meaningful for
members to be attending. Without definitive norms, pressures also
are absent for getting indifferent and deviant members to apply
themselves to the tasks at hand. As one might suspect, without clear
norms the group has difficulty defining "deviance." Norms define the
kinds of behavior necessary to and consistent with the realization of
group and individual goals. Rational norms cannot be set without a
lucid idea of what the group members are trying to achieve. Therefore, group goals need to be articulated clearly if group norms are to
facilitate their attainment.

The *situational* approach to leadership becomes a meaningful
perspective into how training groups formulate and implement their
goals.

In order for a member to take the initiative in attempting to

serve a group function, at least two conditions appear necessary: (a) He must be aware that a given function is needed;
(b) He must feel that he is able to perform it, that he has
enough skill to do so or that it is safe for him to attempt to do
so. (Cartwright et al., 1960)
In the situational approach, the leader is regarded as a group member
who comes to the fore in situations in which he possesses more skill
than other group members. However, for unitary leadership to
emerge, not only must an individual possess task skills but he must
also be capable of communicating to the group the attractiveness of
maintaining activities in which he is skilled. Therefore, as a certain
activity becomes more and more a regular part of the group's routine,
the group member who possesses skill in that activity becomes more
consolidated in permanent leadership.

In one sensitivity training group in which I participated as a
member, one person proposed that the group "role play" to learn "em-
pathetically" what it means to be a member of diverse types of
groups; another suggested having a seminar in which each participant could offer the group his understanding of group process; and
still another advocated developing skills for resolving work problems.
Presumably, each of the persons who made these suggestions possessed skill in the area he proposed and sought both to perpetuate his
interest and assume leadership at the same time.

In a sensitivity training group an aspiring leader's inability to
communicate the attractiveness of a project to the consensus of the
group spells doom to a sustained and concerted attention to a single
group goal. Where aspiring leaders are unable to communicate the
appeal of their interest to the group, concerted goal activity and stability of leadership fail together. The collapse of stable leadership and
the lack of goal attainment are, in essence, the failure of a group of
individuals to function as members of a supra-individual endeavor.
Personal incentives difficult or impossible to attain individually are
blocked insofar as group goals founder. A pervasive dissatisfaction
among the members results.

The participants contrast their floundering with the well-ordered
world outside the group and they speak openly of the consultant's
failure to provide a worthwhile laboratory group experience. They
claim with heated emotion that if the consultant had been concerned
and responsive to their helplessness he would have demonstrated
what they must do to improve their behavior in outside group associations. Because the consultant refused to heed their helplessness he
threw them unaided into a situation in which they feel like rejected

orphans. It is the consultant's fault, they claim, that they are dependent. Some of the group members suggest that the participants remove themselves from the consultant or the consultant be asked to leave. This, they claim, will free them from their dependency on the consultant and enable them to work as mature individuals. Quickly strong pressures are evoked from the other members to counteract the suggestion of patricide. There arises in the group a seeming compulsion to cling onto the consultant. Without an external object to blame for their plight, the participants would have to take personal responsibility for their depleted labors.

 At this point the participants frequently report a parallel between their helplessness to master the complexities of the group training situation and their impotence in influencing the social system in which they seek a livelihood. The inhumanness of the work situation is likened to the consultant who is seen as cold, sadistic, and manipulative. No one cares about them as people, they claim. All that is expected of them is to produce. To hold in check the strong feeling of futility resulting from their "inability to accomplish anything," participants try to disavow their ego-involvement in the group. They sit back with a bored expression, contending that they never actually had high expectations of what a training group could accomplish. They participated, they claim, to find out what all the fanfare about sensitivity training was.

On the instrumental level, the failure of the participants to formulate goals results in a short-circuiting of group process and a lack of continuity from one session to the next. Issues and discussion interesting and involving to some of the group members in one session are dropped and apparently forgotten in subsequent sessions. The group frequently goes through the tedious and stultifying process of resolving problems which members had been led to believe were worked out in previous sessions. This lack of continuity, or "lapse of group mind," reflects the absence of norms and rules for group procedure.

On the expressive level, the failure to formulate goals and develop leadership results in the emotional reaction of dissatisfaction and indifference. Goal attainment, after all, is the group's reason for existing. Members' satisfaction in large part comes from successful goal endeavor. In the absence of goal accomplishment members question the sensibleness of attending to the unpleasant adaptational demands of the group. Members depart en masse and the group ceases to exist. If a group is to survive, it must justify its existence. It does so by achieving its goals and/or nurturing the expressive needs of its members.

The foregoing has been an attempt to formulate a model for predicting issues and concerns that have applicability for all (including therapy) groups. Effective leadership requires a conceptual model which encompasses group functioning in its entirety; otherwise, we miss the forest for the trees. Without a comprehensive model of group functioning we cannot effectively generalize from one group situation to the next. We are confined by the limitations of our own personal experience and intuition to face each crisis and group problem anew as a unique and idiosyncratic dilemma. Without sound theory, blunders corrected, insights advanced through trial and error, trends observed by a generation of group leaders are irretrievably lost.

Our model shows that the effective leader, by anticipating the sequence and pattern of group prerequisites and concerns, can, at the appropriate time, utilize the inherent resources of his group members for instrumental and expressive achievement. In the same way, those incumbent leaders who view leadership as a prize need not fear the encroachment of emergent leadership within their group. By effectively pacing and coordinating their subordinates' leadership, they can stabilize their own position while at the same time promoting the aims of the group and the inherent leadership strivings of the rank and file.

A process group

"has no topic nor any formal way for
finding an 'appropriate' one, it has to
'move' to find out where it wants to
go before it can get where it wants to
be."

R. R. Blake
"Group Training versus Group Therapy"

THE PROCESS GROUP TECHNIQUE—7

THERAPIST AS PARTICIPANT–OBSERVER

The therapist serves as a participant–observer in a therapy
group. His formal knowledge, training, and previous experience as a
group member and leader provide him with both a theoretical and
experiential frame of reference from which to view and appreciate the
transactions taking place. Knowledge of himself gained in his own
therapy and as a helping person to others enables him to respond sen-
sitively and intelligently to the needs of those with whom he works.
Neither aspect of the participant–observer role is sufficient in the
absence of the other. A participating, nonobserving therapist responds blindly and unintelligently; an observing, nonparticipating
therapist responds unfeelingly.

The therapist's task as an observer, as I see it, is to look at the
participants' behavior not as a series of discrete events but as a
process which has a beginning, a middle, and an end. Each behavioral
event cannot properly be explained in terms of any given moment in
time but must be conceptualized in the context of what has gone on

before and what will follow. The theoretical orientation of the therapist need not be of foremost concern provided he feels comfortable
with his conceptual model and it does not force theoretical prejudice
on his perceptual faculties. The therapist initially must attempt to
view the behavioral field with a naïve or common-sense phenomenological attitude. He attempts to look at what the group members are
doing as simply as possible, allowing himself to respond to them and
taking into account his own reaction. He tries to make clear to himself, with the help of his reactions, what the group members are doing
to one another. When he feels he has accurately and comprehensively
described for himself what is going on, he attempts to explain it. In
rendering interpretations, the therapist intervenes only at such times
as he believes that he will illuminate what he sees happening in the
group or in a part of it. He therefore seldom tries to explain individual or group phenomena until he has some evidence (whether it be
cognitive or experiential) on which to premise what he has to say to
the group.

In this respect, the therapist generally has an advantage over the
group members. They are involved in an intensive emotional encounter, impinged upon by a welter of confusing and unclear ideas, feelings, and sensations. The therapist, by employment of a conceptual
model built upon a set of generalizations derived from a series of
comparative situations, is enabled in these instances to grasp the essence of the perceptual process, which is

to strip away some of the redundancy of stimulation, to describe or encode incoming information in a form more economic than that in which it impinges on the [group
members'] receptors. (Attneave, 1954)

The economy of this process often permits the therapist as observer to
uncover the essence of what is happening in the group.

A therapist cannot be effective in a group if he is prepared only to
acknowledge his cognitive experiences. It is not realistic, to say
nothing of the waste of valuable data, for the therapist not to be emotionally activated by the tensions, anxieties, frustrations, threats,
and ambitions of group participants. Vicarious experience must guide
and shape his work. His viscera is a barometer of the emotional climate in the group. He is trained to be sensitive to varying nuances of
emotion and ideation and is capable of identifying behavior and examining it in light of the group reality at the precise moment he feels
it is facilitative to specific individuals or to the group as a whole.

The therapist needs to present interpretive material to the group
members in a manner in which it can be digested. By constantly eval-

uating to himself his role in the group, the therapist can at any point question the role the group members have placed him in and the role he has apparently assumed. From these data the therapist may question the motives he may have in permitting the group members and himself to avoid looking at some important process taking place in the group. This difficult introspective task may be performed, as our analytic teachers have impressed upon us, by dividing our ego— which is both a perceptual and emotive organ—into observing and experiencing selves. As an emotive self, the therapist "participates" and affectively responds to the tensions existent in himself and, by extension, in the other group members; as a "trained" cognitive self, he interprets and makes sense of what he is experiencing. The therapist or group leader who perceives himself as merely another member of the group "free to be himself and do his thing" is not capable of making this valuable ego division and, as a result, negates his effectiveness as a trained observer. The need to assist patients by becoming personally involved with them may justifiably override the therapist's value as an observer at certain junctures. However, to relinquish his function as a trained observer for long periods is to negate a crucial aspect of his therapist role. Being aware of and able to conceptualize his feelings, the therapist can use his experiences as a tool to assess and explain the phenomena into which he, himself, has been drawn.

Therapists have come to believe that "gut" feelings are often more trustworthy guides to working with patients than figuring out "what they're about" from one's head. In my view, neither "gut" feelings nor theoretical notions about patients are sufficient in and of themselves. Integrating the various demands made upon a therapist in a group is not an easy one. It is difficult for a group therapist to respond to the individual concerns of seven or eight highly agitated patients and simultaneously pay attention to the various group process as well as his own personal reactions. Despite this difficulty, the therapist must be aware of group phenomena and personal reaction.

I have found that experience as a consultant or group leader in sensitivity training groups is valuable to the education of a group therapist. Ways in which groups operate that are often ignored in treatment groups may be studied in sensitivity training groups. The discussion in this chapter is confined to one type of sensitivity training group, the process group. Theoretical and experiential material has been employed in this chapter to convey how a consultant to a process group behaves and the rationale for his conduct.

GROUP INTERACTION: A NEW EDUCATIONAL ORIENTATION

A process group, as I employ it, is a designed educational experience. Perhaps the single most significant development in American education in recent years has been the shift in emphasis from the individual student to the small group as the focus of the learning experience. Presenting facts and theory in a formal lecture is no longer considered the most effective method of teaching. Education today tends to downgrade authority and expertise. Each student is expected and encouraged to formulate and validate his own point of view through exchange and discussion with his peers. Moreover, the student himself is no longer content to acquire factual knowledge—he quests after firsthand experience. He wishes, in addition, personally to help resolve pressing social problems. He tends to order his present and future goals in terms of their social relevance rather than their logical consistency and well-reasoned premises.

Factual and theoretical knowledge about group process and human behavior does not automatically enable us to function effectively in our daily social roles. Applying our knowledge about people to real life requires direct experience. Sensitivity training maximizes the current demand for experiential learning by focusing upon the group members' immediate feelings generated in the on-going interactive situation in the training group. The need to make immediate decisions in order to get on with the business of living prevents us from experimenting with new modes of relating to others and with exploring our inner potentialities. The process group is intended as a respite from expediency and the habitual modes of interpersonal functioning.

GROUP TRAINING VERSUS GROUP THERAPY

The goals of sensitivity training have been inconsistently and nefariously stated both in the professional literature and in popular usage. Professional and layman alike are generally confused about the purpose of this hyperbolically touted enterprise. Many of us are especially befuddled about whether or not sensitivity training is another form of psychotherapy. The confusion about the usefulness and appropriateness of sensitivity training as a treatment modality has, in my opinion, contributed to the incidence of serious emotional upsets in sensitivity training participants. Many persons joining training groups implicitly or expressly seek treatment. Depending upon which group they, largely inadvertently, become members of, they may receive no direct psychological treatment, attention incidental to their most pressing concerns or, in a large number of cases, outright incompetent and dangerous treatment.

Professionals who have participated in training groups report that participants and nonprofessional leaders frequently allow their enthusiasm and shrouded personal motives to carry them into areas of the individual member's behavior that even trained clinicians treat carefully. The result can be disturbing to a group member with a precarious psychological balance. Compounding these inappropriate group behaviors by participants, many group leaders are personally and professionally poorly prepared to conduct treatment groups. These leaders may fail effectively to intervene, if they intervene at all, when group members unwisely and unsuccessfully try to behave as psychotherapists.

The process group is explicitly intended for group training, not psychotherapy. The purpose of my training group is to study and develop skills in working with group process and group functioning. Many practitioners fail to recognize that the concern with how participants function as group members is a legitimate aim of sensitivity training. Having made the assumption that sensitivity training should concern itself with individual psychodynamics, such psychotherapists as Emmanuel Schwartz slip easily into assuming that sensitivity training is therapy, which it is not, or at least does not necessarily have to be. Since these practitioners regard psychotherapy that concerns itself with group dynamics as bad therapy, they claim that sensitivity training concerned with group dynamics is ineffectual sensitivity training. But sensitivity training in the form of group training is as valuable and legitimate an endeavor as is psychotherapy. Each of these methods provides somewhat different but no less cogent data about the individual as a psychosocial being.

Sensitivity training as I practice it is therefore not another form of group therapy. Unfortunately, many group leaders as well as their critics have not seen that the goals of group training as enacted, for example, in a Tavistock group or my process group and those of group therapy and encounter groups differ. Whereas most individuals may derive some psychological gain from group therapy, sensitivity training (which requires the individual group members to take a considerable measure of responsibility for himself) seems contraindicated for persons with a tenuous grip on reality. It is best indicated for persons seeking to explore new kinds of interpersonal functions rather than for those needing psychological support in order to maintain themselves. Persons who enter group therapy are impelled by pain and those drawn to sensitivity training should be propelled by joy. (Goldberg, 1970) In sensitivity training the emphasis is on conscious readjustment of social roles in an interpersonal situation. Readjustment is founded on the insight and feedback about oneself accrued from the "here and now" confrontation of participants. Traditional group psychotherapy is seen as restorative. Group sensitivity training on the other hand is proactive in that it is concerned with what the participant purports to be currently seeking for himself as a psychosocial being. If sensitivity training is therapeutically useful for the participant, this is merely a bonus. Modifying psychodynamics is not the goal of sensitivity training.

A process group may provide beneficial interpersonal experience that enables the participant to identify and work through interpersonal conflicts and distortions in his everyday dealings with others. If this is what is meant by psychotherapy, then therapy can and does take place in a process group. But all interpersonal situations have a potential for corrective and enabling psychosocial experience. The task of process groups is not to deliberately encourage and influence the resolution of personal problems that have seriously hindered participants from adequately functioning in their daily dealings with others. Process groups are not for people who are already hurting to the extent that they are not adequately functioning. Interpersonal learning, on the other hand, is encouraged in terms of what it means to be a member of a group—what social and intrapsychic forces bear on a group member and how the members may more consciously utilize group forces in concert with others to achieve group and personal incentives. Every participant, therefore, has the opportunity to observe both his own and the other participants' behavior, the implementation of diverse, personal, and interpersonal strategies, sentiments and attitudes in relating to others, and the effects these interchanges have on the task of the group. Each participant potentially can gain a greater appreciation of himself from the reaction of others to how he performs in the group.

The prerequisites for the development of these flexible and realistic interpersonal strategies in training groups (which might be one measure of success of the training experience) are: (a) the participant must be able to assess his effectiveness in implementing his goals in the training group; (b) difficulties in communication and other group problems need to be explored in an experiential and stimulating manner rather than dealt with by didactic and non-ego-involving exercises; (c) the participants must feel a strong incentive to engage others in the group and take into consideration their reactions. To accentuate the immediacy and ego-involvement in the group situation, emphasis is placed on how participants function as group members—not on past history, speculation about childhood experience, or problems members have with persons outside the group.

The emphasis described above is a distinction that I, myself, make in working with training groups but it is not necessarily representative of what other sensitivity leaders hold to. Some group leaders and psychotherapists are wildly enthusiastic about the possibilities of the encounter group as an intensive and sufficient modality of treatment. Others like Morris Parloff are cautious about the use of sensitivity training groups as a treatment of choice, but nevertheless propose that sensitivity training techniques may be valuable in fostering the required interpersonal skills as well as creating the necessary group climate for making psychotherapy viable.

The conceptual base from which my work in groups is formulated is that all enabling endeavors are designed to provide an arena for dealing with the existential concerns the group leader is interested in. The purpose of a sensitivity training, as Thomas Greening has indicated:

is to provide an existential setting in which participants can intensively review and possibly revise their basic views about man's natural group behavior, and the roles and processes necessary for accomplishing tasks with others.

A person may be regarded as acting irresponsibly to the extent that he fails to question his socially induced roles and the sanctions that reinforce adherence to role demands and expectations. The agendaless simple structure of the process group, in contrast to well-ordered settings of everyday life, forces the participants to come to grips with his deep-seated reasons for coming together with other people. No individual can develop a durable value system and philosophy of life without coming to terms with the values and norms of the groups in which he holds membership. Understanding these values and norms also allows him to appreciate their effect upon others. (Goldberg, 1970)

Unlike such critics of training groups as Schwartz, I do not believe that sensitivity groups are designed to level personality through the pressures and demands of the group. On the contrary, group sensitivity training enables the participant to develop more flexible and realistic strategies on the basis of his effectiveness in implementing personal and interpersonal goals in the situation that confronts him. Realistic goals can be developed only when the participants come to appreciate the effect group norms, values, and process have upon group members' sentiments and actions.

Creating meaningful and effective values and goals requires experimentation with real persons and real situations. Sensitivity groups are artificial in that they are not natural groups in which people carry out their daily transactions. In a more important respect, sensitivity groups are real if they generate the same feelings, attitudes, and behavior that the participants experience and struggle with in their daily existential world. Sensitivity groups are "essential luxuries" in that they allow us a reprieve from the pressures of having to solve problems immediately. We are generally not afforded opportunities in the everyday world to find out what we are about in terms of relationship with others. Group training, no less than group therapy (although in a rather different way), is designed to provide this opportunity. The quality of a sensitivity training group, the quality of any group for that matter, depends upon the way the group functions on three levels: the intentional, the ephemeral, and the subtle.

INTENTIONAL ASPECTS OF GROUPS

The intentional refers to the planned goals of the sensitivity training experience and the methodology the group leader employs to achieve these goals. A process group has no preset agenda nor any formularized structure. It is unstructured and leaderless in that none of the usual parliamentary work procedures found in task groups in Western society are present. (Blake, 1957) Moreover, the participants are not told what should be discussed beyond initial instructions to the effect that, "We are here to study how we function as a group." When participants are not certain about what is expected of them, they are forced to negotiate with one another to develop some viable means of coping with their presence in a highly unstructured and uncomfortable situation. This stark climate lays bare the importance of group contract and the setting of clear and definable goals, the effectiveness or ineffectiveness of various kinds of negotiations, as well as the importance of underlying tensions on the work of the group.

Having said this, I must also observe that the process group does have some delimiting structure—features that both curb and order the experience for the participants.

THE FORMAL STRUCTURE OF A PROCESS GROUP

A host of behavioral cues and limiting conditions informs the process group situation. The single most important determinant of these delimiting conditions is the group consultant. How the group consultant may influence the structure of a process group to maximize the training experience in ways he deems desirable is discussed in this section.

1. *Size and composition of the group.* I generally work with eight to twelve persons who participate in a continuous group; that is, a group that meets regularly (for example, weekly). I wanted a group that was large enough that no one felt constrained to speak and small enough that no one would have to wait his turn to be heard. The process group should be of such size that interaction can freely and spontaneously ensue. The membership of my process groups is heterogeneous. Diversity of personality styles within a group enables the separate, dissociated selves within each of the participants to identify with real objects. These selves, enacted in reality rather than in fantasy, can be tested on the basis of their effectiveness in one's own and others' behavior and consequently modified and more satisfactorily integrated within the central self of the participant. Group training as I conduct it is not a means for homogenizing diverse individual differences among the group members. Indeed, these differences, in part because they are contradictorily represented in all of us, must be meaningfully challenged and dealt with.

Heterogeneity is desirable for a procedural reason as well. Variance in the background of the participants serves to insure that they will attend to the exploration of group tensions. A group composed of participants with similar vocations and personal interests frequently spends considerable time and energy conventionally (and wastefully) chatting about their commonalities outside the group. This only serves to reinforce already existing behavioral patterns. Under these conditions the participants avoid exploring and relating to covert issues influencing the present group situation. In heterogeneous groups members will only rarely tolerate a few participants who pursue issues which fall beyond the pale of the present group situation, for these are issues which generally are of concern to only a minority of the membership. The group is more amenable to exploration of the present group situation because it, not extra-group situations, is what they have in common. A group begins seriously to work together as an ensemble at the point that members become aware of common feelings rather than common experiences and future goals. (Mann,

1953) Henry Thelen summarizes the points made about group composition:

> Group growth, although not directly related to the growth of each individual is, however, in the last analysis, dependent upon the kinds of people in the group. The basic emotional dynamics of the group is a working-out of the changing strains in the network of relationships among the members and trainer [the consultant in a process group]. For example, if everyone in the group were thoroughly content to be forever dependent on the trainer for all decisions, the trainer would find it very difficult to teach the group very much about the nature of dependency, its uses, forms and causes. Training is much easier when some people in the group are satisfied with being dependent and others react against the feelings of dependency. Under these conditions the trainer can help the group see that some of its conflict centers around the finding of an appropriate balance between dependence and resistance to dependency.

2. *Physical setting.* The place where the group convenes is of small importance, provided that the setting is relatively comfortable and free of distractions. Single chairs arranged in a circle with ash trays available are preferable to couches. Studies of small groups suggest that the seating arrangement may and frequently does influence group process. (Hare, Borgotta & Bales, 1955) The configuration and size of the group are important as well as the spatial distance among the group members. For instance, in an interpersonal encounter, the closer two persons are to one another the more likely it is that aggressive as well as sexual feelings will be activated. On the other hand, if the distance between people is too great they generally don't feel related to one another. Consequently, in any encounter a certain degree of spatial closeness is necessary for the participants to feel obliged to relate to one another. The threshhold for comfortable as well as threatening interpersonal postures varies culturally. It has been observed that when the psychological space between group members is disturbed there will be accompanying adjustments of physical space as well, for example, rearrangement of chairs. (Foulkes & Anthony, 1957) During periods of tension when it is difficult for the participants to widen spatial distance between one another, they often make use of what Erving Goffman has referred to as *involvement shields* to keep the others at a distance. One participant may hide behind a newspaper or book. Others may symbolically prevent involvement by drawing their legs close to their bodies, crossing

their arms tightly across their bodies, or pulling into themselves in mute withdrawal.

3. *Frequency of sessions.* I generally schedule process groups in one of two ways. For a staff training group I schedule as many sessions as possible within a concentrated period of time and call it a group sensitivity training conference. (Goldberg, 1970, pp. 68–70) If, on the other hand, the group is heterogeneous, for the mutual convenience of consultant and participants, I schedule the sessions once a week on a regular basis, usually for a period of ten weeks. Some participants drop out and others are added to the group every tenth session. In addition, I have conducted weekly for two and a half years three training groups (one of all professionals and two comprised predominately of paraprofessionals), and another weekly training group for over three years. Whether a more concentrated schedule offers a more effective experience than a diffuse schedule or vise versa has yet to be determined by research.

4. *Duration of session.* My process groups have lasted anywhere from one hour to two and one-quarter hours, but I find that a two hour session works best. The initial hour and a half is given over to free discussion. After that period, the discussion is stopped to allow for recapitulation. Every process group has a summary phase in which the consultant and the participants together try to explain, "What happened during the session?" In groups where the summary is followed with psychodrama, (Goldberg, 1970, pp. 150–54, 160–68) I generally terminate the free discussion after an hour and ten minutes, spend ten to fifteen minutes summarizing the session, and move into psychodrama. A session lasting less than one and a half hours usually results in a group having to break off in the heat of encounter. Parkinson's law of temporal structuring, to some degree, shapes all interpersonal endeavors. To the extent the reader accepts this "law" he may wish to regard temporal consideration of groups as mere artifact.

5. *Outside relationships of participants.* I take no stand on this issue in accordance with my conception of the consultant as a nonauthority figure in the group. Notwithstanding, I feel that both participants and consultant must relate outside contacts of the members to what is going on in the here and now. Consequently, I seek to explore with the participants what is currently transpiring in the group that induces them to bring up and discuss their outside activities with other participants. For that matter, we probe into the tensions generated in the group that induce the participants to engage in outside activities with one another.

EPHEMERAL ASPECTS OF GROUPS

The ephemeral aspects of a process group relate to the issues group training raises about the group members' and consultant's role relationship. Some concerns are: the kind of experience the participants are being subjected to, the risks involved, and the roles and responsibility the consultant is willing to assume in the sensitivity training experience. At the onset of the group experience the consultant states to the process group members the group contract, the terms under which they enter the relationship to achieve certain specifiable goals. A description of a few moments of the first session of a process group I held in a community center some time ago will illustrate the process outlined above. This first session is probably typical of the first session of any process group.

The room is not very large—a circle of chairs occupies most of the space. Seven or eight participants have arrived and sit dispersed around the circle. Two or three participants are inevitably late and will probably arrive shortly. It is now 7:00 P.M.; I enter the room and seat myself facing the door. I light a cigar as the apprehensive eyes of the participants attempt to engage mine. The tension in their countenances concedes a plea for me to lead them, to tell them why they have come to the group. They are asking me what they should do to abate their anxieties about what is expected of them. As I examine their faces, one thought from among many takes hold:

Even if I should choose to lead them and try to resolve their
dilemma, I would certainly disappoint them. How is it possible for one person to resolve another's dilemma? Who can
tell another person how to live and what *he* need not fear?

Casting aside these reflections, I said in an even voice, intentionally devoid of affect, "I am Dr. Goldberg. We are here to study groups— that is, we are here to study *how we behave as a group*." Again, my eyes canvass the group, resting for a moment on each of the participants in turn. The group is already in process, although to the participants, my definition is perceived as rather insufficient direction and preparation for a task in which they are beginning to wonder if they wish to engage.

My initial statement to the process group does contain cues which the participants may use to proceed with their task. "We are here to study how we behave as a group" defines the group's task as learning about what happens in a group by studying how the assembled participants operate as a social unit. Futhermore, the statement also structures the role relationship of the consultant vis-à-vis the participants. Studying group activity is a joint project of the consultant and the participants (implied by the pronoun "we"). But, by using his professional title, the consultant intimates that he will not participate simply as another group member. The consultant also implies, by saying "how we behave" rather than "how we have behaved" or "how we should behave," that the task is not a prepared one nor a retrospective or purely intellectual activity. The participants should be attending to how they behave as a group in the here and now, which is an ongoing, continuous activity.

The absence of an agenda and rules for procedure is intended to mitigate the stereotyped roles and role relationships that frequently serve as defenses against recognizing underlying group process. When habitual, stereotyped roles from the everyday world are stripped away, the feelings and interactions of the members become the focus of the group's attention. Without the shackles of habitual role expectations, each participant has the opportunity to explore what he really thinks and feels about himself and about others. He may at the same time experiment with ways of making his personal strategies less self-defeating and more gratifying. The process of understanding one's transactions with others in the group begins with the exploration of shared feelings about being a member of a group and progresses as far as the participants are willing to take it. The consultant attempts to create an atmosphere of openness in communication by trying to help explain what the participants are expressing to one another.

In training groups emotions tend to be regarded as dangerous and upsetting. There is a rather desperate undercurrent, which frequently sounds like a plea, that people come together exclusively to perform tasks, not to learn about themselves. The participants insist that they are really well aware of what they are doing, that their behavior is clear and quite reasonable to them. That the consultant seems to feel compelled to make statements about the group's emotional state as if the group were an organic entity instead of ten relative strangers who actually feel rather differently about things (or else why would they have so much trouble working as a group?) is very suspect and they resent a canned endeavor to get some rise out of them. The consultant, they claim, may be an expert on group dynamics, but when he starts describing the group his description has nothing to do with them as individuals. After all, they insist, who knows them better than they know themselves?

In brief, the consultant's interventions are sneered at by the participants as wholly inferential and not representative of what any of the participants are experiencing. For some mysterious reason they have the preconceived notion that their personality develops in a social vacuum and is uninfluenced by anyone else. They think that all that occurs within the group is quite intentional on the group members' part and need not be scrutinized for hidden and unconscious motives. It becomes evident to the disinterested observer that the group that denies its emotions becomes exploited by them. This reality needs to be reiterated time after time to the group members because it lies at the heart of their inability to function effectively as a mature group. The group will reject this kind of interpretation initially, as the concept of a group's acting irrationally is a strange idea for most persons. Sooner or later the participants, having suffered boredom, experienced unmitigated conflict generated by hidden agendas, and a general inability to make any concerted effort toward working together as a group, will, from sheer frustration, begin more seriously to apprise the consultant's observations of their group emotions and wonder if indeed his observations have some validity.

THE PROCESS GROUP CONSULTANT

The role of a consultant to a training group is best understood in the context of how the consultation process traditionally has been utilized by community institutions. The consultant does not belong to the institutional system that engages him; instead, he is an outside expert—at least those who confer with him generally regard him as such. He is called in to offer assessment and assistance in the form of recommendations for internal system problems. As an outsider, he has neither the formal authority nor the responsibility for making decisions or for seeing that his recommendations are carried out. Being an outsider without preferential attitudes arising from relationships with system members or vested interest in the consequences of the institution's actions, he is regarded as more impartial in making observations and rendering judgments than are members of the system.

Because he is generally known to the members of the system by reputation rather than as a person, his opinions are generally more respected (although not necessarily better liked or more likely to be acted upon) than are those of others in the system who are known as persons and therefore are known to possess all the human frailties. If at any point his recommendations are felt to be inadequate, the system members may dismiss them; however, due to his status his opinions probably at least will be heard and considered regardless of how the system decides to employ them. The consultant's relation to the system is regarded as temporary. He generally works with the system in such a way that the autonomous resources of the system may eventually take over his function.

The following is an excerpt from the protocol of a process group session. The group was formed about a year and a half prior to this session. All the participants in the group are professional mental health workers who meet twice a week. The present group consists of three females and a male. Another group member, Ann, dropped out of the group about one week prior to the present session.

PAULA: *(to Marion)* You consistently have presented the group with kind of something painful that hangs over us, and I keep wanting to say to you, "Hasn't there been something comforting, hasn't there been anything [in the group] to offset it? Sure I know it won't do anything to change your mind or anything. I can just keep trying to say that ... but I feel very interested in wanting you to stay. *(Marion has talked about the difficulty keeping her commitment to the group has become for her.)*

MARION: The pain is *(pause)* I don't know if it *means more* ... where it stands in the ultimate balance of things.

GRETA: *(laughs)*

TOM: *(asks Marion whether she wants to mend her ways)*

MARION: Trying to change, Tom? No! Somehow I tend to look at the pessimistic side or something. I can shelve the comfort and remember the pain.

GRETA: Part of the problem is that I don't know where you're at. Are you staying or leaving?

MARION: I'm leaving.

GRETA: Definitely? *(no answer; group laughs)*

TOM: You say you are leaving. I could have believed that ten to twenty minutes ago, but it hasn't been sounding like that in the last few minutes.

GRETA: That's it!

TOM: That is why I can't do anything with it.

MARION: What am I supposed to do with you all?

TOM: It just doesn't sound to me like you're ... if we asked you to stay and talk you would stay.

MARION: No!

TOM: No, it just doesn't add up right. It just doesn't feel right.

MARION: *(sounding final)* I'm leaving. This is my last meeting.

TOM: I still am surprised at you, Marion. I don't know how you can come in and someone says something and keeps on you, and you say real quick that you're leaving and just leave it at that.

MARION: How would you like for me to leave it?

TOM: It seems to me that you are just arbitrarily making it dramatic and taking off in the wilderness before someone can say something to make you stop and think and change your mind.

MARION: That's probably warm.

[Tom and Greta don't accept Marion's evasiveness.]

MARION: *(excitedly)* OK. It isn't the greatest decision that is black or white. It isn't! I have feelings about leaving, but I just . . . I don't know what you want. I feel frustrated.

CONSULTANT: I have the impression that the frustration the group is experiencing has something to do with the way the group handled Ann last week.

GRETA: That may be very true!

TOM: There could have been things operating in the group, but I don't see how we could have stopped her. I thought the group tried to stop her.

CONSULTANT: I wonder if the group has been sort of giving up on Marion because look what happened with Ann.

TOM: I don't think we gave up on Marion. What we were saying . . . no matter what we say . . . I mean, if she says, "I'm leaving no matter what you all say," what can we do?

GRETA: Just a minute ago I had a fantasy of seeing Marion getting up out of her chair and walking out.

In the excerpt above, Marion appears to represent the group members' conviction that their unresolved feelings about members who left the group prevents them from dealing positively with threats of additional separation and loss. The participants in the group are expressing their unwillingness to admit that there are any real problems in the group. The group needs to render Marion's dissatisfactions as her problem rather than as a symptom of group dissatisfaction. In fact, the other participants need to see Marion herself as being a specific problem. Marion is apparently in collusion with this latent group objective and feeds into the group expectation by describing herself as moody. In a collusive relationship, there are no innocent victims. Marion's statement suggests an important reason for the group's frustration with her. She tells the group that she is unhappy and suggests that she is unwilling to let the group help her with her problem. Tom and Greta subtly have been encouraging Marion to leave the group throughout the session. In Greta's last statement this directive is revealed in a wish-fulfilling fantasy.

SUBTLE ASPECTS OF GROUPS

The subtle aspects of sensitivity training concern the interpersonal and group processes which operate in all groups. There are a host of preconceived assumptions and expectations made by the group members (as well as the group leader) about what should happen in a process group. These assumptions and expectations are frequently mental fairy tales. They are based upon what an individual would like to happen or fearfully fantasizes may happen in the group rather than what he actually has found to be the case in his previous group experiences. These unconscious notions become pooled and shared by the entire group membership, often in very subtle and obscure ways. It is on the basis of these unconscious notions that group members operate in rewarding and rejecting one another's behavior.

"Common group tensions" may block the group from working effectively. These tensions are the shared, covert aspects of group process in which the needs and defenses of the members are at odds with one another. The manifest content of group discussion may embrace any conceivable topic, but regardless of the manifest content, there always rapidly develops an underlying group tension or emotion that the participants are unaware of but which significantly influences their behavior. It is the task of the consultant to indicate these group tensions and delineate their meaning to the work of the group.

In poorly conducted training groups, group tensions remain hidden agendas. This leads to group regression and depersonalization of group members. If the task at hand is avoided because of the primitive emotions it evokes and the participants are unable to communicate these feelings to one another in an open manner, frustration, anger, and contagion break through in full fury. The consultant needs to pay special attention to such notions as: the group can survive only if its members act simplistically and conformingly or, on the other hand, that members must avoid being influenced by others and, therefore, need to deny that they can work in concert in a mature and rational manner.

How does the consultant undo the participants' proclivities toward acting on the basis of untested, invalid, and preconceived assumptions? He may interpret to the group what it is that they are doing and the function these behaviors serve. I will be more specific about how this is done.

In the same session of the process group discussed several pages previously, Edna, a heavy, bosomy woman with a painted smile and furtive glances, and Harry, a middle-aged, stiff executive, expressed their resentment and disappointment at the consultant for not doing what was clearly his job to do. They contended that if the group experience was not to be a waste of their time, each of the participants must learn ways of becoming more interpersonally competent outside the group. The rest of the group agreed with them that the consultant's job was to lecture the group on social behavior. In this endeavor the consultant was supposed to point out to each of the participants what he was doing to alienate other people. The consultant at this juncture intervened and indicated that he had said or done nothing to convey the idea that he was supposed to lecture them or to make them more socially competent. He wondered out loud where these ideas came from. Since he did not introduce or suggest them to the group (the consultant frequently may refer back to the task at hand when he feels that the group is attempting to avoid confrontation with the goal for which they have convened—a study of what is going on in the here–and–now.), he supposed these ideas must have been brought in by the group members. He suggested that perhaps the members of the group would prefer to be told how to behave rather than struggle with their own undefined intentions and silent fears about being intimately involved in an interpersonal encounter. The participants reflected upon the consultant's words and soon fell into desultory discussion. After a while tension was felt to be building up in the group. The participants again mobilized for another assault upon the consultant's apparent lack of responsibility in performing his task. They claimed that they could not work on the task at hand (as yet undefined) because they did not have the resources to do so. They disclaimed possessing training or knowledge about groups, certainly they denied having the technical knowledge the consultant imputedly possessed but was rather arbitrarily and selfishly withholding. They blamed the consultant for the group's failure to get something accomplished.

The consultant pointed out that the group was insisting that he feed them by telling them what they were supposed to be doing. He shared with them his impression that, ironically, when he did feed them they ignored what he said and continued to insist that he was depriving them of his skills and knowledge. He pointed out that he had observed people in the group smiling and nodding their heads in approval of what he was saying even before he had completed enough of his statements to put his point of view across. It was apparent, the consultant noted, that the participants did not want to hear what he had to say. The consultant raised the question of whether the participants actually wanted advice and guidance or an approving pat on the head.

As the incident reported above should suggest, in his statements to the group, the consultant cannot simply describe what he observes to be transpiring. He must at the same time offer an explanation of the behavior. The consultant deals with the emotional tendencies the members of the group appear unaware of but which are significantly influencing their behavior as members of a social unit. He also tries to clarify the mobilized feelings they are aware of but cannot fashion into words. Articulating their feelings would allow them to compare their attitudes and sentiments with the observations of others and thereby test the validity of their view of themselves and of the world.

Experience remains largely unconscious and inaccessible to rational action unless it is conceptualized. In general, the sensitivity training movement pays little attention to cognitive processing of affective experience. Too frequently, group leaders circumvent resistance by participants and by the group as a whole to the conceptualization of experience by simply ignoring the issue or getting the members involved in a nonverbal exercise. They seem to feel that if people put their feelings into action then there is no need to explore these feelings cognitively. Once emotion is expressed, it is dropped. The objective in these groups is apparently to induce participants to express emotion but not to learn what the emotion is all about or to attain a sense of mastery over one's feelings. (Goldberg, 1970)

I have often been asked if there are times in groups when the members can be said to be efficaciously applying themselves to the task at hand. Bion referred to this as the work group assumption. From Bion's writings may be derived some intellectual appreciation of a work group prototype. I have endeavored, however, to specify the precise expression the work mood takes and have found it a most elusive task.

From time to time participants in particular groups seem to be working more realistically at the task at hand than at other times; they appear more appreciative of the irrational and preconceived notions they have been, or currently are, operating under; they are able to relate to one another with what appears to be sincerity and candor. Nevertheless, I am still at a loss to delineate precisely what expression the work theme takes at the moment it occurs. Perhaps the very words I use to state the problem are inaccurate and misleading. Like pleasure, our effective psychosocial function might not be one discrete moment or specific act, encapsulating appropriate emotional expression or constituting the sophisticated cognitive activities referred to by Bion. Effective psychosocial functioning may be a general feeling that aspects of one's self have been met head on, hopes and aspirations articulated and pursued. The participant fully engaged in mature work activity may have an accentuated awareness of feelings about himself and others. This awareness permits an immediate and open contact with the otherwise fragmented processes of his ego that typically shield him from and compartmentalize his human experiences.

A group is doing its work when each participant knows clearly and explicitly how he regards each fellow member and how he actually reacts to him. Each group member also should be aware of how the other participants in the group feel about each other. To achieve this understanding, knowledge of how a group uses its members to serve its purposes is a prerequisite. Participants unwittingly replace lost objects from their past experiences by relating to the recovered objects (strangers) with the same intentions, affection, and perception originally cathected to the earlier object. A study of this process should lead to insight into the dysfunctional requirements the participants are making upon themselves and their recovered objects in order to maintain inappropriate object relationships. With insight, the participants will be better able to control their need for distorting perception, denying communication and feedback from others, and become aware of intrapsychic signals that are contradictory with conscious perceptions and purposes. With improved communication and clearer understanding of one's intention, the provisions for more meaningful encounter and mutually gratifying negotiation can be established.

A process group is a created situation in which each participant is:

encouraged to bring his own beliefs and attitudes into open debate, and in which those beliefs and attitudes might be objectified, integrated and tested by the standards and methods that a *group* can develop with more authenticity than a single mind can be trusted to do. (Powell, 1949)

The hallmark of the process group is achieved through the shared development of a common method of approach to problems and conflicts emanating from the clash and interchange of different perspectives of the group members.

Society has never been willing to admit its ills. It has sought out individuals to whom to it could attribute its malevolence. In this way, society avoids taking responsibility for the adverse events and practices which all of us participate in and subtly encourage. Our inability to apply the same Nuremberg standard to our behavior as we have to others, in respect to the atrocities of the Viet Nam conflict, for instance, is but a too obvious and tragic example. Our victim-scapegoats are interned in special institutions set apart from the community where their malevolence is not seen as a part of each of us. The employment of process groups and other such groups will, hopefully, help the community view the interrelationship of pathology in its deviants and the pathology that is encouraged by each of us in such a way that scapegoats are no longer created.

> "The characters in Sartre's play *No Exit*
> decide that even though they have been
> thrown together by some unknown agent
> and have no natural liking for one an-
> other, they can perhaps improve upon
> their situation by taking down the bar-
> riers and becoming known. Similarly, in
> a therapy group . . . "
>
> T.C. Greening
> "The Transparent Self"

THERAPIST-PATIENT RELATIONSHIPS—8

EXISTENTIAL-ANALYTIC GROUP PSYCHOTHERAPY

How do I experience myself in an existential-analytic group differently than I did in the psychoanalytic groups I was trained to conduct? In an existential-analytic group, I am less curious about interesting psychodynamics. I feel less like a trained scientist and
technician and am more willing to interact and reveal myself. I experience the demands upon me for relationship more immediately and
genuinely than in groups I conducted psychoanalytically. Reik has
written that in the empathic congruence between patient and therapist, without which therapy cannot occur, the therapist shares the
experience of the patient not as if it were his own but as his own. I,
too, attempt to participate in the experience of the other. However, I
also concur with Roger (1949) that empathic understanding of the
patient must come from the therapist "sensing the client's internal
reference without the therapist losing his own emotional existence."

Although I take up the experience of the other, I need to make
clear to the other what I am and what I am not. I do not wish to stand

for someone else—a father, a mother, a son, a daughter, a teacher, or a former therapist. As a person involved in a relationship with another I wish to have impact on the other as a real person rather than as a fantasied figure. On my part, for this to occur, I must be willing to regard myself as a real person, capable of foibles and human errors, rather than a judge or a detached observer. Arthur Burton (1964) has aptly said:

> Transference and counterference are insufficient as complete therapeutic formulations in themselves. I have always felt that they lacked sufficient breadth and scope as parameters for a most complex relationship phenomenon, and now firmly believe that not all of the psychotherapeutic relationship is a transference neurosis, and not all of the feelings of the therapist are countertransference.
>
> There is a part of the psychotherapeutic interview which is not historical and which is not transference. That is, the reaction of the patient to the therapist, and vice versa, is *pour soi*—for itself—and may have no reference to past figures. . . . Some of the most transcending of human relationships . . . have *immediacy* and *presence,* and their effects are not necessarily altered by an analytic attitude or by analytic applications.

In agreeing with Burton's point of view, I also admit to being no less wary of my own motives in therapy and those of my patients in relating with one another than my psychoanalytic training taught me to be. Motives do not spring forth new, virgin, unfettered by unresolved trappings of fantasied and former relationships. This, however, in no way denies the relevance of the spontaneous, immediate interpersonal encounter with those with whom I work. Inspection of the patient's history is an appropriate endeavor for an existential-analytic group insofar as it frees the being together of patient and therapist, patient and patient, and patient and himself in terms of the present interactive encounter. If the inspection of the patient's past allows the group to avoid dealing with the present situation it is irrelevant to the purpose for convening. Crises occur in the life of each of the patients from time to time and, of course, they are explored. At all times, nonetheless, attempts should be made to relate these crises to the manner in which the patient handles himself in the group.

In an existential-analytic group I am concerned with perceptual distortions and inappropriate emotional reactions among the group members insofar as they impede satisfactory relationships with others in the group and insofar as they are a concern of the patient displaying these behaviors. An existential-analytic group is not concerned with the meaning of relationships in terms of the past but with their meaning in present and proactive strivings. The experience of relating to another person in the group is valuable for itself without having to uncover transference material. Dysfunctional behavior patterns are worth studying insofar as they prove to be obstacles to the patient's developing a conscious conception of what he wants of himself and others in the group, and his reaching out and getting what he seeks.

The following is an excerpt in which the therapist in an existential-analytic group uses cues from other group members and from a particular member, Bud, to attempt to dissolve Bud's passive–aggressive personal strategy: acting only on the basis of other people's acts toward him, and, on the basis of insufficient data, assuming people aren't very interested in him.

BUD: I'm not sure what is happening with me—but just that as people are shooting things at me I'm beginning to feel all—all confused —inside.

THERAPIST: Are you feeling confused now?

BUD: Yeah! . . . You know, like the feeling I don't want to be bothered . . . feel like I don't want to let anyone in. I have sort of planned out my mental activities. I guess I'm always confused about what people think of me.

SALLY: This is the first time I heard you say you don't want to be bothered.

BUD: —can't get involved—

JANE: *(asked if Bud had any fantasies about the group when he was out sick for two sessions.)*

BUD: No, but saw Murray [another member of the group] outside and he told me what happened the last couple of times and I guess I missed being here.

THERAPIST: Sounds like you're a spectator. You want things to happen in the group but I'm not sure what you want in terms of yourself. I'm less clear about you than anyone else in terms of what you want for yourself in this group.

JANE: *(reports that the last time she was in group before leaving for a trip to Chicago she had gone around and told everyone what she thought of him. She mentioned that Bud confused her when she turned to him in that session.)*

BUD: *(mentions he went through a period when he did a lot of work in the group and then for some reason shut off and hasn't been able to work lately.)* I haven't even been thinking why—but I will.

THERAPIST: But you still have time tonight. *(Therapist suggests that Bud go around the group [as Lucy did] and find out what each person thinks of him—since he professes not to know.)*

Bud was put in a position in which he had to initiate risky interpersonal encounters. Moreover, in formulating what he felt each of the other group members harbored about him, Bud was forced to get in touch with his fantasies about himself. He was able to check out the validity of his fantasies by finding out how others in the group actually experienced him. He became less prone to use qualifying adverbs, which were an indication of his extreme caution, and more apt to employ active verbs, suggesting that he was ready to actively deal with himself and others.

THE PROBLEM OF COUNTERTRANSFERENCE

I do not take groups and make contacts with patients for my own growth, development, or therapy. If I did, I would have no right to call myself the therapist and charge a fee; instead, I would be another group participant rather than the designated therapist. One reason that group therapy is preferable to individual psychotherapy is that the group members serve as guards against the therapist's countertransference. They enable me to act more appropriately and more spontaneously in the present group situation. They alert me against carrying over biases and expectations from my relationship with persons who are not members of the present group.

This is illustrated in the following group protocol:

HELEN: *(discusses her former therapist)* Whenever he said things he put it in terms of himself and I was so impressed with that because it made him so real to me.—I guess I wish you could do that, too!

THERAPIST: You want to hear more about me?

(other patients "protect" therapist claiming the therapist has been responsive and supportive of them.)

THERAPIST: Well, what about Helen's statement? She would like to hear more about my experiences than I have revealed.

HELEN: It was a question of the way you put it. Dr. Sprite, in the other group . . . every once in a while he would mention that this was an experience he had. It was natural.

THERAPIST: Uh-huh. What does this do for you?

ABE: [*a patient who also wanted the therapist to talk about his own experiences*] Well, I think it makes it real. Well, the problem we are all struggling with are the problems of people no matter when, where and how . . .

MURRAY: You seem to be saying I wish you could do that, too. I think you are saying I wish you were Dr. Sprite. and I think that this is a difference in personality. *(Helen tries to break in)* Wait, let me say, I feel very comfortable with the way he [*the therapist*] handles the group, comfortable with you [*the therapist*] and if you choose to tell more about yourself I guess I would feel comfortable about that, too. . . .

From this discussion the therapist realized that he had self-protective feelings caused by events outside the group. He came to a clearer understanding of his reactions in recent weeks to patients in his groups. The therapist is not always the person who is most in touch with each of the patients' needs.

One outstanding value of group experience is that there is often at least one member of the group who is personally stirred by the expression of deep feelings and who closely identifies with the person expressing the feelings. (Haigh, 1968)

It is these group members who help monitor my over-reactions as well as under-reactions to patients in the group. The therapy group utilizes the strengths and resources and also clearly crystallizes the weaknesses of patients and therapist. Nonetheless, I have no false modesty about why I conduct a group. I am the therapist—trained, experienced, and, I feel, personally fitted to facilitate enabling processes among and within the persons with whom I work. If I seriously doubted my abilities, I would step aside and try to find out more about myself.

Being intimately involved in an ameliorative endeavor, with its heightened human drama, its challenges, its penetrating philosophical issues, its playacting and personal pathos is comparable to being involved in the creation of the world's greatest art. It is a most exciting, albeit often ungratifying, experience. In addition to his wish (need) to assist others, the psychotherapist is both personally and intellectually curious about the intricacies of human drama. Probably it is both these qualities conjoined with favorable personality attributes which make him an effective therapeutic agent. After all, it is the opportunity for personal involvement and intellectual stimulation that attracts therapists to their profession. But these rewards must remain as incidental payoffs, not the raison d' être for being involved in an ameliorative endeavor with another. Unless I am concerned primarily with assisting my patients rather than with satisfying personal curiosity, I am not fulfilling my contract with my patients. Hurvitz and others have claimed that self-help groups are more efficacious than those that are professionally conducted. If investigation demonstrated conclusively that leaderless groups are more efficacious in enabling patients to heal themselves, it would be meaningless and dishonest to label myself "therapist" and refer to the participants as "patients" and charge them a fee for the experience of being with a person who has no more to offer than does any one of them. To date, the claim has not been substantiated. (See Chapter 14) Until it is, my experience of helping to enable others in groups I conduct to come to terms with their human condition justifies my presence.

FOSTERING TRUST IN AN EXISTENTIAL-ANALYTIC GROUP

The early development in the group of a warm, accepting involvement sets a climate of trust that allows the patient to reveal himself and engage in a growth-seeking venture with others. Trust is agreed to be a sine qua non of effective group experience by social scientists with rather different orientations to the study of groups; for example:

Trust is the pacemaker variable in group growth. From it stem all the other significant variables of health. That is, to the extent that trust develops, people are able to communicate genuine feelings and perceptions on relevant issues . . . with themselves and others and to form consensual goals. To the degree that trust is present, people can be truly interdependent. (Gibb, 1967)

Actually self-disclosure and open expressiveness is not something that is very likely to occur because of one's motivation; that person will also generally require a particular setting conducive to openness and some form of open receptivity on the part of the recipient of his disclosure. (T.C. Greening)

Moreover, studies of small task groups suggest that the group leader's influence on the goal of the group is neutralized in a group that is disturbed and where the members do not have a strong positive regard for one another. So much time is spent establishing a semblance of order that the leader's task functions are neglected. (Fiedler, 1963) This finding may apply to designed groups as well.

In order for trust to develop, the therapist needs to explore those realistic and imagined conditions in a group which retard trust.

THERAPIST: There seems to be a bit of depressed feelings in here. I sense it has something to do with trust. I'm beginning to wonder if we know each other as well as we thought we did. Do we trust each other? Do others in the group trust us?

RITA: What made you say that? I was just thinking about that.

OLIVIA: That is what I was thinking about last week.

RITA: This has been the most devastating week of my life. *(she goes on to describe husband's telling her that he has found another woman.)* I was thinking this afternoon I would like to bring it up this evening but I didn't know how I would be able to. *(Father pulled same trick on mother and Rita said she never trusted him again.)*

THERAPIST: Rita, when I was talking about the lack of trust and if we knew each other as well as we thought we did, did you think I was referring to people outside the situation here?

RITA: I took the roundabout way of bringing it up to express distrust that I probably brought into the group with me.—I hate to bring it up since he is not here, but there is something about Marty. I didn't trust his words—like the time he brought up games he claimed people in the group were into. I didn't understand. But I didn't bring it up because I was afraid of what he meant.

The therapist explored with the group their fears and the conditions they felt were necessary to experience trust in one another. From this and subsequent discussions the patients began to realize that feeling trust was not a mysterious process. A climate of trust must be created intentionally—it does not just magically occur or fail to occur but requires concerted effort by the group members.

THE EARLY SESSIONS IN AN EXISTENTIAL-ANALYTIC GROUP

Although what should occur in a particular group session is neither sensible nor possible to specify, I do offer certain processes occurring in the first few sessions of an existential-analytic group as a tentative frame of reference for the reader.

The interview. Each patient should be interviewed prior to entering a group. The patient's goals and the therapist's conceptualization of what goes on in a group are explored. The patient is encouraged to articulate what he wants from the group experience: how he perceives a group experience helping him; what he has to offer the group; and the roles and functions the therapist, other patients, and himself need to assume in order for him to reach his goals. The therapist must not permit the patient simply to express his therapy goals to the effect: "Here are my goals. I want therapy to do something about ———." Instead, the therapist probes for the ways the patient believes therapy can deal with his goals. Without examining the quality of the patient's conceptualization of problem-solving it is difficult to assess his motivation for intensive group experience. Above all else, the therapist needs to impress upon the patient that the group meets to work.

Initial session. During the first session, the therapist probes the kinds of commitments to the group the patients are willing to make. If all the patients are new to the group, he explores how long they feel the group should meet. In an open-ended group, he asks how long each of the new patients feels he is able to commit himself to working in the group. The commitment, of course, is not irrevocable; but getting a patient to make a commitment to the group helps him involve himself with the others (and vice versa) in a mutual endeavor. The announcement of a commitment in the presence of the group, rather than in private to the therapist, helps the other members throughout the course of the sessions deal with a patient's resistance in claiming he is through working on the goals for which he came. For the therapist with a flexible schedule it is preferable for a new group to decide during the first session how frequently they should meet together. To assist the members in this decision, the therapist relates from his own experience the advantages and disadvantages of meeting frequently, reminding them that they are expected to attend every session, and fees are charged accordingly. The therapist stresses that the patients are expected to level with others in the group and openly share their decision-making. Most importantly, they are asked to specify what they expect of themselves and others in the group.

Because the first session is usually taken up with administrative and group concerns, the therapist has an excellent opportunity to survey the group processes and normative values operating from the onset. It is my impression that in an existential-analytic group the patients' strong identification with one another and with the therapist's goals tends to create a warm, accepting climate, making therapy a viable endeavor. This kind of identification most often has been absent in therapy groups I have observed and conducted in psychiatric hospitals. In groups comprised of paranoid schizophrenics and character disorders, so much time is spent fighting one another and the therapist that too much hurt is unscabbed for tender feelings and identification to surface.

Second session. Clear attempts at forming relationships are discerned in the second session. The therapist is interested in what each of the patients wants from the other and what each does about it. The forming of relationships foreshadows the yet unformulated normative system in the group. The therapist looks, for instance, for the group member who best expresses the feelings of the group as a whole and for the person who is permitted to remain a stranger. Some attempt to discuss the therapist's role is usually made in the second session. I may suggest to the group members that my role is open for negotiation.

Resistance early in the course of the group must be dealt with swiftly as it sets a tone for the future. For instance, patients who report they will miss some particular session are testing the group by seeking to elicit the group interest and concern.

Third session. This session often focuses on the emergent role system in the group.

Initially, group members' activities are rather idiosyncratic. They reflect the norms, values, and culture of the participants' previous and existing membership and reference groups. Only when the participants' characteristic ways of responding to other participants in the group become regulated through a process of modification to the membership of the present group does a grouping of people become a group with a feeling of involvement and identification. The individual member's regulated actions within the therapy group, referred to as a role, cannot be explained on the basis of his personal disposition and past history alone. In isolation from a social system the concept of role is meaningless; a role can be understood only in relation to other regulated modes of behavior by other role occupants. Behavior is a function of the psychosocial field that exists at the time of enactment. (Lewin, 1951) A role in psychosocial terms is a compromise between how the role aspirant wishes to present himself in the group and the mode of behavior that the other group members impress upon him as being available and appropriate to the group. I particularly wish to explore into which kinds of roles the group casts its members.

Frequently, patients categorize one another according to the severity of their symptoms in an attempt to find solutions to the existential question: How do we get to know another person? (For example, in terms of his symptoms, his needs, our feelings toward him, or in some other way?) Since patients utilize values, standards, and beliefs from their previous psychosocial experiences, the therapist needs to explore with each whether or not these standards from the past provide the ways he now wishes to get to know others. I encourage the patients to react to another as they experience him and to compare their present reactions with their fantasies, associations, and "knowledge" about the other.

Fourth session. An important function of the existential-analytic therapist is role-modeling. He, in fact, role-models behavior from his initial contact with the patients. In brief, role-modeling may be defined as a situation in which the therapist attempts to present himself in such a way as to convey effective interpersonal strategies and problem-solving skills. The aim of role-modeling is to give the patient an opportunity to observe and, if he chooses, imitate alternative and more effective interpersonal skills than he presently possesses.

The therapist may intentionally hold back efforts to develop relationships with the group members until he feels that they have struggled with their relationships with one another. Otherwise, he will be subverting his efforts to their dependency demands.

The group is a place where patients can learn to build relationships and develop them—not merely a place where they can understand something about their relationships outside the group. For instance, if a patient has difficulty with his wife at home, he should explore his relationship with the women in the group rather than spend the entire session discussing his wife.

Because in the beginning of group treatment I feel that I have more evidence about group process than about individual psychodynamics I tend to make more group interpretations and fewer individual interpretations. Moreover, early in the group I am primarily concerned with fostering positive group forces and with the specific group norms that emerge. Whenever possible, I interpret the participants' behavior on the basis of what I infer to be their group norms and encourage discussion about these emergent and convert norms. It is the resulting awareness among the members of common feelings, rather than common problems or goals, that is the first step toward working seriously together. (Mann, 1953)

THE DYNAMICS OF EXISTENTIAL-ANALYTIC GROUP PSYCHOTHERAPY

To understand the dynamics of a psychotherapeutic situation one must locate the person who creates movement in the group. In a sense it is I who pushes in the group. I do not do so in an intrusive way (at least, not often), and I actually let the group guide me. I try to sense with whom the group tensions reside most intensely and focus my attention on that person, group, or sometimes, the entire membership. I try to canvass the group, asking myself what each group member's attitude is toward himself and toward others in the group at that point. The therapist may allow his unconscious full rein as his apperceptive faculties engage the patient's choice of words, facial expression, bodily posture, and so forth. The therapist's impressions may take the form of images and fantasies but they are not helpful to the patients if they remain entirely in his head. Only from actions are people really known and fully understood. The therapist must let the deeper recesses of himself contact and respond to the other. He cannot predetermine what effect speaking or acting in a certain way will

have on himself or the person to whom he is responding. As an un-
moved observer, one remains an armchair philosopher not a facilitating person. Only by responding emotionally as a participant and
reflecting upon the effect of his behavior can the therapist properly
assess his influence and impact upon others and adjust his behavior
accordingly, as is illustrated in the following group protocol:

Jane is an appealing, slight girl with large brown eyes often
filled with panic. More than others in this group she lacked meaningful relationships in her life. She claimed to have a number of fears
but was unable to specify any. She was also quick to sense danger in
the group when others seemed comfortable with the mood. She became very agitated if "wounds" inflicted during one session remained
unassuaged until the next. As Jane had been unable to name and
challenge her fears, she could do little more than flee from them.

I fantasized about her in the group. I imagined a large bulky
figure pursuing her, waving a crooked finger at her. I felt my heart
pumping rapidly. I looked at Jane speaking from my fantasy. "Have
you had enough punishment, Jane?" She didn't answer with any
sounds, but her eyes pleaded "Yes, but how do I stop the pain?" I said,
now more consciously aware of my words, "You have a right to tell
that part of you punishing you to 'cut it out!'" Out of the welled recess
of her repressed feelings poured memories she claimed to recognize
only from dreams. She described when she was an adolescent slap-
ping her mother and cursing God's name after finding out that she
was adopted. She had felt unloved since that day but until that moment had not remembered why.

On the basis of my images and impressions, I ask myself what
the others' emotional needs are at that moment and with which group
members the need is most pressing. In Karen Horney's terms, I specu-
late about which objects, ideation, and affect each of the group members is moving toward, moving against, and moving away from. I suspect that the therapist is more discerning about a group member's
emotional need whereas the other group members are frequently
more perceptive about who has the most pressing need in the group at
that moment. With these assumptions as my compass I wait for the
group members to locate the patient with the most pressing need and
I work with the patient, or, more ideally, with the group, to enable
him to structure his affective resources in such a way that he can
make his needs known to himself and to the others. Sometimes I disagree with the group about who is most needy. Because I have confidence in their ability to discover distress, I feel it is important to dis-
cern why we disagree.

"We are the hollow men
We are the stuffed men . . .
Shape without form, shade without
   colour
Paralysed force, gesture without
   motion."

T.S. Eliot
"The Hollow Men"

THE FOCAL PROBLEM GROUP TECHNIQUE—9

All designed groups, regardless of the leader's theories for explaining behavior and the techniques he uses to influence improved psychosocial functioning, are essentially concerned with the manner in which the participants deal with their problems of daily existence. The focal problem group emphasizes active problem-solving but may not appear to be a very exciting approach because it does not deal with fantasies or dreams, nor does it concern itself with seeking the symbolic meaning of aberrant behavior. The focal problem model uses action techniques such as role-playing rather than delving into soul-searching and attitude change.

Unlike other groups using action techniques, the focal problem group seeks to avert the stimulation of transference, conflict, and heightened affect among its participants. In the focal problem group the leader assumes that task performance and rational learning are maximally induced when the participants are unfettered by anxiety, stirred emotion, and inappropriate reactions to one another. The focal problem model, therefore, provides no more glamor than attending to the same task day after day while steadily seeking to improve one's performance on the job. The focal problem model has considerable utility, particularly for the wide spectrum of clients who find themselves not profiting from reconstructive therapy. A good number of clients seeking ameliorative assistance "are not readily reachable by abstract, conceptual, or symbolic intervention." (Minuchin et al., 1967, p. 246) Unlike the more literate and the better motivated clients, these individuals

> are generally action-prone, concretistic, and restricted in the use of verbal symbols. They have difficulty in producing and sustaining rational and coherent dialogue; their modality of talking is more informative when one "reads" behavior rather than verbal content. (Minuchin, op. cit.)

These clients, unreachable by the modalities therapists have employed traditionally, challenge our ingenuity for new enabling approaches such as the focal problem model.

I have made varied and extensive use of the focal problem model. For instance, in a large federal psychiatric hospital, I used it in orienting new patients to a hospital service and in preparing both adolescents and adults (some hospitalized for thirty years) for their impending return to the community. In addition I have utilized the focal problem model for following-up patients on convalescent leaves and for dealing with crises in inpatient services such as drug smuggling and usage in a drug rehabilitation program. Most recently, in conjunction with a new community health program, I employed the focal problem model in training high school, college, and professional volunteers for a "hot line" community service.

I feel that much emotional disturbance results from the chaotic, disorganized, and dysfunctional approaches clients have to problem-solving. The focal problem approach is particularly relevant to people who suffer chronic unmitigated frustration and psychological impotence—to people who have not experienced themselves constructively affecting their environment and do not have confidence in being able to do so in the future. The focal problem approach is predicated upon sound principles of critical thinking, decision-making, and problem-solving. However, I do not contend that a cognitive approach to life problems is a substitute for personal insight or intensive psychotherapeutic experience.

In reconstructive therapy the client can generalize to a wide spectrum of life exigencies what he learns about his internal processes and how they affect whatever situation he is in. Although sound problem-solving principles are universally applicable, the client in focal problem therapy is learning more about approaches to external reality than acquiring knowledge about his own subjective reality. The usefulness of what he learns in focal problem therapy therefore is more confined to problematic situations in which past and present are closely related.

Notwithstanding, any therapeutic endeavor that does not encourage the client to develop and utilize some model for effective problem-solving is not comprehensive nor sustaining. Many intelligent and motivated clients are seriously lacking in proper problem-solving techniques. Therapy that encourages introspection and the accruing of insight but tends to ignore effective methods for resolving problematic situations is missing a central goal of psychotherapy: to help the client become less dependent upon others by becoming more effective and self-sufficient in meeting his needs. Being able to solve his own difficulties builds self-esteem, a sine qua non of successful therapy.

Since a focal problem group has specifiable goals and foci, it can generally be conducted on a short-term basis, with the number of sessions specified at the onset. Today we realize a need for an ameliorative method which is short-term and designed specifically to teach problem-solving skills since intensive psychotherapy is not available —and in many cases is not the treatment of choice—for a considerable number of our clients. A large percentage of clients hold regular employment and are required to attend family and community functions. The amount of time they can spend away from their social duties is more limited than for the major classes of clients in the past: the isolated schizophrenics who idled away their life in a state hospital or clients with financial leverage and professional status who could more freely arrange their therapy hours.

Therapists often encounter patients who are resistive to therapeutic endeavor that threatens exposure of certain guarded areas. These areas may be severely conflict-ridden and the client deficient in resources to deal with their ascent into consciousness. As a result, the therapist may encounter a floodgate of ebullient affect ruptured when he probes too deeply. Probing too deeply in these areas may evoke in short a psychotic episode which requires the patient's hospitalization. Rational approaches, because they are less threatening and require less probing of these disturbed areas, are more acceptable to these resistive clients.

Although the focal problem model, a rational approach to personal difficulties, is not the treatment of choice under ideal conditions, rarely do ideal conditions exist in working with difficult clients. Rational models in solving personal difficulties offer the therapist an approach to clients whom he otherwise might not be able to assist.

I will describe psychodynamically Mrs. Jones, a patient who in many aspects is an ideal candidate for a focal problem group. Mrs. Jones, a fifty-six year old alcoholic patient with numerous psychiatric hospitalizations, was evaluated for intensive psychotherapy and was found to be not a good candidate for insight therapy.

Mrs. Jones lacks insight and the ability to reason analytically. She appears overly concrete and does not seem to have sufficient ego strength to form a relationship in which she must tolerate critical scrutiny of herself as a person and disclose her painful and threatening feelings to another person. She needs to form a dependent relationship with a therapist in which she is given advice and counsel amalgamated with considerable support and acceptance. The therapist might focus on getting at her strengths in order to help her consolidate her resources. Once she develops trust in her therapist and some self-esteem, she might be encouraged to expand her energies into new areas of functioning.

THE FOCAL PROBLEM MODEL

The focal problem model is an ameliorative approach concerned with the "hows" rather than the "whys" of behavior. It is a directive technique whereby the group leader and the client, with the help of the other group members, explore the client's current problem-solving skills and difficulties. The participants join together to develop specific sets of procedures to improve the client's approaches to decision-making and problem-solving.

Short-term training in problem-solving frequently becomes bogged down because introspective inquiries such as "How come————?" or "How would you explain————?" open isolated avenues of insight and awareness. The group leader in a focal problem group stresses the enactive modality, challenging the client to show him how he can improve on his previous performance rather than probing why the client could not perform effectively in the past.

Insofar as the focal problem approach is a group technique, it is defined by the characteristics of the participants who comprise the group. This technique may be modified for individual counseling session or adopted by task groups to solve community (group-wide) problems. Unlike an individual counseling session, in which a client presents a concern to the therapist and may expect his attention in dealing with it, the group setting requires that each participant consider only the concerns that are shared by the entire group. In a heterogeneous group a range of psychological sophistication and presenting complaints offers each of the group members counter arguments, defensive alternatives, and dystonic emotional reactions —in short, a wide array of alternatives to problematic situations. In a focal problem group, on the other hand, the group leader is concerned with fostering the shared concerns of his clients: those issues with which all have encountered difficulty in the past. A group that has too much diversity in terms of interests, problems, and skills has considerable difficulty deciding upon shared concerns. Therefore, the group leader initially selects clients highly similar in presenting symptoms and complaints or, in the case of a task group, with congruent backgrounds (for example, a group might be composed of teachers, or supervisory managers, or blue collar workers). As a result, commonality of personal concerns is highly probable when the clients convene as a group.

At first, during the *assessment stage,* the therapist encourages a free discussion of the concerns that brought the clients for professional assistance. He encourages the participants to find common concerns among themselves. He helps clarify what is being discussed, but more importantly his role in the initial phase of the group is to be supportive of free and comfortable interaction among the participants. The leader must create a group climate in which each of the participants can communicate his problems and concerns in such a way that they may be addressed. He may foster group interaction by what R.C. Dubois and M.S. Li have referred to as "group conversation." A *group conversation* is designed to create a mood of well-being, mutual regard, and liking among the clients from their involvement in a topic of concern to all. The participants are asked to freely associate to what is being discussed and relate, if they wish, their earliest memories of the issue under discussion. In this way, intimate experiences are shared with others in the group. Regression may be noted in the group and is not unwarranted in the early stages of a focal problem group. The therapist must initially reduce the clients' anxiety in order to permit ego-involvement in a shared endeavor. Each member of the group is asked to freely relate to the topic being discussed in the group. Each participant is encouraged to furnish the discussion topic with whatever recent or early experiences he feels may be useful to the other group members in understanding where he as a person stands in terms of the topic.

Occasionally, even with sufficient warm-up and support, some clients will narcissistically refuse to accept the notion that some of their most pressing concerns are similar to those of others in the group. Where resistance to locating and accepting shared concerns is widespread, the therapist may wish to be more directive and indicate problem motifs that appear to him to be common to the complaints of the participants. The therapist may interpret, according to his theoretical system, that certain complaints and symptoms refer to a particular, underlying dynamic which he believes is the group's shared concern.

It is advisable that, in addition to theorizing about the content of the discussion, the group leader be sensitive to existent group tensions. For instance, on theoretical grounds the leader may infer that under the circumstances of being in a hospital where, as at home, people provide for them because it is their duty and, paying no fee to participate in the group, the participants' discussion of loss of employment is an expression of dependency and is a shared group concern. The therapist may also note nonverbal cues, as when a patient expresses anger and threatens to leave the group after having admitted that previous group experience has been helpful to him and when another bitterly reports that his mother still calls him at the office to see if he is dressed warmly enough while, as he is reporting his complaint, he is smoothing his obviously expensive suit. The group leader may regard these nonverbal behaviors as counter-dependent manifestations—the participants expressing the need to deny that they can't handle their difficulties alone.

Both the manifest and latent group processes may be viewed as being concerned with the issue of dependency. The client's counter-dependent need causes resistance toward avowing shared difficulties and concerns. In the group described above, the therapist confirms the dependency motif derived on theoretical grounds in terms of manifest content by responding to the covert tensions in the group. Attention to these covert tensions helps to account for the participants' refusal to accept explanations of their behavior. Being cognizant of the common group concerns and the specific mechanisms the participants employ in handling their concerns, the therapist explores with those everyday situations in which the inferred shared group concern has impeded their adequate functioning. Unlike in a reconstructive group situation, the group leader may specify his theoretical sources and assumptions for the inferences he renders. Intellectual tools are valuable because the participants are required to perform a rational task in a focal problem group.

Often in a focal problem group, the participants' resistance to avowing shared interests is not extirpated simply through the therapist's interpretation of the group discussion. In a focal problem group, unlike in reconstructive therapy, individual and group resistance is generally regarded simply as an obstacle rather than an issue which is important to explore. In reconstructive therapy, the therapist uses interpretation to enable the patient to understand the function his defensive stance serves.

The technique of interpretation is discouraged in focal problem groups. Instead, a *contract* is employed to resolve resistance to concerted group endeavor. The contract may be established through verbal agreement between the group leader and each of the participants in a dyadic interview prior to the initial group session or among the participants during the first session. The contract specifies the roles of the client and the group leader. The client is expected to do homework to participate actively and report on it to the group in group discussions and so forth. The group leader is defined as an expert in problem-solving who expects the client to abide by his suggestions and advice. Also outlined are the number of sessions the group will meet and ways in which the client may be helped by the focal problem approach.

During the course of the group, the client's unwillingness to abide by the contract is grounds for his being requested to leave the group. Whenever possible, of course, the client's obstreperousness is dealt with in the group so that the client will not have to leave. In a focal problem group, the group leader makes the final decision for a person to leave the group. But the experienced group leader in handling a client's resistance does not rely solely on the working relationship contract or upon his own assessment of the situation. He asks for feedback on his own and the resistive client's behavior from the other participants. If the in feedback is congruent with his assessment of the situation, he asks for support from the other group members. Critical confrontation from the other participants makes it difficult for the client to disregard having to deal with his aberrance.

Once a common group concern is decided upon, training in problem-solving commences. In the inventory phase, which requires the group leader's active participation, participants are asked to share their previous experience with the focal concern at hand. Participants are asked to describe all aspects of the problem (for example, when it started and who was involved). Naturally, no one is able to describe all aspects of any problem. Nonetheless, the requirement that he discuss everything he knows about the problem enables the client more consciously and rationally to consider aspects of situations which, while crucial in the outcome of his endeavors, he tended, for various reasons, to regard as incidental and insignificant.

Reviewing how problems were dealt with in the past helps the leader and other participants assess the problem-solving abilities of each client. Strengths and resources, as well as weaknesses and faulty work habits, are brought under scrutiny. Probing for the reasons—the inner needs and psychic determinants—for dysfunctional performance is not encouraged. The focal problem group is concerned not with reasons but with the ways in which problem-solving techniques proved unsuccessful in the past. However, any spontaneous insight the client gains about his behavior has potential value in facilitating the unlearning of old habits of thought.

Having assessed what went awry in the past—the environmental conditions and demands that weren't met—the group has reached the inspiration phase. Members explore possible resources for getting the appropriate information and skills for developing efficient strategies to handle previously unmet demands.

The group leader does as much as he can to enable the participants to identify and to put to immediate use whatever tools they have acquired for solving problems. An excellent method for getting started is partialization of the problematic situation. As a whole, a problem may be perceived as overwhelming and insoluble. By dividing the situation into steps, each of which requires some definite and structured tasks and procedure, order is introduced into the problem-solver's confusion.

A brief illustration from my work with a group of management interns from the Department of Health, Education and Welfare during a group relations conference, will summarize what I have said about the focal problem mode. The group leader and management interns decided in discussion what the major concern was they shared in common. The shared concern was: How are we going to explain to our supervisors that there is a better way of making decisions than the offhand way they now make them. Second, to locate resources, the participants were referred back to their recent group training experience for tools which would be useful in dealing with the problem at hand. As a lead, the group leader said:

> It seemed to me that this group felt that their way of working on problems could not be improved upon by sensitivity training earlier this week. You people seem to feel differently now. What has happened that changed your opinion? Is there anything you learned from this week-long conference that might be helpful in effecting a change in your agency's system similar to the change you have here experienced?

The group leader then demonstrated how the participants could apply the concepts and experiences acquired in the conference to the group's central concern.

> What have we learned about how people change their attitude and begin to engage in honest dialogue with others during this conference?

In other situations, the group leader may give each participant a project concerning a problematic situation outside the group. Clients are required to obtain information, locate resources necessary for making decisions and trying out new alternatives, and report how they got on with the group. In their report, they are expected to relate accurately and in detail what happened; to evaluate their performance only after fully describing objectively what happened; and to diagnose errors and delineate their plans for the next step in dealing with their problematic situation. In this project the participants are learning to become sensitive and objective observers of their own and others' behavior. Role-playing is frequently used.

The thrust is upon generating within the individual alternatives to problematic situations through a greater appreciation of his own and others' reactions to these situations. The client through experiential learning appreciates emotionally what he knows intellectually: any one problem can be viewed in a multiple of perspectives. Hence, problems can be solved in any one of many ways—there is no correct way for everyone. Freed from the need for absolute certainty and correctness in solving his problems, the client is better able to discover what is "correct" for him. This focus is derived from an existential-analytic position.

The recommendation phase is concerned with decision-making: how to decide when it is most opportune to act; the risks that are involved in each decision and how these risks may be evaluated. The decision-making skills that have been discussed may be employed to handle group as well as individual problems. Decision-making skills may be applied to problems in reconstructive therapy as well as to everyday matters. The following is an example of the focal problem approach to handle poor group attendance in a reconstructive therapy group.

In attempting to conduct a therapy group in a large psychiatric hospital, I was hampered by an insufficient number of patients attending on a regular basis. Several of the patients who had agreed to attend the group did not appear; other patients approached were "not interested in joining another group." An existential position suggested that making group therapy a viable venture was not my responsibility alone. I therefore expressed the opinion to the group that lack of membership was also their concern. I brought up what was obvious to the patients but was not openly being discussed and dealt with because it was regarded as the therapist's problem: we were having difficulty getting a group started because we did not have enough patients showing up for sessions. I asked the patients why this was happening and refused to accept their "I don't knows." I pointed out that the concerns that were keeping the other patients from coming to the group were probably the same kinds of concerns with which the present group members were wrestling. If these concerns were not brought into the open and dealt with, some of the present members also might stop attending sessions and the group would cease to be.

It was suggested that each group member had an investment in the other members showing up and that the sessions would be attended regularly only when the members shared their concerns openly. A discussion followed about how we could help one another relate our concerns openly in the group. Once it became evident that each of the present group members had an investment in the missing patients attending sessions, they were encouraged to work out ways they could get one another and the absent patients to show up regularly.

In subsequent sessions, we discussed finding new patients for the group. We considered what people get from a group experience, who profits from the experience, and who does not. Some group members suggested that outsiders, such as spouses and relatives, be invited to attend sessions; others suggested patients on their ward. The members were asked to discuss how they best might approach others and offer the group experience to them. The patients had to decide how long and on what basis a visitor would be permitted to sit in without committing himself to the group and on what basis visitors would be acceptable as regular group members.

In the evaluation phase the participant is concerned with assessing his performance and deciding how he can improve upon it and what follow-up is necessary. The evaluation process requires progressively integrating the observer role with that of active participation in decision-making. The goal here, as in other types of psychotherapy, is to attempt to maximize a participant's "ability to observe, without limiting his ability to participate." (Minuchin et al., 1967, p. 246)

Finally, in the follow-up phase the therapist attempts to help the client develop strategies for the transition from the focal group to whatever other group or situation the leader and client have decided best meets the client's needs. For example, having developed problem-solving skills and having reduced his initial anxiety about treatment, the client may be ready for reconstructive psychotherapy, to seek a job in the community, to responsibly care for his family, or to pursue other goals not available to him heretofore.

THE GROUP LEADER

As the group progresses, the leader attempts to fade from active leadership and encourages the participants to take over the leadership function. In the ideal development of focal problem model, the leader evolves into a group consultant who offers assistance to the group only when he feels the participants do not have sufficient resources to handle certain difficulties that arise. He concerns himself more with the expressive and group dynamic aspects of leadership, leaving to the participants the instrumental functions of the group and the development of problem-solving techniques.

The function of the leader in the focal problem group is to facilitate group communication through his understanding of and skill in group dynamics and learning methodologies. The leader uses his training and experience to guide the participants in employing the most effective methods for imparting information and deciding on work strategies among themselves. Because time is limited, the therapist must teach problem-solving skills in an efficient as well as effective manner. To do so the leader must initially take a more active and directive role than he would in reconstructive therapy. The role of the leader is an important learning feature in the focal problem group. In reconstructive therapy, the focus is on intrapsychic and interpersonal processes. In the focal model the emphasis is on the role model the therapist presents. By working on individual and group concerns in a rational and considered manner (for instance, questions which elicit data necessary for formulating plans and making decisions), the group leader demonstrates to the participants the steps necessary for developing and implementing their own goals.

"Junk is perfect, it is god, it is the best thing of life, even as it kills. Take a shot and you feel no pain, no anxiety; no one or no thing can hurt you. What else could give such bliss? Can his mother? Can a wife, or a father offer such total protection, absolute comfort?" (statement of a veteran addict)

Washington Post

GROUP THERAPY WITH DRUG ADDICTS—10

In this chapter I have attempted to avoid excessive use of technical and slang jargon because the use of jargon is an intellectual defense which insulates affective experience from conscious awareness by condensing and distorting it. Experience described by jargon is not directly or personally perceived nor kinesthetically registered. The first person who used such terms as "feeling uptight," "hung up," or "copping out" probably gave a pretty vivid image of his emotional state. I doubt, however, that the professional who wishes to show the addict that he is "with it" or the neophyte drug user who thinks he can "swing" only by using such terms has much of a gut feeling about what is going on in himself. I have attempted to describe the addict's view of himself and others phenomenologically.

Drug addiction is an inordinately entrenched emotional disability which requires an intensive and a prolonged period of withdrawal and rehabilitation. It is well known that the treatment and rehabilitation of the "acting-out" character disorder, particularly that of the hard-core drug addict, has not progressed in terms of treatment philosophy nor effective practice to the extent that neurotic and psychotic disorders have. (Casriel & Deitch, 1966) We cannot afford to write off this state of affairs as merely a psychiatric embarrassment. A modest estimate is that there are 250,000 active heroin addicts in the United States today—and their ranks are increasing daily. It has also been estimated that the majority of crimes committed in this country are perpetrated by people who have drug related problems. Some people may argue that this is an exaggeration but there is no denying the growing magnitude of the drug problem in the nation today.

The psychiatric profession has attempted to remove the taint of its embarrassment in not being able to correct drug addiction by expounding in theory and practice the notion that drug addiction is incurable. (Casriel & Deitch, 1966) This tactic is reminiscent of the treatment of the mentally ill during the latter half of the 19th century.

Freed from having to treat patients who were considered incurable, some physicians sent patients with drug related problems to the federal public health hospitals at Lexington and Fort Worth and, more recently, to the teaching centers located in some of the larger medical schools and hospitals. Other physicians and concerned paraprofessionals have seized upon methadone

> as the treatment for heroin, in a manner reminiscent of the way heroin was employed in the treatment for morphine at the close of the last century. [Moreover] society in its desperate battle to protect itself from the addict has passed more and more laws with harsher and harsher penalties. But the threat of long prison sentences has not attenuated the process of this malady which is reaching epidemic proportions. (Casriel & Deitch, 1966)

The confrontational approach described in this chapter is useful for working with people with character problems. The technique is based on a resocialization and learning process which enables some people to escape from a self-destructive subculture and explore, with the help of the reality-testing of people with kindred difficulties, a more consciously realized existence.

CONFRONTATION THERAPY WITH DRUG ADDICTS

Some of the best work being done with the hard-core drug addict —many observers contend, the *only* effective therapeutic work—has evolved from a group procedure rather different from traditional approaches. I will present the salient features of this confrontation approach, along with my own thinking about existential-analytic group therapy and group process, in order to provide a frame of reference for establishing an inpatient drug addiction rehabilitation program for metropolitan based hospitals.

The confrontation approach is concerned neither with drug symptomatology nor with speculation about the causes of drug behavior. An existential-analytic approach to working with drug addicts is as follows. In working with the addict, I, the therapist, wish to avoid long, rambling, unfruitful tales about the addict's way of life and his obsessive–compulsive documentation of procurement of and habituation to drugs. Insofar as a drug-free program is maintained, I make the assumption that the patients were once active addicts but are not so at the present time. My concern is with the addict as he currently is functioning. The focus, consequently, is the experiential here-and-now. When he was an active addict, his entire existence was imbued with his drug habituation. I am now concerned with the addict as a person.

It is frequently ignored that, in addition to his drug symptomatology, the addict is a person. It is by the simple reality that he and I are both people who have experienced problems in living and are attempting to cope with them that we relate to one another. (Unless an addict knows he has difficulties in addition to his addiction, any therapeutic endeavor with him is fruitless. Similarly, unless the therapist can acknowledge to the addict that he hasn't found any "golden road" to the problems of living, he will not be able to relate to the addict.) If I accept the contention that the addict is a different kind of person, (The addict tries to turn off the professional therapist by viewing him as "a dumb bastard who doesn't know what junkies are talking about because he doesn't know the scene, because he hasn't been there.") a person to be understood only by fellow addicts, I reinforce his narcissistic disturbance while at the same time fulfilling the prophecy that only an addict can work with other addicts. (I have found that a program that blends the training and systematic theory of the professional and the experiential knowledge and empathy of the ex-addict is preferable to a program that relies exclusively on either for staffing.)

If I can convey the idea that I am concerned with problems in living which he has in addition to his addiction, the addict becomes like other people. Whereas addiction is his means of coping with stress, the affective states that activate him are not necessarily different from the fears, hopes, and ambitions that those who work with him also harbor. Rather than exploring with him the tenacity of his will power (whether he will or will not return to drugs), the therapist needs to help the addict examine his inability to secure a gratifying existence without drugs. (According to addicts who are willing to tell it like it is, discussions about will power are academic. One addict reported, "My family kept telling me all it would take was will power. Will power doesn't have a damn thing to do with it. I needed drugs like a diabetic needs insulin." Said another addict, "A junkie has no will. He is a puppet, and junk pulls the strings. But she pulls so sweetly, so well, that he loves it and will deny he has no choice.") The addict must be led to realize that by rejecting societal guidelines for securing society's goods and services, his life style has been forged on getting without learning the process of getting. (Yablonski, 1965)

Ninety percent of the individuals addicted to hard-core drugs, according to Robert Sharoff (1969), are from disadvantaged backgrounds. They feel that their opportunity for achieving status, satisfaction, and self-esteem in society at large is rather slim. On the other hand, drugs give the addict the illusion of having immediately what other men spend a lifetime striving for: pleasure, power, and security. (Ginott, 1969) It is small wonder, therefore, that the addict's life style is imbued more with illusions than with reality-tested attitudes in regard to achieving satisfaction of his wants. The addict's efforts toward achievement are inconsistent and self-defeating. The addict doesn't seem to profit from experience; he repeats the same stupid, self-defeating acts, patterns, and attitudes over and over again. (Yablonski, 1965) ("I do not look on an addict as one who is sick. He's stupid. A dope fiend is one who never accepts responsibility. All maturity—in the normal way—stops when you stick the needle in," said Fred Phillips, an ex–drummer, ex–sailor, and ex–dope fiend who is the director of the Alexandria, Virginia Community Mental Health Center. (*Washington Post,* Summer, 1971) The addict claims that there is no one in the world who is going to tell him what to do. The irony is that there is probably no class of people on earth who are told more what to do than the addict and his fellow deviant life stylers. (Yablonski, 1965) The commodities the addict wants from life are reasonable: security, status, self-esteem, pleasure. But the ways he has of getting them are all inappropriate.

> To be psychologically dependent upon one or another substance leads, in itself, into a vicious circle of more and more immature wishes and frustrations, and with that, into a more and more compulsive seeking of escapes. (Wurmser, 1970)

The addict believes himself to be a clever "con artist," a person who can get whatever he wishes from others without working as the "square" people do because he, unlike others, knows what the game of life is all about. In reality, the addict doesn't know much about the kind of life in which he can secure the things he wants. His narcissim keeps getting in the way. *Narcissim* is a characterological scab that binds around an emotional wound suffered during the early developmental years. It coagulates with the most tenacity as a result of social and emotional deprivation. Narcissistic attitudes are characterological strategies used to compensate for injury to a person's ego, particularly to those parts of the ego that are involved with autonomy and self-exploration.

If a child discovers early in life that he cannot depend upon significant others in the family, and in time "[if] the commitment to a close person is profoundly betrayed, it is replaced by a commitment to a thing, namely, a drug." (Wurmser, 1970) Not only does the youngster learn to distrust others when his needs are, without clear reason, irregularly attended, but lack of responsiveness from others causes him inwardly to fear that there may be reason not to trust himself. Because he essentially lacks confidence in his ability to test reality, he needs to test others to find out how much he can get away with. Under a manifest bravado lurks disturbing doubts about his own self-worth and critical faculties. Despite these fears, and because he doesn't trust others, to survive he must depend entirely upon himself.

Since others treat the narcissist as a means to their own satisfactions rather than as a person who possesses intrinsic self-worth, he observes that manipulation has a payoff. He comes to realize, without actually giving it much thought, that his fear of others induces him to pay off. The person with a character disorder is also a reactor and a game-player. He rarely initiates the setting of rules for his relationships with others, but he uses to his advantage whatever rules and standards they employ with him or with third parties. As a game-player, he holds firmly to fairness in following rules. He justifies employing threat-imposing strategies with others by projecting onto them his own mistrust of himself, claiming that no one can be trusted, that everyone is out for himself, that a man needs to dupe the other before he, himself, is betrayed.

In this regard, the psychotherapist who works with "acting out" characters may be subtly manipulated into feeling and acting as if the therapy endeavor is exclusively his responsibility. This is demonstrated in a psychotherapist's account of his first experience working with addicts in a forensic unit of a psychiatric hospital:

> The group finally got started fifteen minutes late. Five of the
> nine members were present. Two being on sick call, another

decided against joining the group. The subjects discussed during the session dealt mainly with how I could help them get out of the hospital or have their charges dropped. This they felt was the primary purpose of the group because this was their major problem. They expressed feelings of being rejected, of hostility and frustration at the whole legal and forensic system and particularly with the doctors in the unit. They felt that there was nothing wrong with them and that the doctors were there only to draw their pay. I felt that the conversation was directed toward me, for my benefit: letting me know what I could do for them. There was interaction, though the patients followed a single theme pretty much in an orderly way. I tried to hold back from responding to them directly. I felt it was a life or death gripe session. I was conscious of being quite anxious during the whole meeting, *wanting* to hold the group together, *to give them some reason for being there* and not wanting to fail in this attempt.

In a rehabilitation program the addict's manipulative, deviant life style and attitude must be halted if he is to acquire the commodities of life he desires in the community at large. He must develop those social skills and abide by those social norms which lead to the satisfactions he seeks. The interpersonal competence that has maintained his addictive life style in the drug subculture is not functional in society at large. Resocialization for the addict is mandatory. Establishing a clear and definitive contract with the addict is one of the most helpful ways of teaching him new social skills. A rehabilitation contract is an agreement in which the services, responsibilities, and obligations of the parties are defined.

An effective rehabilitation contract provides a consistent and rational baseline for setting treatment goals and expectations and specifying how the change agent and recipient are to contribute to the endeavor. Included are safeguards to protect both the program and the recipient from exploitation and irresponsibility by the other party. The contract specifies on what grounds the agreement between the parties may be discontinued and the procedure taken in terminating it. In an effective rehabilitation program, the recipient learns more about himself and the mechanisms of learning and resocialization and becomes more appreciative of the areas of himself he wishes to work on. He then, through negotiation with the staff, rewrites his contract with increased specificity and detail.

All rehabilitation contracts must contain rules without which the integrity of the program and the well-being of the addict are in serious jeopardy. Physical violence or threat of violence and the use of narcotics or other chemicals are automatic causes for dismissal from the program. Because staff are in the rehabilitation business not the detective business, they do not have to offer proof of violation. Suspicion that an addict has used chemicals or has assaulted another patient is sufficient for dismissal. If standards were not consistently maintained, the addict would have respect neither for the staff, the program, or himself. By involving himself in a desperate venture that failed, he would turn on staff and other addicts "like a wounded animal because he allowed himself to hope and his hopes died, too." (The statement of a veteran addict.)

In a drug group Julius Loschile (a patient described in Chapter 2) became furious at the therapist when he was told that he was once more behaving as he had last week—as if he felt very sorry for himself. Loschile leaped out of his chair, ran over to the therapist and raised over him, threatening to slug him. The therapist told him to sit down or he couldn't continue in the group. Other patients pointed out to Loschile that the group contract, agreed upon by all, precluded acts of violence. Loschile picked up an ashtray, left the circle, and flung the ashtray against the wall. He returned and sat down. He said to the therapist "You lying bastard, are you going to tell me that I'm not a man?"

He was told by the group that he certainly wasn't acting like one at the moment but was behaving like a child who wouldn't take responsibility for his actions. Someone rather wisely asked if Loschile were not to be judged on the basis of his actual behavior, on what other basis were we to judge him? This seemed to reach Loschile. He pleaded that he really wanted to be a man and wanted to assume adult responsibility. The therapist gave him an opportunity by pointing out that since he was rather upset he had the responsibility to decide for himself whether he was able to continue the session in a rational manner or preferred to leave. He was told he could return when he felt he could handle critical assessment of his behavior. He chose to leave. But he left without sulking or impotent rage. He returned the next day appreciative that the group had not permitted him to get away with acting like a spoiled child.

In addition to serious violation such as violence, there also may be a number of lesser violations which patients and staff agree to regard as detrimental to rehabilitation. If these violations are brought up in the group meeting and freely explored by the person who committed them, the matter is dropped by staff unless the patient group decides the issue should be handled in some other way outside the group. Staff however has veto power for activities occurring outside the group meeting. On the other hand, if a violation is brought to the meeting by a third party, the persons involved are summarily dismissed from the program. To rend the collusive criminal code of not reporting rule violations it is made clear that if patients are aware of violations in the program and do not report them in the group meeting, staff will clear the ward, dismissing everyone. The program challenges the addict to stand on his own feet and share in the responsibilities and concerns of his community. Without applying himself and mastering this crucial challenge, the addict is interned forever in the addict subculture.

THE REHABILITATION PROGRAM, A TOTAL COMMUNITY

The rehabilitation program is a closed community in which the residents provide all the services necessary to maintain their existence. They do their own cooking, housekeeping, and repairs, and provide entertainment and educational activities for their fellow residents.

CONFRONTATION GROUP THERAPY

The confrontation approach is concerned with the entire social system of the ward. The addicts meet as frequently as possible as a group. In that the whole resident group meets together, the program should contain no more than fifteen addicts. Therapy in its most intensive form, which I refer to as "perpetual stew" (after Synanon), is an ongoing twenty-four hour a day session. At all times at least one staff member is available to meet with as many or as few residents who desire to "rap" about their personal or drug rehabilitation concerns or simply to converse.

A key point of these sessions is an emphasis on extreme, uncompromising candor about one another. No holds or statements are barred from the group effort at truth-seeking about problem situations, feelings, and emotions of each and all members of the group. (Yablonski, 1965)

The group has the right and responsibility to question one another on any aspect of their functioning, whether it be the addict's dealings with others in the program, his self-concept, or his delusions and distorted views of the world.

The addict in the program is not merely questioned. He is confronted and verbally pushed, time after time, until he levels with the group and tells it "the way it is" rather than the way it sounds good. The confronted patient must be made to realize that he has tried every conceivable form of "medicine" to "cure" his interpersonal and intrapsychic conflicts. His presence in the program is testimony to the futility of drugs and suppression for solving his difficulties. He therefore is expected to confront his problems directly with the help of his fellow addicts. Until now the addict has been unable or unwilling to see himself as others see him.

Those who have worked successfully with addicts have found that the addict cannot afford to lie.

Any slips of truth on [the addicts'] part can be deadly. If [they] do not level with each other, [they] add more guilt to [their] already heavy load. This would fester and [they would] split and go back on dope—[they] have to be honest to stay clean. (Yablonski, 1965)

Pat pseudo-psychological answers or any other alibiing or rationalizing of one's behavior are confronted and attacked if they persist.

Frequently the addict will try to get individual psychotherapy because he anticipates that the analyst will ask him leading questions about his childhood and will then discover the "cause" of his addiction. Having thus found the "reason" for his habituation, the addict believes that he will be freed from his drug obsession and can at will stop himself from further usage. Such a slanted view of psychotherapy in which he is the passive recipient of the therapist's magic, belies a reluctance to look at his current uncertainties about himself and deal with his feelings constructively. It also suggests magical thinking where the analyst (as Father Surrogate) undoes the injustices done to the addict (as injured child) in the past and refurbishes him, rendering him for the first time in his life a complete person (a fully functioning adult).

In my opinion, the addict manipulates the well-intentioned therapist in individual psychotherapy into "psychologizing"—giving psychological reasons for his behavior. Then because the addict "knows why" he uses heroin, he doesn't have to do anything about himself. Because of this consideration, individual therapy is counterindicated.

As long as there are "reasons" for using drugs there are also "reasons" for continuing to use them. The addict can consequently abrogate personal responsibility for his behavior by pointing to a number of quasi-reasonable excuses for his drug usage—aversive external conditions, lack of education, a poor home situation, a prison and drug record—all of which have prevented him from getting a job and leading a regulated existence which would accure the respect and self-esteem he desperately desires. Therefore, the therapist should not be concerned with the addict's obsessive-compulsive ruminations about why he became the way he is, but with what he feels as he is being confronted. The addict's feelings in the here and now govern his dysfunctional behavior rather than the rationalized reasons he prefers to offer.

MODALITES FOR CHANGE

All ameliorative endeavors are predicated on one of three general modalites of change: (a) direct change; (b) suggested and trial change; (c) self-change from emotional and/or congnitive shifts in meaning.

In the first modality, the change agent directly modifies the client's situation so that the client is induced to change his own behavior because the environmental conditions either enable or force him to do so. The need for change may or may not be explained to the client. Examples of this modality range from providing children and distressed adults living under aversive conditions with a healthier and better regulated environment to imposing "cold turkey" on drug addicts and "drying out" alcoholics. Under the direct change concept, the client is regarded as incapable or restively unwilling to modify his dysfunctional behavior on his own under the present aberrant environmental conditions.

In the second modality of change, the change agent may ask the client to give new behavioral alternatives a trial to see whether or not they are more gratifying and functional than the strategies the client has habitually employed in the same situations. (Lippitt, 1959) Again, explanations may or may not accompany the client's endeavors. Correspondingly, explanations, if offered, may precede or follow the implementation of a new behavior. Whether or not explanations are offered for trying particular kinds of behavior, the client is urged to proceed on the advice of the change agent.

The change agent presents himself as an expert or authority in these matters. Firm, but generally nonoppressive, pressure is applied in persuading the client to try out new behaviors. Undesirable consequences from continued use of the old strategies are enumerated with more recalcitrant clients. In the process the client may be goaded, needled, or cajoled into making modifications in his behavior. Generally, however, the client's faith in an authority who takes it upon himself to plan the client's new life style allows the therapist to effect some modification (albeit often temporary) in the client's behavior.

The change agent in this modality proceeds upon the assumption (not implicit in the first and third change modalities) that it is more amenable, functional, and, perhaps, even more ethical for the change agent to suggest changes in behavior rather than to induce changes in affect and attitude. At such time as new behavioral patterns are developed it is assumed that corresponding attitudes and sentiments will become integrated with new behavioral patterns. This assumption is supported by considerable empirical data that suggest when new ways of responding have become increasingly more gratifying but are in conflict with what a person has habitually believed about himself, the client will modify his attitudes so that they are more congruent with his new behavioral patterns. (Festinger, 1957) Examples of the trial change modality are found in traditional education, psychodrama, encounter groups, and behavioral modification.

In the third modality of change, the change agent attempts to modify the client's attitude and values by bringing out the emotional and functional purpose they serve. Knowing the reasons behind his behavior, the client, it is assumed, can better deal with them. It is further assumed that once the client understands what he is really seeking, he will come to realize that his present behavior is an inferior compromise predicated on subjugating his feelings that he is neither capable nor deserving of the things he seeks. The change agent, by being sensitive to the needs and ideas of the client, creates an atmosphere which enables the client to discover the advantages of change for himself. Reconstructive psychotherapy such as psychoanalysis and existential therapy (see Chapter 8), as well as process group training (Chapter 7), are examples of the self-change modality.

Every therapeutic approach generally contains elements of all three change concepts. Confrontation group therapy initially relies on direct change and subsequently employs the other two change concepts in succession. In the drug program the therapeutic agent directly modifies the addict's situation by removing him from the old environment and his source of drugs. The environmental field, therefore, is so modified that the addict can no longer resort to habitual strategies in attempts to handle anxiety and noxious stimulation and feelings. Not having the old strategies available, he either must seek innovative means of handling anxiety or undergo the stress without relief. Before the patient's anxiety is reduced, he must examine what he is experiencing, how it is affecting him, and what he does to relieve it. Otherwise, he would learn nothing about his maladjusted strategies for handling stress and would not have the opportunity to develop more effective ones.

It is recommended that time-binding activities that do not require interaction with other patients, such as watching television, are
not available in the program. The addict, with the help of his peers
and staff, must acquire interpersonal skills to handle stress and anxiety. The addict cannot acquire these skills by losing himself in a solitary, passive activity. The addict sees an insurmountable abyss between his dreams, ideals, what he expects of himself, and what
resources he has. Through drugs, his disillusionment with himself
gives way to the illusion that he is successful, gifted, unique, and
untouchable by the fears and chafe that afflict common men. He is
subverted by cultural attitudes (fostered by mass media) favoring
passive reception of stimulation. Instead of actively challenging his
disillusionment, he dreams himself into a blissful fantasy that everything is as he wants it to be. (Wurmser, 1970)

However, once his patterns of passively accepting his current
state of being is challenged and new attitudes and values are acquired, insight-oriented psychotherapy (the self-change modality)
may be indicated. Insight therapy with "acting out" persons generally
has been unfruitful prior to the patient's making behavioral change.

GROUP DYNAMICS IN WORKING WITH ADDICTS

Frequently in working with patients with severe narcissistic
character disorders, the therapist finds himself pressed by the group
to defend himself. Often the therapist may wonder just how he fell
into this plight. He remembers entering the group to help the patients work on their problems and before he realized it, they were
working on him. It is important at such times for the therapist to not
lose his perspective and permit his integrity as a therapist to be
threatened. His words, and especially his interpretations, may be distorted, ridiculed, and denied by the patients. Nonetheless, the therapist's manner and the impact it has upon the group will be hard to
deny and will linger on long after the associations to the therapist's
words have been extinguished.

By his manner, no less than his words, the therapist conveys his
feeling that the group are desperately trying to work on him in order
to avoid looking at themselves. They react to the therapeutic situation as though the therapist were trying to do something ill-advised
to them. They project their own feelings of inadequacy and confusion
about their intentions onto the therapist. There is the hope that if
they stay active and put the therapist on the defensive, he will not be
able to pass judgment on them—a fear that their whole life style is

characterologically designed to avert. For the addict "treatment is a game of upmanship; an arena for practicing his confidence-man skills." (Bassin, 1968)

By remaining reclusive and associating with others only to meet pressing physical and emotional needs, the addict avoids intimacy and the threat of letting others down and being rejected in turn by them. Daniel Casriel and David Deitch (1966) point out that the addict, rather than using the flight or flight adaptive responses that most of us employ to gain pleasure and avoid pain, employs "detachment," a more primary defensive mechanism.

Just as a turtle puts his head into a shell, so do [addicts] withdraw from the pain of awareness, [which] they experience as the danger of everyday functioning.

By successfully removing themselves from the pain of reacting to stress, they have detached themselves and spend their energy reinforcing, by encapsulating, their isolation to a nonpainful state of functioning.

Thus the patient takes flight without fear into a fortress in which he feels secure, but in which he is quite isolated, incapacitated, and imprisoned. The longer the individual stays in his own jail, the thicker the walls become by secondary encapsulation, with the result that the individual is less and less able to cope with the problems of everyday living.

Confrontation in the group generally occurs between individuals. Nonetheless, the therapist who expects to work effectively with a group must be aware of and able to work with the common group tensions that are continually influencing the issues discussed and the manner in which group members react to them. The confrontation approach cannot come into being before the addicts, as a group, recognize it as viable. The addicts must accept the necessity of confronting one another and themselves as the only hope they have of jarring themselves from their suicidical-directed life style. (Castriel & Deitch, 1966)

The therapist helps lower resistance against the group as a therapeutic agent by enabling the patients to understand its influence on each member. This method rests upon the group dynamic theory that it is usually easier to change individuals who are part of a closely knit group by modifying the values and the normative structure of the group than it is to change members of the group individually. Initially, the function of the therapist in the group is to facilitate group communication. He must be able to point out how the group, as well as its individual members, resists doing the work for which it has convened.

CRISIS

My work with drug addicts has pointed up the character disordered person's real inability to control his anxiety. Unlike the neurotic who internalizes his agitation, the "acting out" person externalizes the unacceptable parts of himself and acts upon them as if they were real threats imposed by external reality. This would suggest that addicts are relative babes in the wood in effectively handling crisis situations whether they occur in the street or in the designed therapeutic community. Crisis serves the important function of making staff and patient alike squarely face what each has done to cause a quagmire in the program. (Yablonski, 1965) The drug addiction rehabilitation program is built upon confronting, learning to understand, and working through conflict. Without learning to appreciate how he influences and participates in the many conflicts that permeate his existence which in the past he has sloughed off as not his fault, the addict will do as he has always done: reject responsibility for the situations he gets into and project the blame onto society. In essence, the tragic flaw in the addict's character is that he acknowledges nothing that happens to him as his own fault—

not his addiction, not his degradation nor his desperation. He is convinced he has been thrown into life without the armor and weapons that others have. Heroin enables him to escape from the unfair battle. (Bassin, 1968)

The addict uses

the sense of social ostracism caused by drug abuse as a rationalization for his position in life. He can now blame all his problems on a society which mistreats the addict and makes no effort to understand him. His failure is something that society has forced him into; and he thus has a facile excuse to abandon the struggle for growth and maturity. (Sharoff, 1969)

CHANGING SUBCULTURES

Advocates of each of the three change modalities agree on at least one point. There is a need for social reinforcement and support for the client upon leaving the change experience. Without the support of a power-field (Lewin, 1951), an induced field that continues to reward the client for maintaining new and emotionally more risky behaviors, there is little hope that these new behavioral patterns will be stable or longlasting.

In leaving a rehabilitation program the addict is caught in a dilemma. In the community in which he grew up there was

only a weak sense of belonging, the adherence to one of the drug cults and to such a "groovy group" lends to the member a sense of solidarity, a mutually confirmed identity. (Wurmser, 1970)

If the addict is to avert his rehabituation to drugs, he must escape from the addict subculture. Yet, at the same time, he feels himself unwilling or unable to move into the "square" world. He seeks a reference group of ex-addicts whose goals are similar to his. Too frequently, the addict fails to find a congenial ex-addict group and returns to drugs to escape his loneliness and desperation. Therefore it would seem advisable for a group of addicts to enter the rehabilitation program together. Not only would being in the company of friends probably increase each addict's commitment to the program, but once they left the program together they could offer mutual support to one another.

ROLE MODEL

One of the most tenacious problems a rehabilitation program for drug addicts has is trying to dispel the magnetism of the "successful" drug pusher as an ego-ideal for the addict.

The quest for heroin is the quest for an identity and a meaningful life. The deeper meaning of "hustling" lies in the gratification of accomplishing a series of challenges, exciting tasks, every day of the week. (Wurmser, 1970)

A successful rehabilitation program requires the presence of ex-addicts.

The change agent most likely to be effective with the junkie is another addict who has made a commitment to himself, one who is prepared to use himself as a role model and become involved with his "brother". (Bassin, 1968)

The role model is a living example of what the newcomer in the program can become.

[He] points out why and how he is no longer deviant or misbehaving. This permits the newcomer to identify with someone who has experienced the same internal conflicts as he is currently feeling. In addition, the role model provides some preliminary information about problems that the new-comer can anticipate. (Yablonski, 1965)

It is important that the addict also have access to non-addicts as role-models. The professional staff person best serves as an "ideal" in terms of his problem-solving skills. He demonstrates to the patients the steps necessary for them to develop and achieve their goals when they are on their own by working on problems in the program in a rational and considered manner: asking clear and meaningful questions which elicit relevant material necessary for formulating plans and rendering effacacious decisions.

Confrontation therapy encourages the "acting out" person to level with himself and others.

It helps him to see himself as relevant others do. He gains information and insight into his problems. . . . A participant . . . is forced to examine positive and negative aspects about himself, as well as some dimensions he would never have considered on his own. This leaves him with a clearer view and a greater knowledge of his inner and outer worlds. (Yablonski, 1965)

An addiction rehabilitation program as outlined here may be one of the most inexpensive, efficient, as well as effective, programs a hospital or halfway house may operate. Little or no medicine is required. Few staff are required because drug addiction patients, in contrast to confined psychiatric patients, can assume their day to day maintenance. Addicts who successfully complete a period of rehabilitation may (at little or no salary) be trained as addict counselors. Addict counselors work with active drug users on the street or in agencies dealing with addicts, as well as provide staff and role-models for the inpatient hospital program from which they have recently graduated. Such a plan, combining treatment and job training simultaneously, is both economically efficient for the program and socially reinforcing to the addict.

Drug rehabilitation programs maintained chiefly by professional workers have little hope of stemming the tide of drug abuse. Experts have suggested that as many people become initiated to drugs in a day as are cured of their habit in a given year.

"All the world's a stage,
  And all the men and women merely
    players:
  They have their exits and their
    entrances;
  And one man in his time plays many
    parts,
  His acts being seven ages."

W. Shakespeare
As You Like It

NONVERBAL COMMUNICATION—11

In present-day society each of us is required to participate in a large and ever increasing number of natural groups. (Bradford et al, 1964) Within these groups the individual may be required to assume various social roles which are not part of his social repertoire. When the individual is not able to adapt to new and more complex social demands he thwarts existing and potential interpersonal relationships with other members. Consequently, if our activities in groups are to be intelligent and productive, we need

to understand the dynamics of effective group thinking and
action and to . . . [become] masters of the skills of effective
member and leader functioning. (Bradford et al, 1964, p. 4)

In short, the "stage" has become more complex and it becomes increasingly more difficult to remain a mere player, with set exits, entrances, and pre-established roles.

Behavioral scientists indicate that we have become an overly verbalized society. The problem, these scientists point out, is that verbal communication is only one of the many ways we communicate information and attitudes. For many of us in modern Western society, nonverbal communication remains an unstudied and unintentional source of information about how we experience ourselves and what we wish from other people. However, awareness of nonverbal language recently has been promoted by such best-selling books as Julius Fast's *Body Language*. Fast has been able to popularize his book by indicating the practical advantages that knowledge of body language, or *kinesics* (its technical name), has for success in dating, a more effective performance during employment interviews and other facets of living that the modern American values highly.

As with other popular trends, a "jumping on the band wagon" phenomenon has arisen. Not only have a great many publications on kinesics appeared, but, correspondingly, the "correction" of social inhibition has been attempted by means of new parlor games such as "Body Talk," "Sensitivity," and "Black and White." Let us look at one of these games briefly. *Body Talk* consists of fifty-two cards representing thirteen emotions and four modalities for their expression. Each player must render his gestures to express a given emotion. The other players take turns guessing which emotion the protagonist is portraying.

Whether or not one agrees that the body language movement achieves its aims by promoting parlor games, it is clear that the recent stress on kinesics has made the public more appreciative of the existence and impact of nonverbal communication.

What nonverbal communication is can be observed most clearly in the developing child. The infant, possessing few words, expresses his wishes and fears through his body posture and facial gestures. Even as a toddler, the child continues freely to express his emotions kinesthically. When the child enters school, his characteristic gestures and postures become salient factors in the way others view him. Awkwardness, lack of coordination, and physical torpidness are, therefore, impediments to his success in school. (Middleman, 1968)

As the child matures, he becomes increasingly aware of culturally designated ways of using his body. In the school setting, for instance, massive restraint of bodily expression is required. Rewards are achieved by the child for increasingly complex and abstract verbalizations. The result is a child who displays great skill in using words about words with no real feeling for, or image of, concrete phenomena. (Middleman, 1968) Awareness of body language is relegated to the preconscious or is entirely lost. Consequently, in most educated adults, communications are consciously most often transacted on a verbal level. Indeed, a person might regard it as rather unfair if any but his verbal and conscious communications were taken as his real intentions.

To the extent that our reactions to others are beyond our conscious awareness, our success in adapting to new and more complex social situations is predicated more by chance than by design. Dr. Omar Khayyam Moore indicates that every society has puzzles, transmitted by folktale, allegory, proverb, and so forth, which express ideal interpersonal relationships and the payoff for successful interpersonal functioning as viewed by that society. Every society has also games of chance in which the outcomes of interactions are determined by factors external to the intentions of the players. In addition to games of chance, Moore cites games of strategy in which the outcome depends upon each of the players taking into account the potential actions of the other players. In short, success in the game of strategy, unlike the game of chance, is due to a player being aware of what he wants from the other players and how they react to him, and this success is determined by intentional and purposeful activity.

An enabling experience helps group members move from the game of chance to one of strategy. I propose the use of nonverbal language for enabling the individual to move into new roles and functions as a more effective group member or leader, predicating his adaption on strategy rather than chance.

Most writers who have discussed kinesics have concerned themselves predominantly with the solitary individual in his social microcosm. In this chapter the principles of nonverbal communication will be extended to both natural and designed group situations. In terms of natural groups my focus will be on social gatherings and chance encounters. Designed groups dealt with are a clinical seminar, a nurses' staff meeting, and psychodramatic group situations. I will then discuss the more technical aspects of nonverbal communication drawing from my experiences with patients in dyadic and group modalities including patients in the ward of a large federal psychiatric hospital. Finally, I will describe some exercises or games which I have found helpful in increasing awareness of body language.

THE PROBLEM WITH WHICH KINESICS SEEKS TO DEAL

In social situations people frequently employ words to obscure, from themselves as well as others, how they actually feel. A verbal facade mitigates the stress and discomfort a person experiences in placing his vulnerable feeling under the scrutiny of others. Man seeks to protect himself emotionally no less than physically. He employs words or, conversely, silence toward this end. We generally enter social situations with a number of preset perceptions, expectations, and preferred roles. In most social situations we try to create a certain picture of ourselves in the minds of others. Unfortunately, our expectations often blind us to others' real feelings and are more detrimental than facilitative to the ends we aspire for.

A typical party situation may be illustrative. A young man enters from the left and pauses, scanning the room and adjusting his tie. He sees an interesting looking girl sitting on a sofa alone at the side of the room. Her eyes are lowered; her hands folded in her lap. The young man quickly and cheerfully approaches. He sits beside her on the couch failing to note her slight recoiling movement, her stiffening shoulders, and clenched fist. Unaware of the effect of his assertiveness on his intended partner, he continues to inch closer and reaches out to touch her arm to emphasize a point in their conversation. He does not detect her deft withdrawing movement as she crosses her arms and covers her chest. Feeling from their verbal exchanges that he is making considerable headway, he proceeds, not heeding her crossed leg which is swinging more and more rapidly. When she breaks into the conversation and suggests that he get a drink for her at the bar, he gladly complies. On his return he is surprised and dismayed to find that she is nowhere in sight.

Nonverbal communication is that which is expressed by a frown, a pensive face, the provocative way a person walks, the inquisitive tilt of the head, a smile of recognition, tightly clenched fists, sweating palms, or eyes filled with tears. Learning to read nonverbal cues may be worth a thousand words because nonverbal communication is never terminated, unlike its verbal counterpart.

Let us further explore nonverbal communication by observing two friends, Kathy and Elaine, young women who are in their midtwenties. Both are vivacious, outgoing, bright, and attractive single girls. Of the two, Kathy seems more competent in developing heterosexual relationships, although she has a number of close friends of both sexes. She is, we will observe, a person who has no difficulty getting her messages across. Elaine, on the other hand, maintains more superficial relationships—often feeling that she has been taken advantage of in more intimate relationships. Aware of her difficulty, she expresses concern about her inability to make herself understood and get her messages across. Although objectively Kathy and Elaine are equally bright and attractive in heterosexual relationships, Elaine is seen as "flighty and scatterbrained" whereas Kathy is considered to be more "feminine and mature."

First, let's take a look at Kathy in a rather typical social situation. Kathy enters the room slowly, looking around to initially assess which social groupings appear open and approachable and which appear closed. She proceeds to scan the open groupings for someone who appears interesting or for someone who has been watching her entrance more attentively than the others. Kathy will join the group by approaching with a slow, easy gait, hands swinging loosely at her side. Her facial expression appears interested but subdued. Kathy places herself on the periphery of the group taking the role of an attentive listener. Although Kathy is verbally quiet, she is extremely expressive. She has lovely eyes and knows how to use them. She will canvass the group and when one of the members returns her glance, she will maintain eye contact and draw that person toward her with her seductive smile. Kathy seems almost to swallow people with her steady, interested gaze.

In addition to her quick and ready smile, she moves her head constantly, periodically reinforcing the speaker's message with nods or shakes. Kathy's hands also move freely as she speaks, and she often reaches out and lightly touches a person's arm to emphasize a point in the discussion. All the while Kathy gradually moves into the core of the gathering and casually becomes an important part of the discussion. In brief, Kathy knows how to join a group. Her expressive cues are clear, consistent, and warmly reinforcing to the others in the group. In dyadic encounters, because of her close attentiveness Kathy's partner usually feels that he or she is the most important person in the room.

In contrast, Elaine approaches a group rapidly, barging in, and immediately trying to make her presence felt. Her gait is rapid and tense and connotes some aggressiveness. Elaine's arms are in constant movement, but the movements are too rapid to appear natural and comfortable. Elaine also uses touch frequently but puts little effort into guiding the effect of her touch on her partner. Somehow Elaine's touch often seems obtrusive rather than pleasing. The quality of Elaine's eye contact is ubiquitous. Elaine takes in everyone but sees no one. Often she scans the room to see who else has entered the party, abruptly retiring from the person with whom she was engaged, or, frequently, she will stare for long moments at her hands or bracelet. Elaine's partners have commented that they feel as if they didn't exist for her. Not surprisingly, Elaine often leaves a party disappointed though she does feel concerned about the baffling effect she has on people.

To appreciate the crucial factors involved in the situations described above, the reader should be aware of at least two levels of communication. The first is the content level—or what is actually being stated. The second, and more covert, level is the attempt by the persons in an encounter to set up a relationship. Furthermore, these levels must be discerned not only by what is being conveyed verbally but by a myriad of nonverbal signals. A person misunderstands what is being communicated when he is alert to only one level of discourse.

It is possible that Elaine has mixed feelings about what she actually wants. Often people simultaneously want contradictory commodities. This in part may be due to our constantly changing picture of ourselves and others and our contradictory feelings about ourselves and others. Principles of logic usually cannot be applied to these conflicting feelings. The result is often a great discrepancy between what one thinks he is saying (the content) and what the other is picking up (the quality of relationship). Since communication difficulties often result from contradictory messages being transmitted on different levels, obviously the two modalities of meaning must be coordinated in order for effective communication to take place. Elaine, for example, often verbalizes a wish to get closer to people, but her nonverbal cues erect thorny barriers to intimacy with others.

CONCEPTS ESSENTIAL TO NONVERBAL COMMUNICATION THEORY

The three areas I would like to focus on in more detail in terms of Kathy's and Elaine's behavior are territoriality, touch, and the influence of first impressions.

Territoriality. Julius Fast states that no matter how crowded a physical setting may be, each person tries to maintain his own characteristic domain (the area of space he usually regards as his own, intrusion into which he regards as a violation of his personal territoriality). Most of us have experienced in everyday life that groups that meet, over time, tend to parcel out to members certain areas of personal domain. Group members tend to take the same seats week after week and are sorely annoyed if their territory is violated (perhaps by a new member who does not know the "geographic" boundaries of the group).

Edward Hall has maintained that man's use of physical space has a pervasive bearing on all his relationships with others. Kathy successfully gauged her movements in regard to others' territoriality; Elaine did not. Hall explains how physical distance makes a difference in a person's response to others in an encounter. The closer two people are to one another physically, the greater is the need to respond to the other emotionally. Moreover, when people stand in an intimate range to one another, each is more likely to be overwhelmed by an awareness of the other and the need to protect his territoriality. An intrusion into one's intimate territory is perceived as a peril. Intimate distance in our society usually is regarded as within four feet of the other person. Distances of about seven to twelve feet are generally regarded as proper for formal, social, or business relationships, being more protective and impersonal. An intermediate distance of about four to seven feet is reserved for informal social gatherings where people are attempting to get acquainted with others but do not know and trust the others sufficiently to interact on intimate terms. Fast indicates that knowledge of the differences in impact of communication from various physical distances is salient in successful interpersonal accomodation. Whether in a social interchange one person will react in an aggressive or tender manner is influenced by the distance between the two. As the first illustration in this chapter indicates, close, intimate interactions between persons of the opposite sex who are not sufficiently acquainted with each other to have fostered mutual trust leads to increased defensive reactions. This is something Elaine appears unaware of and results in her aggressiveness which her partner experiences as intrusive and uncomfortable.

Knowledge of personal space also is extremely important in appreciating large group phenomena. For instance, whereas decreasing physical space creates intimacy—the desired mood for a party or a therapy group—increasing physical space may serve other kinds of social objectives for larger groupings. Hall, for example, speaks of a teacher moving fighting students to a larger room where the fighting ceased. Remember, too, what happens to an angry, closely confined crowd as it begins to spread out and disperse in a less congested area.

Touch. Also with Kathy and Elaine, a second area of difference between them is in their use of touch. Fast speaks of touching and fondling as a potent signal, the common and most obvious form of nonverbal communication. But to serve its desired aim, touch must come at the right moment, in the right context. Elaine's frequent use of touch was not consistent with her other signals and was experienced by her partners as confusing and insincere. Elaine also was not aware of feedback on the effect of her touch. Rather than being seen as creating intimacy or even as a friendly gesture, it was often seen as an invasion on her partner's territory and reacted to with defensiveness.

First impressions. The importance of dress as a first impression and powerful nonverbal signal has largely been neglected in the professional literature with the exception of the work of Flugel. "A man is what he wears" may sound like a trite and commercial phrase, but it holds a certain kernel of truth. Most people, whether consciously or not, dress to present a certain image to other people. Elaine dresses in a modish but somewhat overdone manner; her clothes are too stylish, too fashioned, her hair too much in place, creating an almost artificial air. Kathy, on the other hand, dresses in a stylish but casual manner, her hair straight and hanging to her shoulders. This casual look is not by chance, however. It is a look which she spends considerable time, effort, and money in achieving and which is consistent with her other personal signals.

In therapy settings, too, nonverbal signals transmitted by dress may provide extremely important information. For instance, one of my patients, essentially rather shy and inhibited, could not understand why everyone called her a flirt and viewed her as sexy. An examination of her appearance quickly reveals what the patient has overlooked. She wears heavy cocktail makeup and her hair in long curls. Her frequent gains in weight are contained in clothing that is already tightly fitting and, although appropriate for a day in a large city, not suitable for the casual way of life in the rural area in which she lives.

Fast states that besides having faces for every occasion, we have, as well, masks and cloaks for the entire body (that is, makeup, dress, and so forth). He also points out that in a situation in which an individual feels invisible, his need to wear a mask is gone and the mask may be dropped. This often can be observed with mental patients. Deterioration in mental processes is usually accompanied by deterioration in physical appearance. Marked change in the physical appearance of a patient may provide an important nonverbal cue to the therapist as to possible change in the patient's self-concept and mental attitudes.

These considerations can also be extended to business and work situations. We have been told that people in their business roles are generally more guarded and more resistive to role transition than in most other aspects of their existence. It is generally not difficult to guess a person's occupation from his attire. Each profession and trade has its own uniform. These uniforms represent restrictions on the individual's expression of his individuality.

People in the business world often are so absorbed in achieving success that they claim to have no time for examining their non-work oriented behavior. They also fear what their associates would think of them if they revealed their true selves and their deeply felt needs.

These are, however, the factors that make action training, a branch of sensitivity training using nonverbal communication, a valuable approach.

Even many mental health practitioners, who are trained to work with expressive disorders, often are oblivious as to how they present themselves to others. We will illustrate.

Somehow, Dr. Densspake couldn't understand what had gone awry at yesterday's clinical seminar. His speech had been brilliant, as usual; his references to the psychiatric literature had been numerous and erudite; his points elaborate and carefully prepared. His talk apparently had been so precise and clear that no questions had to be asked of him. In fact, his talk was taken in complete silence by the students. But yet the same clinical errors in assessment and treatment were being made. The same questions he so carefully had answered in his talk were coming up again. Hadn't they heard a word he said? Had he misjudged the effectiveness of his delivery? A quick review of yesterday's seminar might have provided Dr. Densspake with some clues to his quandary.

Tom smashed his cigarette against the side of the ashtray and reached for another cigarette. Tom rarely chain smoked. Gloria crossed and recrossed her legs, squirmed in her chair and glanced continually around the room. Marv gazed with intense occupation at a flamenco print on the wall, tapping his fingers on the table in a slow steady motion. George squashed his third page of scribbles into a ball and aimed for the ashtable–a perfect shot. Pat showed facial indications of losing a long battle to stay awake and slumped in her seat.

At some time or other each of us has participated in a similar meeting, class, or group session in which the speaker seemed totally oblivious to what he was failing to convey to his audience. Often when the speaker realizes his failure, his retort is "But no one asked any questions!" Perhaps the speaker is looking for the wrong kind of feedback. Dr. Densspake was unaware of the students' nonverbal communication. In the situation described above, the students were giving the speaker a nonverbal indication of their thoughts, feelings, and mood. If Dr. Densspake had been attuned to these cues and had been able to relate them to his presentation, his lecture might have achieved better results.

Because the nonverbal communication of a group has received little attention in the group literature, I feel it is worth exploring further here. On entering a group to present a workshop or a lecture, I first take note of what the members as a group are saying without words. The group members' body language gives me some indication of what they expect. I notice whether the group is seated close to the front or is huddled near the rear of the room or next to the largest exit. If the group is seated too far back to be responsive to my communications, I suggest that they move up, carefully noting how the request is received. The very movement of the group often warms up the participants to the presentation. Next, in terms of posture and bodily position, I notice whether the group as a whole appears alert and interested, whether they are sitting straight up with arms relaxed and legs planted firmly on the floor and faces held up and toward the speaker's chair. Often participants are slumped in their seats with their arms folded across their chest and knees tightly crossed. This may be a hint that the speaker is the last person on earth they wish to be listening to at that moment.

Two other bodily cues have been valuable to me in assessing the mood of a group. The first is facial expression, particularly the kind of eye contact. A yawn or a fixed, wide grin are, of course, easy to identify. As I look over the group, I notice whether my gaze is returned or if the group members look away or whether they fixedly stare at me, at the podium, or at a far wall.

The second cue is the quality of a handshake. In the United States, handshaking most often occurs among males. In a small group, men often begin their interactions by shaking hands. Is the handshake firm and strong, or weak and limp? Are the palms sweaty? Sweating is frequently a sign of tension and anxiety. As you extend your hand does the other person come forward and grasp it, or does he step back and hesitate? Although the handshake is regarded as an automatic courtesy, it also is an important source of information about the handshaker's emotions.

The principles I have been discussing helped to facilitate the stated goals of a group of public health nurses. The spokesman of the group had requested my help in opening up channels of communication among the nurses. I was flattered to hear that the nurses were looking forward eagerly to my presentation. But when I entered the group, one glance revealed that I had been misinformed. The nurses' legs were crossed, their arms folded and barricaded across their chests. There was little movement or interaction among the group members. Their eyes were staring straight ahead and through me. The few attentive group members seemed to be concentrating on the refreshment stand. There appeared to be a general mood of apprehension, which, indeed, proved to be true.

In light of my initial reception from the nurses, I abandoned my vague, preconceived plans and commented on the climate of the group and asked what the nurses had expected to accomplish in our time together. Essentially, the nurses had heard that I would run a sensitivity group and had been frightened by this unknown prospect. Furthermore, these nurses rarely met as a large group and felt uneasy in being together as a group. Talking only seemed to increase their apprehension. In order to put the nurses at ease, I suggested a series of nonverbal exercises. As the exercises progressed, anxiety and apprehension diminished and interaction correspondingly increased. At first, the nurses had sought safety by clustering with those they already knew and felt comfortable with. Noting this, I added the proviso that further pairing in the exercises must be with people they did not know.

After a while, when the nurses were asked to reassemble as a large group, they seemed reluctant to leave their new groupings and to terminate the exercises. Only a few nurses returned to their former chairs. Instead, chairs were drawn more closely together in several large groupings. After the session, instead of congregating around the punch bowl and then the door, the nurses stayed in groups and conversed past the end of the work day. This made me feel that I had succeeded in my task of reducing social inhibitions and promoting increased communication among the nurses.

EMPLOYMENT OF NONVERBAL COMMUNICATION IN PSYCHOTHERAPY

Until rather recently, therapy had been primarily on a verbal level. As Milton Ehrlich (1970) states:

The mainstream of analytic writing since Freud has consistently placed enormous faith in the power of the word to set man free; that is, verbal insight or intellectual understanding is thought to be liberating. This emphasis has seldom been challenged. One exception is Frieda Fromm-Reichmann who appreciated how much the patient needs an experience and not an explanation.

For a more complete account of the development of the use of nonverbal techniques in psychotherapy, I refer the reader to Ehrlich. Here it suffices to state that Ehrlich speaks of Reich as paving the way for the importance of nonverbal communication in therapy.

Reich's concepts of character armor and character resistance were based on his understanding of the meaning of the body image and the changing postural model in a given individual.

Reich found the content of a patient's communication to be secondary in importance to how the person expressed it. He alerted other therapists to the importance of expressive movements, postures, and gestures. Ehrlich reminds us that Freud's pleasure principle was based on viewing the ego as first and foremost a body. That is, reality is experienced through an individual's body; the more in touch a person is with his own body, the stronger are his feelings of identification with reality. This concept has been found to be useful in working with schizophrenic as well as neurotic patients. As Connie Moerman (1968), a dance therapist, states:

> Part of their being out of touch with reality is a loss of contact with their own bodies, which movement and the dreaming stimulated by movement can help to restore.

Many of the thoughts and illustrations in the following pages were drawn from my work with regressed schizophrenics in a large federal psychiatric hospital. At that time the treatment modality I found to be useful with these severely incapacitated patients was psychodrama. More recently I have become increasingly appreciative of psychodrama as applicable to and extremely effective with nonpsychotic persons. The core concept that nonverbal action therapies are built around is that a person can never not communicate. Indeed, Sigmund Freud, the master of the "talking cure," once wrote:

> No mortal can keep a secret. If his lips are silent, he chatters with his fingertips; betrayal oozes out of him at every pore.
> (Davis, 1969)

In the following pages are some guidelines for using nonverbal therapy. The therapist looks for characteristic patterns of body communication, typical responses of a person in a particular context. Interpretations of isolated gestures or observations of single events are generally spurious and do not help define a patient. The therapist must remember that communication, nonverbal as well as verbal, is a two-way process in which the therapist's body signals heavily influence the interactive process between him and those with whom he works.

Knowledge of the principles of body language are crucial in the practitioner's work with groups. Nonverbal signals often transmit powerful and urgent emotions from member to member, from members to the group as a whole, and to the therapist. The emotional climate the therapist senses in a group, but often cannot verbally define, is the result of a powerful social contagion being transmitted by body language. Nonverbal signals illustrate the *psychic economy principle* in that they are reflexive in nature, not requiring the concentrated endeavor of the central nervous system. Because they are rarely, if ever, cognitively processed, they may consist of intentions rather inconsistent with our professed attitudes and beliefs. Nonverbal communication may consequently lie at the heart of double messages and double bind situations. As a matter of fact, nonverbal communication is the organism's vehicle for expressing his ambivalence and is a door to the unconscious. (Goldberg, (b), 1970)

As a psychodrama trainee I learned methods of translating body language into conscious, verbal communication. One of the most salient roles a psychodrama trainee learns to assume is that of a *double*. A double is a participant who takes the role of the *protagonist* (the person with whom the psychodrama is focusing upon) from the double's empathic (intuitive) understanding of the protagonist's feeling and attitudinal states. The double is "playing the role" of the protagonist but is not the protagonist. It is this which enables him to express deep-seated and conflict-ridden thoughts, feelings, and actions which the protagonist experiences intensely but cannot himself articulate. In order to respond more intimately to the feelings of the protagonist, the double assumes the identical bodily postures and mimics the gestures of the protagonist.

In a recent psychodrama, a young man discussed his intense feelings toward his father, emphasizing the difficulty he has always had in understanding his father's actions toward him. In recreating the situation psychodramatically, the director (the therapist) asked the young man to select someone from the audience to play his father. In the interchange with the person playing his father the young man became increasingly more agitated, expressing considerable frustration. Here in the psychodrama, just as in real life, he couldn't reach his father, he reported.

The director asked him to change roles. On assuming the role of his father, he changed his entire posture and bodily expression. He seemed almost bent in half with woe, shoulders rounded, arms clutched tightly between his legs which were spread and planted firmly on the floor. Someone from the audience called out softly and with much feeling, "You seem to have the weight of the world on your shoulders." "Yes," the young man responded (with an increased appreciation of his father), "it seems that things have been so difficult in the past few years. . . . " He continued speaking with intense, but apparently liberated, emotion about the important episodes in his father's life.

This illustration shows that bodily posture is often an important clue to attitudes and feelings. From time to time in traditional verbal therapy, I mentally assume the body posture of my patients. I believe doing this helps me in establishing an empathic bond with them.

In psychodrama the patient must be taught to appreciate his own and others' bodily cues. I offer here an illustration.

A female patient who wants to explore her conflict-ridden relationship with her husband has set the scene in her home, an apartment in a large city. The time is 5:00 P.M., the hour her husband usually arrives home from work. The husband enters the apartment and is greeted by his wife's perfunctory hello. They sit down opposite each other without another word. She then begins the conversation, asking him about his day but receives only monosyllabic replies. When she finishes her unproductive efforts to relate to him, he in turn asks her about her day. The conversation is marked by long silences. One particularly long silence is broken by the wife's discussion of their eleven year old son's destructive behavior at school. Throughout this long conversation, the therapist notes that both spouses have sat in extremely tight and uncomfortable body positions with crossed arms and legs, rigid backs, and almost no eye contact. The therapist mentioned this to them and asked how their body positions made them feel. "Holding on," said the husband; "holding things in," said the wife, "as if I had a bad ache or pain."

"I wonder," continued the therapist, seizing on these cues, "if the holding in might be a holding in of your feelings about each other and the discomfort the discussion of family problems induces? I wonder if you don't try to escape these feelings by focusing on your child?" Here body language confirmed what was an important conflictual motif in the life of this troubled family.

Later in this same session, in discussing aspects of themselves they claimed to want to change, the wife skillfully avoided discussing herself, preferring continually to interpret her husband's behavior or ask him, "What's bothering you?" The therapist pointed out that the wife was holding tightly onto the back of her chair as if for dear life. The psychodramatist asked, "What are you feeling?" She replied, "I feel like if I let go I will fall and fall. ... " The psychodramatist added, "I have an idea that this says something about how you hold onto feelings and control them by focusing on your husband."

VARIATIONS OF THE NONVERBAL TECHNIQUE

Working with deaf-mute and severely psychotic patients at a large federal psychiatric hospital made me realize most clearly the need for nonverbal treatment modalities. Few practitioners will happen to work with deaf-mute patients but therapists will, at one time or another, come in contact with psychotic patients who are unable to articulate their needs. One useful way of working with these patients is through *movement* or *dance therapy.* Connie Moerman, a clinical psychologist and dance therapist, maintains that motion often precedes words. She believes that patients progress faster if they are encouraged to move as well as to speak.

Although Mrs. Moerman employs dance therapy as an adjunct to her more traditional work with patients, she also views dance therapy as having value in its own right. She feels that psychotic patients can benefit from movement therapy because their external movement has been severely restricted. Mrs. Moerman believes that since the psychotic is largely out of touch with reality and his own body, movement, and fantasy associated with movement, helps restore the vibrance of reality. This is reminiscent of the theories of Reich discussed earlier in this chapter. Mrs. Moerman's (1968) final point about dance therapy relates to what has been stressed about nonverbal techniques in general: "People are not able to deny the evidence of movement as they might deny the reality of words."

My dance therapy training sessions with the late Marion Chace left me with a lasting impression of the sensitivity of movement therapists for nuances of feelings in others. Through action more than word, Miss Chace radiated a remarkable sense of warmth and gentleness. She could approach the most withdrawn patient or skeptical staff member with gratifying results. By her very manner she stressed never being artificial or insincere. Her behavior verified that she was as much attuned to her own nature as to those with whom she worked. She approached patients cautiously, stopping immediately when she received some bodily cue that she had intruded too quickly upon their territory. If she came too close and the patient withdrew, she approached more carefully but was certain to convey in word and manner that she was sorry. Then, almost invariably, the patient would begin to relax.

Miss Chace's techniques also emphasized approaching the patient at his own physical level. For example, if a patient were seated, she would also take a seat. I can appreciate the patient's defensiveness in trying to relate to someone who is standing above him and talking down at him. In working with children, awareness of physical level is particularly important. Too often we forget that the child's world is at our knee level. Sitting on the floor or in a chair removes the height difference, making the child less anxious and the development of a relationship more comfortable.

The importance of eye contact in involving others also bears mentioning here. Somehow it always appeared that Miss Chace was looking at all of us at once. She referred to this as wide vision and felt that looking simultaneously at each of the patients gave them a continuous sense of being recognized and accepted. I practiced trying to hold four people in my visual field at once and found it an arduous task.

But a word of caution is in order here. Although to many people eye contact offers encouragement, interest, and recognition; to others, eye contact and the therapist's gaze at times may be rather threatening. The therapist must always be aware, therefore, of the effect of his nonverbal communication on others. Unfortunately, some therapists who are keenly aware of their patient's body language, are correspondingly oblivious to their own. No matter how pure or neutral a transference object the therapist purports to be, as long as he remains within the patient's view he is transmitting myriad signals which patients are surprisingly adept at discerning. If there appears to be a discrepancy between the therapist's words and actions, there may result a serious threat to the sense of trust that has been fostered between patient and therapist, therapist and group.

Following are nonverbal exercises which I have found useful in my work.

When a person's entire body is involved in movement and expression, he is sooner willing to engage and respond to the others in a new group than he would be in a more verbal orientation. I begin by inviting the entire group to participate because in most groups at least several members are resistive to involving themselves in an unfamiliar activity, preferring to use the size of the group to remain safely anonymous. If volunteers are requested these members need only remain silent to preserve their nonidentity. However, if the entire group is involved in action, the only way to remain anonymous is to join in. Thus, initially involving the entire group in action serves to foster a sense of camaraderie as well as making it easier and less threatening for the more resistive members to join in.

A good beginning technique preferred by many movement therapists is *milling*. The group members walk around the room at whatever speed they choose and come in physical contact with whomever they wish for as long as they wish but they do not speak. When they reach a spot in the room where they feel comfortable, they are asked to "freeze." The participants are alerted to be particularly aware of their own and others' nonverbal cues. They are also asked to remain aware of their feelings while encountering the other group members. The exercise usually runs about five minutes. If participants are still milling, the leader may state, "We will have to end now. Find a place where you feel comfortable and freeze."

Milling has several purposes. Schutz (1967, p. 134) states that,

Knowing the structure of the group itself is frequently important for determining the need of various members. If for example, some members feel isolated, it is helpful to bring this fact to the attention of the rest. Often, talking about issues of this type doesn't clarify the situation because people may not know or be willing to admit their feelings. . . . Milling is a way of clarifying these issues.

I find milling to be a quick and relatively nonthreatening means of helping me assess the structure of the group, the isolated members, the cliques, and various closely-knit alliances between members. I agree with Schutz that although words can easily be denied, it is difficult to deny body position.

The way in which people mill is important. Some questions for group exploration and discussion are: Did you come in physical contact with other group members and how did these contacts feel? Did the feelings differ between people contacted? Who initiated the contact and was he sensitive to the other person's nonverbal cues as to whether the contact could be continued? How did you choose the people you wished to remain near? How did you let the other person know it was all right? How did the other person return your message? In terms of your "final place," were you in the center of the group or on the fringe? Were you hiding behind a chair or leaning against a wall for support? Was the group as a whole widely scattered or huddled close for warmth, support, or comfort?

There are many variations of this technique. One simple variation that has stimulating results is a comparison of heights. All of the members who consider themselves tall get down on their hands and knees and all those who consider themselves short walk around on their toes. Participants can then discuss the differences in interaction and affect the new height perspective brings.

This exercise was tried in a recent nurses workshop and resulted in mixed reactions. One of the very tall girls consciously slumped over when she spoke and expressed her great discomfort on meeting someone even taller than she was. When placed in a face to face situation with a smaller girl, she spoke of how she moved back or created distance since from a distance the difference in height was not as obvious. A very short girl was asked to stand up on a chair and speak to the group. She discussed her extreme discomfort at speaking down to people. All of her life she had been used to speaking up to everyone but children. When she met people shorter than she was, she almost automatically treated them as children. Her attitude toward height certainly must affect her patient's response to her.

It is interesting to try milling at the beginning of a group and then at the end, or, if the group is an ongoing one, a number of sessions later. Usually the group configurations will change greatly. Milling highlights the progress of group movement.

Various adaptions of children's games are useful in recovering body skills that have been repressed and abandoned by adults. In a game called "talk down" two participants face each other and are told to spend the next two minutes talking without stopping. The first one to stop speaking loses. At the end of two minutes the participants are asked how they felt. Usual responses are: "I didn't hear a thing he said"; or "He didn't hear a thing I said." The leader may discuss how often in life we encounter situations in which we talk and talk and feel that nothing is getting through to our partners. And how often people leave a party or gathering after hours of chatter feeling empty.

The participants are then asked to spend two minutes getting to know each other verbally. The audience is asked to watch what is being communicated nonverbally, whether it is consistent with or contradictory to the words being spoken, and what effect the nonverbal communication seems to have on the developing relationship.

Finally, the exercise is repeated nonverbally. Participants are given two minutes to get to know each other nonverbally. When the members compare the three exercises, they are often astounded how, when the barrage of words is cut through, the relationship changes.

At this point, with the group warmed up, more individually oriented techniques may be helpful. I begin by pointing out what body areas are most helpful in reading another person's nonverbal communication. I then ask the audience to assume various body positions to see what feelings these positions engender. For instance, I may instruct the group to

> press your back against the back of the chair, hunch your shoulders and cross your arms tightly over your chest, cross one leg over the other and bring your legs back toward the chair. How does this position feel?

The answers usually include "protected, tight, defensive, and holding in."

The group are then asked to plant both feet flat on the floor slightly apart, lean forward, and arch their backs backwards, head thrown back and hands resting on knees. Their answers to what this position feels like usually focus in the area of readiness or alertness.

The group are then asked to shake hands with the person next to them. I ask: What do these handshakes tell you? Who initiated the handshake and who broke contact? How did the body positions change during the handshake? Was there eye contact? Were the other nonverbal cues consistent with the handshake or giving contradictory messages?

Finally, I have members approach each other in a variety of sitting and standing positions. The person approached is usually asked what reaction he had to the various manners in which he was approached. He is asked whether he picked up signals from the other person and modified his behavior accordingly. Most people forget that even before words are exchanged the nonverbal approach and encounter have begun to determine the relationship. For instance, if a person rapidly approaches a seated friend and hovers over him while carrying on a conversation, he will create one effect, whereas the same conversation carried on at the friend's eye level has a quite different effect.

In concluding, one reminder: nonverbal techniques are no more the single best ameliorative method than are the various "talking cures." Each technique has its judicious time and place. The therapist becomes most skilled when he has learned to temper his knowledge of theory and technique with clinical intuition and interpersonal sensitivity.

> "... individuals today have called
> into question the whole process by
> which men are mobilized and used in
> our society for purposes and in ways
> that deny their essential humanity."
>
> J.C. Castreel
> "The Rise of Interpersonal Groups"

SOCIETAL CHANGE PROCESS—12

The consanguine family system in the United States is faced with a serious crisis. Today one in every four American marriages ends in dissolution; the rate is rapidly rising. In some areas of the nation, especially in regard to recent marriages, the trend toward divorce is over fifty percent. Symptoms of the unloosening of the consanguine family bond have been evident for some time. The growing crisis has necessitated serious study and concern about the institution of the family. A good number of remedial measures have been proposed to curb the trend toward family dissolution and many are already in practice.

Marital counseling has been made an adjunct to divorce proceedings, and in some states it is mandatory to receive professional psychological assistance before a divorce finally is decreed. Family therapy and counseling centers are springing up all over the nation.

Trial marriages have become fairly standard in American life. Many universities have erected coeducational dormitories with free access and little or no restriction on visitation. Some of the more radical mental health authorities suggest wife-swapping and extramarital dating to refurbish "tired" marriages. Yet the problem of failing marriages continues to grow. These and other corrective endeavors to hold together the family as a basic unit of society appear to have failed to address certain fundamental issues in modern American life.

That the complete dissolution of the family system is not what is being sought is revealed by the drift of large numbers of "drop-outs" from society, both those who have attained professional skills, expertise, and middle-class goals and those who have not, into collectivities where they live together as a family. These collectivities, or communes, are a form of social movement. A social movement signifies the dissatisfaction of a number of persons with the definition of "the good life" as proposed by existing social institutions.

The proliferation of this social movement is witnessed by the fact that less than a decade ago there were only a handful of these collectivities; *Time* magazine (December 28, 1970) estimated that there were about 3,000 communes in the United States. These communes differ widely in type, including: politically-oriented, socialistic collectivities modeled after those in the U.S.S.R.; peaceful, productive communities modeled after the Israeli kibbutz; the caravan "Four Marriage" families who sojourn the United States "to discover America" and respond to its spiritual needs; and utopian communities established by religious fundamentalists, political radicals, and conscientious objectors. There are also communes at encounter culture growth centers, and drug-taking, violence prone, mystical cults found on the West Coast. I will not attempt to define or differentiate this wide array. But, instead, I intend to address certain fundamental issues in American family life.

The commune as a contemporary social movement is a relatively undocumented phenomenon. While communes only recently have taken on serious importance as a challenge to the consanguine family system, they are, nonetheless, hardly a recent phenomenon in American life. The historian Daniel B. Reibel (*New York Times*, 1969) reports that more than 160 communes were established prior to 1860 in the United States. Few, however, survived long enough to make a real impact on American life. This chapter analyses some of the fundamental ideas that have contributed to the recent rebirth of the communal system.

THE AMERICAN SCENE

At the root of the proliferating movement toward communal living by young people lies the psychogenically disturbed condition of society. Many observers hold that young people today are forced to drop out of society because they have been cast as misfits and condemned for seeking meaning, beauty, and human contact in ways threatening to the highly competitive, materialistic, anti-erotic, and paranoid attitudes of their elders. They have been characterized as fleeing from

> what they regard as the constriction, loneliness, material-
> ism, and the hypocrisy in the straight society and the family
> life on which it is based. (*Time*, December 28, 1970)

Man has pulled himself through disastrous world wars and is beginning to realize that despite the threat of world suicide through warfare, and environmental problems such as overpopulation and pollution (all of which he has the knowledge to correct), he has the technological ability to stabilize life. In short, man's daily preoccupation need no longer be a struggle for survival. Indeed, individuals today find it inordinately difficult to dissolve their own lives. Intensive programs have been instituted to rehabilitate drug addicts and alcoholics; cautions about the dangers of cigarette smoking and the adulteration of our food have become psychologically effective; the study and prevention of suicide are rapidly becoming major branches of the mental health arts.

THE QUEST FOR MEANING

The magnitude and comprehensiveness of modern technology is such that only a relatively small portion of the population, composed largely of scientists and technicians, is actually required to serve the physical needs of the multitude. A century ago, over fifty percent of the American population lived in rural areas and were engaged in agrarian labor. Today, perhaps less than ten percent of the population live on farms; nonetheless, our food production greatly exceeds that of 100 years ago. One obvious reason for our large unemployment rate is that we simply do not require the large labor force of the less technological yesteryear. Economists have indicated that in ten years in large cities, such as New York, a minority of the denizens will support the majority.

An individual may be freely egocentric and asocial to a degree untolerated only a short time ago. Each individual today is not actually required, except perhaps in a moral sense, to maintain a trade and a life style forged on supporting family and kin. In the past, a man's destiny had always been his family—they were the root and essence of his life. Now, with the high rate of divorce and remarriage, a man may not even be required by law to support the woman he took in matrimony and the children he produced. If other individuals do not take up his financial and social responsibilities, large public agencies will. Today, the young person seeks more than the perpetuation of his existence; he yearns for personal and transcendental meaning in his life.

THE CONSANGUINE FAMILY SYSTEM

Few will argue that protection, care, and socialization of the young are the principal functions of the consanguine family system. These functions throughout American history have had strong underpinnings in society at large. With the dissolution of the extended kinship family, the average family has become rather small and generally isolated from kin. *Time* magazine (op. cit.) indicated recently that a small family requires the members to play a greater variety of roles than was necessary in the extended family.

All sorts of roles now have to be played by the husband and wife whereas in the older, extended family they had all sorts of help—psychological support, financial advice, and so on. The pressures of these multiple roles are partially responsible for the high rates of divorce, alcoholism, tranquilizers, etc.

In the past, socialization of the child was the consanguine family's raison d'être. But today, authorities have begun to question the wisdom of the child's socialization being given predominately to the biological family. They recognize that, along with the warm affectional bonds nurtured in the home, the family

is also a place of savage battles, rivalries, and psychological if not physical mayhem. . . . R. D. Laing [a prominent British psychiatrist] . . . finds it hurtful that a child is completely at the mercy of his parents, even to having to accept affection. (*Time*, op. cit.)

The state has found it more efficient and equitable to provide the child's education and, often, medical care. Consequently, the biological family no longer has exclusive title to its traditional normative functions. Some observers, such as the psychologist Richard Farson, have suggested that the biological family "is now often without function. It is no longer necessarily the basic unit in our society." (*Time*, op. cit.) The consanguine family, with its extended kinship system, many believe, served best in eras of economic scarcity and keen competition for goods and services. When the state had laissez faire policies, which were indifferent to the needs of the populace, the consanguine family and its extended kinship system assumed most, if not all, the socializing functions of its members: education, religion, healing, recreation, instruction for a trade, and apprenticeship opportunities, even the contract of marriage for its young. The family now shares these functions with other societal institutions.

THE COMMUNAL FAMILY SYSTEM

The communal family system has been offered as an alternative to the consanguine family. The remainder of this chapter discusses the reasons the communards believe that their system is an improvement over the presently constituted family unit.

1. *The communal system is freely chosen and intentionally designed.*

The person who moves into a commune consciously selects a normative reference group and actively seeks new ideals. In contrast, the culture and socialization transmitted by the consanguine family are usually uncritically assimilated. One cannot choose his natural mother, father, and kin, or their values. The consanguine family system is forged for survival and permanence. It is, generally, unappreciative of life styles that threaten traditional, time-proven ways of behaving. The communal system, on the other hand, is specifically designed to question the foundations of the consanguine family. Some communards, for example, use no last names because they believe that their relationship to one another has more lasting meaning than does a marriage contract. But were that meaning to be dissipated, there would be no point in their being legally bound to one another. "Everyone does his own thing at his own time. They are concerned with flexibility and mobility, not with permanence." (Kanter, 1970)

2. *The communal system calls into question the individual's most basic reasons for coming together to live, work, and procreate.*

Of course, in entering into marriage these same issues must be considered. The marriage contract is, nonetheless, obscurely formulated and institutionally imposed if, indeed, recognized at all as a negotiable contract by parties entering into marriage. A contract for coming together is more likely to be spelled out, rationally negotiated, and reasonably adhered to in a setting where there is less need for permanence, and where there is sincere interest in social experimentation, strong value-orientation, and emphasis on group problem solving and candid confrontation of one another. Influenced by encounter and sensitivity training attitudes and techniques, many of today's communes rely upon small group processes as preferred ways of fostering honest criticism, resolving disagreements, and creating a sense of mutual concern for one another and commitment to the community. (Kanter, 1968) The communards want to create the essential warmth, intimacy and companionship to restore the extended family relationships which have disappeared from the natural family.

The desire is to create intense involvement in the group— feelings of connectedness, belonging and the warmth of many attachments. (Kanter, 1970)

3. *The communal system provides an opportunity for the individual to sort out in the company of peers the way he wishes to conduct his life.*

The individual entering a commune presumably has been unable to express and implement an autonomous life style under the consanguine family system. The communal system permits social and personal experimentation in ways different or impossible in a status quo, survival-oriented society. No longer are people seen as personal property to be hoarded and used economically for goods and services. In an ethic of oneness and community, emotional, as well as physical, private property is banned. One's physical and emotional energies are shared. In some communes "newcomers are given to understand from the outset that property and bodies are to be shared freely, on demand." (Houriet, 1969)

Free love and sexual orgies, considered deviant and immoral by a society based upon private property, are at the very heart of the moral being of a communal family system. An individual experiences guilt when he acts in ways contrary to the values and system of rewards and punishment existing in his community. When an individual engages in extramarital relationships, he usually feels guilty and is generally disapproved of by those who know of his affairs. Indeed, to the extent that he keeps any relationship clandestine he indicates its asocial or even antisocial essence. Group sex in the commune, therefore, is an attempt to create a new social ethic, so that the individual need no longer feel guilty and alienated, so that he is able to share more of his personal life openly with all of the community.

To the extent that one is willing to ascribe a definition of morality to the shared approval of the community rather than to a metaphysical source, group sexuality is seen as moral and sustentative to the community, while private and clandestine relationships are amoral. Exclusive coupling and separation by consanguine families are, in most communes, discouraged or forbidden. In the utopian communities in the past, marital relationships tended to be replaced by celibacy; in today's communes, by group marriage and free love. In the "Four Marriage" families the children are reared under shared direction, reportedly without jealousy and domination. (Clairborne, December 24, 1970) One communard pointed out that "most children get their sense of reality and of their selves from just two adults." (Houriet, 1969) This, she claimed, is "an egoistic situation, [the children] never learn to share and see the world." (Houriet, op. cit.)

Another communard who shared her husband with others in the family reported:

Group living creates new relationships—not just sexual. I've become close to other men besides my husband. When you can get past the cat-and-mouse stage—the seductive way women treat men—then you can learn to be friends as human beings. There's not much difference between men and women after all. (Houriet, op. cit.)

4. *The individual today leads an "uptight" life in a large, complex, and achievement-oriented society.*

The policy of the social institutions that regulate our daily existence is generally determined only by very influential people. Influential leadership requires sophisticated political knowledge, effective public promotion, economic support, and past achievement. These requirements for leadership generally place the younger person at a decided disadvantage. But, at the same time, young people today are generally more concerned and vociferous about social conditions than are their elders. This wide disparity between youthful energy and political power has contributed to the counterculture of the youth and the "generation gap." The young person today needs to find alternatives to traditional political institutions with which he can more influentially involve himself. The family, youth have found, is a rather poor place to induce social change.

the family has had no long historical experience in dealing with the new rebelliousness. Unlike youths of the preindustrial age, who simply entered some form of apprenticeship for the adult world at the age of puberty, millions of teen-agers now remain outside the labor force to go to college. It is this fact that has made possible the existence of today's separate youth culture, by which parents feel surrounded and threatened in their sense of authority. (*Time*, op. cit.)

The commune is a new social microcosm designed to harness youths' idealism, energy, and wish for change. Some observers believe that the new communal movement began in Southern California and was mobilized by a common aversion to the large city with its political corruption and ecological pollution and the materialistic ethics of the capitalistic system.

Working for a profit lies at the core of the communards' disenchantment with urban life. The capitalistic system forces people into boring activity. It denies the brotherhood of man, making a person an object and alienating him from the simplicity of nature which the communards generally hold in religious awe. Consequently, although the members of most communes do not appear to be opposed to labor, they toil sporadically, generally preferring, it is reported, to be paid in kind rather than in cash. (Houriet, op. cit.)

In contrast to their former life outside the commune in which they toiled to obtain profit and accumulate material reserves as security against the uncertainty of the future, the communards may work only to sustain the family. This work may be as much to nurture the emotions as to furbish the body. For instance, in some ways the commune is seen as a twenty-four hour group therapy session. One communard described life in the commune

> like having to look at yourself in the mirror all the time . . .
> we all came into the family with ego hangups of one sort [or
> another]. Our life together wears down these hangups until a
> sort of group spirit takes over. (Houriet, op. cit.)

In the "Four Marriage" family, if one of the partners is not seeing things straight there are three other persons present to straighten him out instead of one, as in the traditional family. Group problem solving is a way of life in the commune. In the larger community the small family unit feels compelled to try to solve its problems independently of others.

5. *Communal living increases one's personal responsibility by enlarging the individual's ego boundaries.*

An individual's ego boundaries are not confined to the body shell and skin boundaries that delimit his physiology. The automobile driver will agree that his vehicle in short order becomes an extended part of himself (his self-concept). Other vehicles taking him by surprise and violating traffic and informal rules of the road are serious threats to his self-concept as well as to his physical safety. William James pointed out that the self consists of all that belongs to one, all that to which he lays claim: his house and his wife and children are no less properties of the self than are one's own body, ideas, and ambitions. In the consanguine family, then, self is modified by the adjective "my"; one's personal responsibility is limited to what he can claim as personal possession. We do not, therefore, speak of my atmosphere, my solar system, or my ocean; and we do not get excessively disturbed about these physical spaces although what happens in them may have more dire consequences for each of us than events in life space denoted by "my" about which we get rather agitated.

The individual apparently accepts responsibility for events only to the extent they take place in his life space. In the commune, the deviant behavior of "someone else's" child, for instance, is no longer an issue for "someone else" to concern himself about alone. Because the communal life space is a shared possession of all the communards, problems arising in it are the responsibility of all.

6. *Religious institutions no longer have the influence they had in yesteryear.*

Modern man still faces chafing anxieties despite having attained greater psychological understanding of himself. Man is still in search of spiritual guidance. The consanguine family, having relinquished many of its normative functions, has failed to provide leadership in spiritual matters.

The commune, on the other hand, seems to have a strong spiritual and religious life. Life together in a communal setting is a spiritual search for rebirth

> for utopia and community, brotherhood and sharing, warmth and intimacy, participation and involvement, purpose and meaning. Today's utopians want to return to fundamentals. They want to put people back in touch with each other, nature and themselves. (Kanter, 1970)

The usual trappings of formal religion are still visible but are not held as sacred in themselves. Ritual, dogma, and attitude are borrowed freely from Zen Buddhism, psychedelics, metaphysics, and mysticism, as well as from formal Christianity, modified and improvised upon. In this regard, a caravaning communal family reported that its odyssey across the continent was "to see America and at the same time speak out publically at a time when the country is ripe for a spiritual renaissance." (Clairborne, December 24, 1970)

Group happenings enhance the mystical feeling of oneness sought for in the commune. One moonlit night a communal family in Pennsylvania stood outdoors, hand in hand, and chanted, "Hare Krishna"—then they were silent for long minutes, just listening to the sound of their own breathing. Once, in the midst of a thunderstorm they did a rain dance to the accompaniment of recorders, a clarinet, and a saxophone. There were also a few nude love-ins in the creek. "It was beautiful," reported one of the family members. "There was no difference anymore between what you thought and what you did . . . " (Houriet, 1969) Such events appear to be a search for inner tranquility by renunciation of self and a denial of Western man's fear of intimacy and deindividualization. Drug experience as a group happening is often encouraged because through it the family is able to attain "a group high that wouldn't have been possible if [the family members] had taken separate trips." (Houriet, op. cit.)

7. *A communal system is often able to create economic self-sufficiency in the community.*

Today many "communards believe that money and private property create barriers between people." (Kanter, 1970) Property and resources are held in common in most communes. The communards try to produce all necessary goods within the commune so that they need not depend upon the outside world and thus need never be in a position to compromise themselves for these goods.

8. *With the decline of paternal leadership in the consanguine family, the communal system provides charismatic leadership.*

There is rarely a formal leader in today's commune as there was in the utopian communities of yesteryear. Today's communes often are founded on world views espoused by charismatic guru-type leaders. The gurus have become disillusioned with a society founded on hate and competitiveness and instead preach an ethos of love and nonviolence.

It does not seem sensible to evaluate at this time how well the communal system has fared or whether it is a legitimate successor to the consanguine family. It is simply too recent. It is evident, however, that the new communes will have more impact on American life than the utopian communities did in the past. The natural family is in serious crisis. It requires new directions and must offer more alternatives to the young than in the past. Some type of amalgamation of the consanguine and communal system seems certain. Whether this union will produce a family unit which will reestablish the consanguine family as society's essential unit remains to be seen.

> "Group therapy should be viewed as a two-edged sword that can both help and hinder client adjustment.... Therefore, therapists ought to be able to identify their major behavioral assets and liability in terms of their impact on client adjustment, and guide their professional behavior accordingly."
>
> R.L. Bednar & G.F. Lawlis
> "Empirical Research in Group Psychotherapy"

TRAINING GROUP PSYCHOTHERAPISTS—13

Because this book is addressed to the student, the concerned citizen, and the inexperienced group psychotherapist, this chapter deals with the training of the group therapist.

TRAINING PREREQUISITES FOR THE GROUP THERAPIST

Many people in the mental health professions hope that eventually psychotherapy will be both an applied art and a legitimate intellectual and scientific discipline. Psychotherapy is, as yet, more of an intuitive art than it is a science. Yet undefined are those personal qualifications of the psychotherapist that may be more influential in the outcome of his therapeutic work than his methodology (Powdermaker & Frank, 1953). The personal attributes and specific types of training that produce the best therapists are not precisely known. Moreover, it is questionable whether there is a single best type of therapist.

Of course, the personality of the therapist is of immense importance. His personality and character must be such that he can be personally and intimately committed as a therapist. In general, he must be able to be open with others and capable of engendering mutual trust. Nevertheless, very different kinds of personalities have such qualities and may be equally suited as therapists (Foulkes & Anthony, 1964). Furthermore, whereas the very gifted and the poorly qualified may be easily recognized, often it is difficult to differentiate adequate therapists from simply mediocre ones. But the approach to defining a good or adequate therapist may be misleading and fatuous. Therapists have come to realize that no one kind of ameliorative approach is effective with all patients or even consistently successful with the same individual. Correspondingly, every therapist is not equally comfortable and successful with each of the therapeutic tools at his disposal. The therapist's work must be a creative endeavor in which his style and the technique he employs are congruent with his own personality, temperament, and the demands of the therapeutic situation (Foulkes & Anthony, 1964). The question, "What is the best therapeutic approach?" becomes "What is the best therapeutic approach for whom and by whom?" (My opinion is that the personality theories upon which particular psychotherapeutic methodologies are based are not equally applicable for all age groups. Certain psychotherapeutic systems seem more accurately descriptive of particular stages of life: Freudian psychoanalysis does best with childhood; Adlerian individual psychology with young adulthood; Jungian analytic psychology with the middle aged, and so forth.)

Obviously, a trained therapist is a better therapist than one without training. In addition to the necessary personal qualifications, a competent therapist should have training in three areas: education, supervision, and experiential training.

The education of the psychotherapist should not be overly weighted in favor of science and technical methodology. Without the leveling influence of humanism, science tends to become mechanistic and aimless. A serious and continuing interest in history, philosophy, and the arts is indispensable for a practitioner who is required to relate conversantly with people in all walks of life and who are troubled by many of the same concerns that have plagued men from the dawn of time. A practitioner must, of course, have a sound background in the social sciences and scientific methodology. He requires a comprehensive knowledge of theories of personality, theories and techniques of psychotherapy, and theories of psychopathology. The therapist must be thoroughly conversant with studies of group dynamics and small groups (the latter would provide him with an understanding of the vital interrelation between personality development and milieu).

Education in psychotherapy should be designed to provide sound grounding in present knowledge and skills, yet enhance the student's awareness of how current approaches are but a point in historical development. The aim should be to convey knowledge and principles without dogmatism and rigid adherence to techniques *qua* techniques. Acknowledging the inevitability and desirability of change in the field should make it clear to the student that without his future creative and innovative contributions, the art and science of psychotherapy will become stagnant. (Bookbinder & Rosenthal, 1969)

It is hard to conceive of an individual acquiring the forementioned knowledge, which can be regarded as only minimal preparation for being a practicing psychotherapist, without at least a graduate degree. (The California School of Psychotherapy in San Francisco and two or three other professional schools attempt to provide an adequate background for psychotherapists prior to their entering the graduate school level.)

SYSTEMATIC READINGS IN THE GROUP PSYCHOTHERAPY LITERATURE

In my training program for group therapists in a large federal hospital I developed a list of fifty weekly reading assignments designed to acquaint the trainees with important recent and innovative, as well as classical, references relating to the enabling processes in groups. (Because of limitations of space, this material could not be included here. The reader interested in obtaining this material may write the author in care of the Laurel Comprehensive Community Mental Health Center, 217 Main Street, Laurel, Maryland.) This list was intended to provide the trainee with a prospectus of the most influential work in the fields that have contributed to group psychotherapy. This list was prepared "developmentally;" the trainee was taken through a progression of reading material starting with the history of group therapy the first week, going on to a survey of group therapy the second, and then to seminal thinking on social processes, highly technical and specialized techniques dealing with dreams, resistance, countertransference, and so forth.

The trainees were encouraged to use this material in conjunction with group discussions in the training seminar in evolving their own conceptual frame of reference for working with groups.

Emphasis was placed on developing a comprehensive and well-ordered conceptual framework. The trainee chose what theoretical system he wanted to use. Theory was stressed in that many of the people entering the group psychotherapy training program felt that their previous training and education had been atheoretical or confusingly eclectic. Both these orientations left the impression that any theoretical position or treatment technique might be appropriate for any patient and any treatment situation. The beginning practitioner needs to be aware that the personality theory implicit in each system of counseling and psychotherapy was originally formulated from the theorist's clinical experience with a specific client population. This suggests that each system of counseling or psychotherapy is more appropriate for some patients than for others.

Without some consistent and comprehensive framework, much of the clinical data the practitioner needs to understand and deal with fall beyond his ready comprehension. To help them develop a theoretical frame of reference, the trainees were requested to find a group therapy text to be read in its entirety. Each trainee was also to secure a reference text (not necessarily a group therapy book) which especially related to the treatment of the patient or client population which comprised his therapeutic group.

Most mental health educators would agree that expert supervision is required both during academic preparation and during the initial years of a practitioner's professional career. Initially, supervision should be conducted individually on a regular basis, not simply whenever the fledging is troubled by a difficult patient or consciously puzzled by a session. Supervision in a group is also desirable but should supplement individual supervision. Too frequently the young practitioner who is glib is able to cover up his difficulties in a supervisory group. On the other hand, reticent or overly defensive trainees are more likely to receive attention in a supervision group. Group supervision becomes more valuable to the neophyte practitioner as he gains experience and confidence in his abilities and is willing to disclose troublesome aspects of his practice.

The group psychotherapists I trained at the federal hospital already had individual supervision prior to their entering my program and were ready for group supervision. Three hours a week of group experience and formal group supervision are sufficient for conducting a viable group psychotherapy program, although more time, when available, is generally preferable.

During an hour and a half session once a week, the trainees discussed recent sessions of the groups they conducted as therapists. The range of these groups was wide—inpatient groups for geriatric patients; intensive inpatient groups for alcoholics and drug addicts; outpatient, continuation clinic groups; and community consultation in ghetto areas of the city. Problems were handled in supervision, through advice, feedback, confrontation, sharing of experiences, role playing, various group exploratory techniques, as well as through those modalities that spontaneously arise in a freewheeling discussion. Problems and issues concerning the selection of patients, planning, implementing, and conducting groups were brought back to the supervisory group and dealt with among the trainees. Each trainee's problems and concerns served as a learning experience and a jumping-off point for discussing important therapeutic issues for the other trainees.

In presenting problems to the supervisory group the trainee was expected not simply to drop his problems on the group and ask the other trainees what should be done. He was expected to accompany the presentation of his problems with several alternative solutions and his rationale for each. He then could employ the group to help him select the most appropriate of these alternatives.

A SOUND BACKGROUND IN PSYCHODYNAMICS

I strongly recommend that group psychotherapists gain experience conducting individual psychotherapy sessions prior to leading groups. Group work is generally regarded as a more complex and exacting task than is individual psychotherapy. Consequently, working intimately with persons on an individual basis allows the practitioner to familiarize himself with psychodynamics and personality patterns which tend to be obscured or complicated in a group situation. Moreover, the group leader who has had experience in both individual and group situations is likely to be more aware of the multiple levels of functioning operating concurrently in a group. Each group member feels pulls from at least three levels of functioning: the intrapersonal, the interpersonal, and the integral. Inconsistency and contradiction in a group member's behavior or conflict among group members are frequently reactions to antagonistic pressures from these concurrent levels of functioning. Most group leaders tend to emphasize one of these levels rather than to devote balanced attention to all three.

The need for a sound understanding of psychodynamics is not an idle suggestion. Today many group therapists, along with a number of encounter group leaders, apparently fail to realize that an effective group leader must have more than simply the skill to move a group in a particular direction. He also must have the ability to evaluate accurately the psychodynamic status of each individual in the group at any given movement. In so doing, the group leader needs the ability to assess how beneficial is the direction the group is moving in for each of its members and for the group as an ensemble. A group psychotherapist must have thorough conversance with personality theory and the ability to evaluate the unique psychodynamics of his clients.

EXPERIENTIAL SUPERVISION

In many ways, supervision is the pivotal experience for the trainee in psychotherapy. It is the meeting ground between the practical, the theoretical, and the personal. To maximize the effectiveness of their relationship, the supervisor and supervisee need to relate to one another much as the therapist and his patient do in terms of their reaction to one another in the immediate situation rather than in terms of formal principles of therapeutic practice or on the basis of their previous experience with similar relationships. This highly immediate and personal aspect makes supervision a particularly relevant training device for the inexperienced therapist whose concerns go beyond the question of "proper" technique and "correct" understanding of the patient's behavior.

Generally, the most pressing concern of the inexperienced therapist is "what he is all about" as a person in a therapeutic encounter with another. Attention to the immediate personal aspects of psychotherapeutic training discourages an artificial distinction between didactic and practical education. The supervisor should be a good example in terms of clinical excellence rather than on the basis of academic achievement. The supervisor

> must be that which he attempts to teach others to be. It is
> not sufficient for the teacher to be highly competent in psy-
> chotherapy research or the teaching of psychotherapy theory.
> (Bookbinder et al., 1969, p. 4)

Experiential Training. It is my belief that the traditional methods for training practitioners to work with others need to be recast. Emphasis should be on learning through dynamic interaction, learning by participation, both as a leader and as a follower. One cannot properly attend to another's needs if he cannot experientially attune himself to thoughts and feelings of others. Therefore, the therapist should obtain direct experience being "on the couch" as well as sitting "behind the couch." Personal dyadic therapy is highly important to the practitioner, but no less important is his exposure to a wide array of group experiences. While in training he initially should be a patient in a therapy group and then supplement this experience by being a participant in expertly conducted sensitivity training, encounter, gestalt, and other types of new groups.

Group experience has not always been recommended to the practitioner. Heretofore, professional workers were expected to enter individual psychotherapy, particularly psychoanalytic therapy, in order to work out their own personal problems and countertransference. It was thought that this would sufficiently enable the professional worker to become an able practitioner. Unfortunately, this kind of therapy was too long, too expensive, and often did not help develop the skills the practitioner required in becoming an able therapist beyond being sensitive and responsive to his own motives. This became increasingly more evident as professional workers shifted the major portion of their responsibilities from dyadic sessions to working with patients in a group.

For an hour and a half a week, the trainees in my program met together in a process group. In these sessions, each of the trainees had the opportunity to observe both his own and the other participants' behavior, the implementation of diverse personal and interpersonal strategies, sentiments, and attitudes in relating to others, and the effects these interchanges had upon the task of the group. In short, they had the opportunity to study their own behavior as a group.

In the process group session the trainees had the opportunity to experience their own reactions and those of the other trainees under conditions in which they were not certain what was expected of them. They had, therefore, to negotiate with the other group members to develop some viable means of coping with a highly unstructured and frequently uncomfortable situation. This climate lay bare the importance of a group contract, the setting of clear and definable goals, the effectiveness of various kinds of negotiations in a group, as well as the importance of underlying group tensions. These young group therapists were already intellectually familiar with these phenomena although they reported that they were disguised, unclear, or somewhat elusive in the groups they conducted. Clearly, more than intellectual understanding of group dynamics was necessary. A therapist trying to respond to a pressing concern of a patient finds it difficult concurrently to pay attention to group process, to say nothing of intelligently responding to his own internal reactions to what is taking place. Despite the difficulty, the therapist must adequately perform these tasks. Process group experience contributes significantly toward developing this tripartite skill.

In summarizing what transpired in the process group after each session, I found that increasingly the trainees were comparing what they had experienced as participants in the process group with similar situations in groups in which they were therapists. Situations which were experienced as anxious and puzzling in the process group were inevitably situations that these young group therapists had the greatest difficulty understanding and dealing with in their own groups. The realization of what they were doing and where they were getting stuck seemed to be maximized by the process group experience. This is not difficult to understand. Simply knowing about human behavior and group process does not automatically enable professional workers to appreciate what their patients are experiencing in groups and in other interpersonal situations. Thus, each trainee was able to gain a greater appreciation of the phenomenological world of the patient and, at the same time, a clearer insight into his own transactions with others. He gained understanding from the feedback of the other group members and by observing an endeavor in which he, himself, was intimately involved. Efficacious training for the practitioner requires supervision in exploring relationships with peers as well as in conducting patient groups.

The supervisor acted as a consultant helping the trainees understand their behavior as a group. The last fifteen to thirty minutes of the session were devoted to summarizing and systematizing the events of the session and how they related to what the trainees had been reading in the group literature and to the difficulties they experienced in the groups they were conducting. The experiential group provided the group psychotherapy trainees with the opportunity to observe and interact with an experienced group leader in a well-functioning group.

PERSONAL PSYCHOTHERAPY FOR PRACTITIONERS

Therapy is more than simply a cognitive endeavor. A group leader who is not in touch with his own feelings and is unable to recognize his own inappropriate responses cannot avoid subtly encouraging his clients' resistance patterns, their unwillingness to face up to their own perturbance. A group practitioner who has not confronted his own problems in personal psychotherapy can be expected to be uncomfortable with clients assuming "patient" and "healer" roles in a group he is conducting. On the other hand, a group leader who has had personal psychotherapy is more apt to realize that group experience helps him remain aware of his own countertransferential behavior. Conversely, the group leader without personal therapy frequently handles confrontation deleteriously. He refuses to deal with his own irrational notions when called to task by group members. Instead, he turns these threats to his leadership back on the group members by suggesting that it is their problem, not his.

A well-trained group therapist has a balance of experience and training in all of the areas described in this chapter. It would be injudicious to consider only one or two of these areas as sufficient for competence in psychotherapy or to assume that an abundance of training in some areas can compensate for a deficiency of training in others. Each of these areas of training blend together with the necessary intellectual and emotional equipment into a dynamic gestalt.

> "Group psychotherapy is clearly not a standard treatment in which routine procedures are applied as, for example, in a surgical operation. It is a social interaction ... the processes and outcomes of any psychotherapeutic group will be influenced by its unique combination of members and how they perceive and respond to one another."
>
> H. Walton (Ed.)
> Small Group Psychotherapy

RESEARCH IN GROUP PSYCHOTHERAPY—14

As mentioned in Chapter 1, a number of research studies suggest that a great many patients remain "unchanged" by psychotherapy. Several behavioral scientists have interpreted the same data differently. They contend that it is spurious to regard psychotherapy as having no effect upon patients. These investigators infer that there are two equal but opposite effects of intensive psychotherapy: it is a double-edged process which may either ameliorate or cause exacerbation of the problems that bring people into treatment. (Bergin, 1967; Traux & Carkhuff, 1967)

Evidence clearly suggests that the therapist plays a central role in facilitating patient improvement or deterioration. Psychotherapy in the hands of poorly trained and incompetent practitioners, no less than in the hands of highly trained and skillful, therapists, is a powerful tool. Therefore, it is incumbent upon the practitioner to locate those attributes and technical skills which favorably influence the enabling process. Only in this way can he fashion more effective treatment modalities and help provide intelligent training for students.

In developing better tools research data are indispensible.

Five major surveys of the group therapy literature have appeared in recent years (Yalom, 1970; Meltzoff & Kornreich, 1970; Bednar & Lawlis, 1971; Goldstein, Heller & Sechrest, 1966; Mann, 1966). Of the behavioral scientists who compiled these surveys, only one claims that "a substantial body of evaluative research has been accumulated to confirm the effectiveness of group psychotherapy." (Mann, 1966) Other behavioral scientists are discouraged by the present state of research methodology in group psychotherapy. The current body of information, with few exceptions, consists of theory, case histories, clinical observation, and anecdotes. Group practitioners seem to have had an indifferent attitude toward research investigation. As a result, the group psychotherapy literature has remained at a primitive level of impressionistic observation and inquiry. (Goldstein, Heller, & Sechrest, 1966) The practitioner regards the literature as having little practical value to him in his work. He would prefer a systematic ordering of information which separates empirical data from impressionistic and speculative reports.

It is unfortunate that most practitioners do not realize the value of the empirical group therapy literature. Some empirical work has been conducted in regard to a number of important group therapy issues. The practitioner needs to be aware of these findings; otherwise, he becomes a prisoner of trial and error experimentation. Research data are used to address fourteen basic issues about group therapy in the remainder of this chapter.

The Utility of Group Psychotherapy

An impressive array of empirical studies reports on the responsiveness of group psychotherapy to various psychological conditions. John Mann (1966) has summarized the outcomes of forty-one diverse studies and has found positive change in patient variables in approximately forty-five percent of the cases cited. However, scrutiny of the research designs and methodology employed in the studies reveals such errors as bias sampling, rater contamination, lack of satisfactory outcome measures, and extrapolating individual therapy measures inappropriately to a group modality. Moreover, few better designed studies have been replicated. (Bednar & Lawlis, 1971) Errors in research are not difficult to understand. Group psychotherapy is not a standard treatment method. It is a complex interactive situation which touches upon the widest range of human emotions and relationships. Therefore, an investigation of the unique and elusive features of therapeutic experience will incur serious methodological difficulties. Perhaps one of the most difficult methodological problems in psychotherapy is precise replication studies.

One would expect that the outcomes of a treatment modality which produced lasting changes could be measured by follow-up investigation. Unfortunately, this is not the case. No follow-up studies of group treatment verify lasting effects. The few well-designed studies, such as those by George Fairweather (1963), suggest that patient changes resulting from group treatment are not measurable over time and are therefore probably shortlived.

A survey of the evidence suggests that group therapy often may be a useful tool. But the proponent of group psychotherapy must be prepared to admit that some of the positive results of empirical investigations are due to experimental bias and errors.

The Kinds of Problems for Which Group Psychotherapy Is Indicated

Group treatment appears to have best results when used in conjunction with other treatment modalities. (Baehr, 1954) A favorable outcome from group treatment is considerably more likely with nonpsychotics than with patients with severe cognitive disorders. (Meltzoff & Kornreich, 1970; Bednar & Lawlis, 1971) Severely psychotic patients do better in individual sessions than they do in groups. Conversely, group psychotherapy is more effective for nonpsychotic patients than are individual sessions. Schizophrenics do best in groups when their condition is acute rather than chronic.

The Harmful Implications of Group Psychotherapy

There are sufficient data to suggest that deterioration is often effected by dyadic treatment. (Bergin, 1967; Traux & Carkhuff, 1964) In the group psychotherapy literature both Fairweather (1960) and Charles Truax and Robert Clarkhuff (1967) found that some patients receiving group treatment improved while other patients became worse as a result of group therapy.

The Types of Problems for Which Group Psychotherapy Is Counterindicated

The findings from a number of empirical studies suggest that patients in the following clinical categories should, in most instances, be excluded from treatment in groups: suicidal, paranoid, brain damaged, acutely psychotic, extremely narcissistic, hypochondriacal, drug and alcohol addictions, and psychopathic. My clinical experience, however, cautions against blanket rejection of difficult clinical entities. Some empirical data indicates that carefully designed groups

ul to at least some of the above clinical entities. (Semon &
957; Williams et al., 1962; Sacks & Berger, 1954; Jones &
}; Feifel & Schwartz, 1953)

The Dimensions of Psychological Functioning Which Are Affected by Group Psychotherapy

Empirical data strongly suggest that affect and mood, particularly depression, as well as somatic symptoms, are favorably influenced by group treatment. (Traux et al., 1968) On the other hand, severe thought disorders and marked interpersonal withdrawal do not appear to respond favorably to treatment in a group. Group psychotherapy does appear, however, to influence cognitive dimensions in nonpsychotics. At least three studies indicate some improvement in intellectual functioning in psychoneurotics. (Coons, 1957; Jones & Peters, 1953; Teahan, 1966) Cognitive and affect functioning are, of course, interrelated. The reduction of depression and anxiety as a result of group treatment may lead to a greater experienced capacity for intellectual work rather than increased intellectual development. Unfortunately, there are insufficient data to verify this contention. Some evidence suggests that affective states are improved because group experience contributes to feelings of relief from personal discomfort, self-depreciation, and inadequacy and leads to a sense of well-being and social adjustment. (Reisper & Waldman, 1961; Williams et al. 1962; Boe et al., 1966; Zimet & Fine, 1955; Luria, 1959; Johnson, 1964)

Abundant evidence indicates that in an institutional setting group treatment leads to environmental adjustment, improved behavior patterns which are readily observable, and control over disruptive behavioral patterns. (Wilcox & Guthrie, 1957; Cowden et al., 1956; Semon & Goldstein, 1957; Tucker, 1956; Wilson et al., 1967; Snyder & Sechress, 1959; McDavid, 1964)

The Selection of Appropriate Groups

The few studies that touch on the issue of fitting patients into appropriate groups are investigations of hospitalized patients. Hospitalized schizophrenic patients fare best in group treatment when the group is initially structured (Anker & Walsh, 1961) and group objectives and role expectations are clearly defined from the outset. It also appears that schizophrenic patients will respond favorably to less structured groups if the increases in group-centered activity is gradual. (Bednar & Lawlis, 1971) The now classical work of T.W. Adorno et al., (1950) suggests that emotionally disturbed persons respond more favorably to structured situations. Verbal groups which aim at promoting insight and self-introspection are counterindicated for schizophrenic patients. Not only do insight-oriented groups appear to offer no discernible positive gains, but there are indications that this orientation may actually be detrimental for patients with severe thought disorders. Schizophrenic patients appear to do best in treatment that encourages group interaction and activity. (Meltzoff & Kornreich, 1970) That much more research is required concerning the issue of selecting groups is attested by the fact that group psychotherapy, despite considerable differences in theoretical orientation and therapist styles, is most frequently studied "in its most generic form . . . . Currently group therapy is a very undifferentiated research variable." (Bednar & Lawlis, 1971, p. 814)

Group Size

Very few studies have investigated group size relative to treatment outcome. There is, however, a voluminious literature concerning group size based upon clinical observation and theoretical assumptions, as well as considerable discussion devoted to group size in group therapy textbooks. Also, a number of surveys have been conducted to answer the normative question: "What is the size of actual treatment groups?" (Fidler & Waxenberg, 1971; Rosenbaum, 1965; Rosenbaum & Hartley, 1962) Each of these surveys recommended eight as the ideal number of members in a group. Jay Fidler and Sheldon Waxenberg (1971) suggest that, although the sizes of the groups they studied varied from two to eighteen members

> working with more than eight members in a group may tax
> the therapist's capacity fully to regard each one as a distinc-
> tive personality. Thus, the number eight may be taken as a
> pragmatic optimum.

Most of the studies that experimentally have compared size to group processes and outcomes have been investigations of nontherapeutic groups. In summarizing this literature I find that group size has an important influence on such group variables as leadership, verbal interaction, and relationships among group members. Of course, findings about the dynamics of nontherapeutic groups cannot directly be applied to treatment groups. Differences in orientation and goals between therapeutic and task groups cautions against straightforward generalization. (Goldstein, Heller & Sechrest, 1966) Nonetheless, these data have served as a starting place for some investigation of therapy groups. One such study was conducted by G.F. Castore whose data suggest that group size should be determined by the effect size has upon patterns of verbal interaction in a group. Castore found that nine patients is the upper limit for a group whose members are reticent and have marked difficulty interacting. My own rational for selecting an appropriate group size was discussed in Chapter 4.

The Optimal Composition of a Psychotherapy Group

The issue of group composition may be the one about which the most empirical information is available. The findings about group composition may be categorized under clinical entities and personality traits.

In terms of clinical entities, there is evidence that patients who do well in group psychotherapy are either psychoneurotic or are experiencing short-term psychotic reactions. (Fairweather, 1960) The traits that appear to lend to favorable group treatment outcomes include: cooperativeness and motility (Giedt, 1961) and high verbal interaction. (Heckel & Salzberg, 1967) R.L. McFarland (1962) found that intelligence scores were the single best predictors of what he regarded as positive participation in group behaviors. Evidence from an array of other sources tends to confirm these findings.

The practitioner will probably not regard these findings as very meaningful. That brighter, more capable, nonpsychotic patients respond better to group psychotherapy than do persons with severe problems in these areas is no remarkable finding. Persons with the same attributes also do better in individual treatment. The therapist requires some information about how difficult, uncooperative, and less intelligent persons may also profit from group experience. In this regard, the recommendations about matching up patients in a group stemming from investigations by Powdermaker and Frank (1953) and A. Samuels (1964) offer more promise than does a stereotyped elimination of difficult patients from groups. Evidence is mounting on the importance of matching patients in specific groups on the basis of compatible needs to establish a group balance. There is some evidence that group compatibility may be the essential ingredient in fostering group cohesiveness (Yalon, 1966) Many practitioners contend that group cohesiveness is a sin qua non condition for favorable outcomes. The therapist should evaluate the personality traits of the group members in order to maximize the interactions that are useful to the group processes he seeks to foster.

Thelen has summarized the importance of personality traits to group composition in the following passage:

> Group growth, although not directly related to the growth of each individual, is, however, in the last analysis dependent upon the kinds of people in the group. The basic emotional dynamics of the group is a working out of the changing

strains in the network of relationships among the members and [the therapist]. For example, if everyone in the group were thoroughly content to be forever dependent on the [therapist] for all decisions, the [therapist] would find it very difficult to teach the group very much about the nature of dependency, its uses, forms, and causes. [Treatment in a group] is much easier when some people in the group are satisfied with being dependent and others react against the feelings of dependency. (Thenlen, 1954)

Patients in a Group for Whom the Therapist Should Be Most Concerned

Many theoretical discussions have taken place concerning the silent patient. It is generally advised that overly reticent or underly socialized persons not be placed in a group. Traditional psychotherapy has placed an inordinate emphasis on verbalization. The traditional psychotherapist has contended that patients with underdeveloped verbal skills who are in distress are more likely to act out feelings in a destructive manner than patients who have verbal skills. In individual sessions, it has been assumed, there is greater opportunity for the therapist to support nonverbal patients and encourage them to verbalize feelings.

Research evidence, however, suggests that the therapist's major concern should not be the silent group member but the uninvolved member. The uninvolved patient may verbalize more than others in the group but his commitment to treatment is tenuous and his participation is inconsistent. The uninvolved patient may be readily differentiated from the silent but involved group member by attention to various nonverbal cues such as body movement and facial expression. (Bednar & Lawlis, 1971) The uninvolved patient who drops out early in therapy tends, according to Morris Parloff, to be ranked lowest in popularity by the other group members.

Individual Versus Group Psychotherapy

A controversial issue in psychotherapy is the relative merits of individual and group therapy. The importance of group treatment as a modality in large measure depends upon the demonstration that patients do better in group than in individual treatment. In light of the importance given to this issue in theoretical writings, it seems strange that only a few studies touch upon a direct comparison of individual and group psychotherapy. These studies arrive at the conclusion that there is no systematic difference in overall utility between individual and group modalities. (Novick, 1965; Imber et al., 1957;

Barron & Leary, 1955; Baehr, 1954; Fairweather, 1963) Also these studies have failed to identify the conditions under which individual or group treatment is best indicated.

The practitioner will not be encouraged by these findings. From his clinical experience he knows that often there are definite indications that individual or group therapy is the treatment of choice for a particular patient. However, the practitioner may be heartened by Yalom's (1970) observation that even if the outcomes of group and individual treatment are equivalent in overall effectiveness, one must not interpret this to mean that the results are equivalent. The experienced practitioner is aware that individual and group therapies have different types of results. There are some data to support Yalom's clinical observation. Patients involved in group psychotherapy showed more changes and variability in interpersonal behavior, while patients receiving individual therapy tended to demonstrate perceptual change. (Fairweather, 1960)

The Effective Varieties of Group Psychotherapy

A number of varieties of group therapy have been compared for their utility. Most of the groups studied were composed of hospitalized patients. A canvass of the groups studied reveals a continuum of therapy orientation in these groups from therapist-oriented to group-centered. The most prevalent group was in an intermediate position on this continuum with leanings in one direction or the other. (Meltzoff & Kornreich, 1970) Which of the orientations was most efficacious was not indicated definitively although the evidence seems to suggest that a modified group-centered approach leads to a favorable outcome more frequently than other group orientations. (Coons, 1957; Semon & Goldstein, 1957)

In terms of normative data, the dimensions of interaction most commonly found in all varieties of group treatment by factor analysis fall in the following categories: hostility, attention, seeking control, leadership, support role, succorance, submissiveness, withdrawal, and disorganized behavior. (Lorr, 1966) The concepts most frequently exhibited in group therapy were: acceptance, altruism, universalism, intellection, reality testing, transference, interaction, spectator therapy, and ventilation. (Corsini & Rosenberg, 1955)

Processes Which Lead to Successful Outcomes

The identification of ameliorative factors in group treatment is still a highly complex problem. Insufficient data are available about the interactional effects of therapist orientation and other salient therapist, patient, and group variables which probably accounts for the lack of systematic investigation of essential group properties in relation to treatment outcome. (Bednar & Lawlis, 1971)

A few dimensions which appear significant to group treatment outcomes have been located. There is some evidence that the patient's expectations about the nature and duration of treatment are important. (Goldstein, Heller, & Sechrest, 1966) Other evidence points to the importance of compatibility between patient and therapist expectations in fostering and maintaining a therapeutic relationship.

The atmosphere of the group appears to be one of the more important group processes. The therapist is wise to foster carefully a group atmosphere in which patients experience warmth, concern, and genuineness from the therapist and other group members. (Traux, 1961) The patient also needs the opportunity for expression of feeling and involvement in meaningful participation. According to Yalom, influencing patient expectations prior to the initial group contributes to subsequent positive group behaviors. Patients also do better if they trust their therapist (Lorr, 1965), and they experience as most beneficial those sessions in which they have the greatest participation. (Sechrest & Barger, 1961) The group discussions that patients felt were most beneficial dealt with sexual maladjustment in terms of conflict, anxieties and symptoms, guilt and shame, and efforts to relate these problems to early life experiences. Topics perceived as least useful were those related to people outside the group, money problems, and work problems. (Talland & Clark, 1954)

There are considerable data from nontherapeutic groups showing several central group processes also to be essential to successful group outcomes. (Yalom & Rand, 1966; Goldstein, Heller & Sechrest, 1966) Group cohesiveness appears to be one such factor. Although there are no substantiative data to support the contention, many practitioners hold group cohesion to be as important a curative factor in a treatment group as is the patient–therapist relationship in dyadic treatment. (Bednar & Lawlis, 1971) Data from a study by Frank (1959) suggest that status, ego-involvement, and personal satisfaction in group activity heavily contribute toward an optimal level of group cohesiveness.

Producing Greater Economy and Efficiency in Group Psychotherapy

Most patients who drop out of group treatment do so in the first few sessions. Laboratory and clinical observation reveals that the initial sessions of a group are replete with struggles for establishing norms for future group behavior. (Jacobs & Campbell, 1961) Evidence indicates that patients who establish popularity early in the development of the group express the greatest satisfaction with the group and show favorable group outcomes (Yalom et al., 1967). It may be assumed that the popular group member successfully has learned to maintain himself in terms of group norms. The initial group sessions are clearly essential to outcome. Evidence suggests that pretraining in dyadic treatment can teach patients early interactive patterns. (Goldstein & Shipman, 1961; Frank, 1959) A few studies have demonstrated that patients can be systematically prepared for group therapy; pretraining programs have focused on role expectations of the patient in group treatment. (Yalom et al., 1967; Traux et al., 1968) To develop a facilitative group climate in groups comprised of schizophrenics, patient behavior may be activated by means of physical activity, task-oriented activity, and medication. (Bednar & Lawlis, 1971)

Effects of Leaderless and Alternate Sessions

In recent years leaderless group modalities have proliferated. Much of the impetus for these groups has come from the encounter movement. More venerable are a very large number of leaderless self-help groups founded by such organizations as Alcoholics Anonymous and Neurotics Anonymous. In recent years a number of analytic group practitioners have promulgated the utility of the leaderless alternate group session. The number of leaderless groups currently being held is therefore rather large.

A number of studies have demonstrated the validity of leaderless groups for nonpatient populations. (Bednar & Lawlis, 1971; Berzon, 1968) One study showed that irregular attendance on the part of the therapist has greater facilitative value in comparison to regular or no attendance. (Exner, 1968) Data on hospitalized patients, on the other hand, caution against employing leaderless or alternate sessions with a patient population. Traux (1968) found that alternate sessions influenced patients to see themselves in more pathological ways.

Group psychotherapy is a powerful treatment technique. It rarely has no effect on its recipients. The composition of a treatment group heavily determines the interactive patterns in that group. Patients should be carefully chosen for a group which most appropriately meets their needs and the specific needs of that group. Selection of patients is clearly only an initial step in convening a group. Most patients require orientation and support in developing constructive roles and expectations prior to convening with the group. On the other hand, all patients do not respond favorably to treatment in a group. Early detection of patient difficulties therefore must be stressed. Patients who successfully adapt to the group's norms and expectations early in the course of the group fare best in group treatment. The patient who is uninvolved requires the directive attention of the therapist and the other group members. Lack of involvement in the group may seriously jeopardize group cohesiveness.

The patients who appear to do best in group treatment are bright, articulate, and cooperative psychoneurotics. Patients experiencing psychotic disorders derive optimal benefit from groups that are originally structured and gradually increase in group directed activity as patients become more comfortable in an interpersonal setting.

In reviewing the literature on group psychotherapy research, I observe that, as yet, insufficient empirical data exist to arrive at a firm understanding of what the important ingredients of group psychotherapy are. More investigation is needed concerning the complex interactive effect of therapist, patient, and group processes and properties. However, I, as a therapist, neither plead ignorance nor resign myself to a passive stance. As I have shown, there is much that is known about facilitating the healing in others. Correspondingly, there is also much yet to be discovered. But there is no definitive, universal method or foolproof therapy for all. Each individual must find for himself, be he patient or therapist, who he is and what he is about in his ameliorative being together with another. Only from this highly complex and intimate encounter can the therapist be helpful to the other.

Hopefully, the researcher will work with the practitioner steadily to bring into greater clarity and comprehension the essential ingredients of successful ameliorative endeavor. In this way, group psychotherapy can be transformed from an art to a creative science.

"If there is an answer to the problem of meaning in my life, it does not lie out there someplace, but within me. Life does not present me with meaning. Life merely is. The meaning, the true zest for living, comes from full involvement with life."

H.F. Thomas
"An Existential Attitude in Working
With Individuals and Groups"

CONCLUDING STATEMENTS—15

In this book I have delineated, compared, and evaluated the "traditional" and the new group views of psychotherapy and have described several different group therapy approaches. How should the reader most judiciously select the technique designed for his professional needs? As I have reiterated throughout this book, the "science" of psychotherapy has not advanced to the stage where there is a single best technique for all ameliorative endeavors, although the advocates of schools of psychotherapy would have us believe otherwise. They would have us believe that a book such as the present one, describing an array of treatment modalities, is not required. They maintain that the only necessary text about psychotherapy is the one that describes the single best treatment—their own.

This book was written because, as research findings confirm, the single best technique of psychotherapy has not yet been advanced. The practitioner must select the technique whose rationale is most syntonic with the demands and limitations of his patient population, that conforms to the conditions in which he is working, and that requires skills with which he is conversant. For example, the ability to verbalize is one of the criteria for selecting patients for a heterogeneous group. Unfortunately, many patients are not highly verbal. Must nonverbal patients be excluded from ameliorative endeavors? I would hope not!

Traditional approaches to treatment generally are not prepared to deal with nonverbal persons. Therefore, traditional reconstructive therapy and a number of the approaches described in this volume are not appropriate for nonverbal persons. But innovative techniques such as psychodrama are. What if the patient is a drug addict and pathologically has manipulated all his previous treatment in dyadic sessions and analytically-oriented groups to his own "advantage"? Confrontation group therapy, in my opinion, is the technique best suited for working with drug addicts and other patients with character disorders.

The practitioner with ingenuity need not discard one technique simply to employ another. For example, a practitioner who is responsible for a ward of mixed nonverbal patients—mentally retarded, chronic schizophrenics, and acting-out characters—may decide to use psychodrama. But he will vary the approach to best address each individual patient's need. With some patients he is more supportive; with others he is more confronting.

The practitioner who is skilled in both verbal and action techniques offers his patients a more comprehensive set of skills than the practioner who is confined by training and inclination to only one kind of enabling technique. The essential therapeutic concepts, nonetheless, are transcendental: they are generalizable to any interpersonal setting in which the practitioner works.

In summary, then, there is no single best method of psychotherapy. An effective treatment program requires several kinds of therapy. In selecting a treatment modality, the practitioner must clearly formulate a meaningful rationale for his choice. He must take into consideration his patient's situation in reference to his overall patient population, the conditions of time and space, the availability of other trained personnel, and his own skills and levels of anxiety and comfort.

An innovative technique should not be employed simply because the practitioner and patient are bored with the old program. No patient should be sent to dance therapy, psychodrama, occupational therapy, or any other program simply because other patients on the ward are going or "it probably won't do him any harm"! The therapist and patient together must assess the patient's difficulties, goals, and motivation for ameliorative endeavors. The therapist must work out for himself his notions about human growth and development and a comfortable style (as I have with my existential-analytic position). Then, when he has a clear notion where the patient is and where he is seeking to go, the therapist is in a position to select the program best suited for the goals he and the patient have conjointly chosen. The value of a psychotherapeutic approach is derived from the practitioner's facility in soundly applying the principles of a particular therapeutic rationale to the demands and limitations of his own practice.

REFERENCES

Abrahams, J. Group psychotherapy: Remarks on its basis and applications. *Medical Annuals of the District of Columbia,* 1947, *16,* 612–616.

Adorno, T. W., Frenkel-Brunswick, E., Levinson, D. J. & Sanford, R. N. *The Authoritarian personality.* New York: Harper & Row, 1950.

Angyal, A. *Neurosis and treatment: A holistic theory.* New York: John Wiley, 1965.

Anker, J. M., & Walsh, R. P. Group psychotherapy, a special activity program, and group structure in the treatment of chronic schizophrenics. *Journal of Consulting Psychology,* 1961, *25,* 476–481.

Attneave, F. Some informational aspects of visual perception. *Psychological Review, 61,* 1954, 183–193.

Bach, G. R. *Intensive group psychotherapy.* New York: Ronald Press, 1954.

Baehr, G. O. The comparative effectiveness of individual psychotherapy, group psychotherapy, and a combination of these methods. *Journal of Consulting Psychology,* 1954, *13,* 179–183.

Bales, R. F. *Interaction process analysis.* Cambridge, Mass: Addison-Wesley, 1950.

Barron, F., & Leary, T. F. Changes in psychometric patients with and without psychotherapy. *Journal of Consulting Psychology,* 1955, *19* (4), 239–245.

Bassin, A. Daytop Village on the way up from drug addiction: Stop-over or cure? *Psychology Today,* 1968, *2* (7), 48–52: 68.

Bednar, R. L., & Lawlis, G. F. Empirical research in group psychotherapy. In A. E. Bergin and S. L. Garfield (Eds.), *Handbook of psychotherapy and behavior change.* New York: John Wiley, 1971. Pp. 812–838.

Bergin, A. E. Some implications of psychotherapy research for therapeutic practice. *International Journal of Psychiatry,* 1967, *3,* 136–150.

Berne, E. *The structure and dynamics of organizations and groups.* New York: Grove Press, 1963.

Berzon, B. Self-directed small group programs: A new resource in rehabilitation. Final narrative report, Project Rd–1748, January, 1968. Vocational Rehabilitation Administration.

Bion, W. R. *Experiences in groups.* London: Tavistock Publication, 1961.

Blake, R. R. Group training versus group therapy. *Group Psychotherapy.* 1957, *10,* 271–276.

Boe, E. E., Gocka, E. F. & Kogan, W. S. The effect of group psychotherapy on interpersonal perceptions of psychiatric patients. *Multivariate Behavioral Research,* 1966, 1 (2), 177–187.

Bonner, H. *Group dynamics: Principles and application.* New York: Ronald Press, 1959.

Bookbinder, L., Fox, R., & Rosenthal, V. Minimal standards for psychotherapy education in psychology doctoral programs. Unpublished report, American Psychological Association, October 12, 1969.

Bradford, L. P., Gibb, J. R., & Benne, K. D. *T-group theory and laboratory method.* New York: John Wiley, 1964.

Burrow, T. The group method of analysis. *Psychoanalytic Review,* 1927, *14,* 268–280.

Burton, A. Beyond the transference. *Psychotherapy: Theory, Research and Research and Practice, 1,* 49–53.

Burton, A. (Ed.) *Encounter: The theory and practice of encounter groups.* San Francisco: Jossey–Bass, 1969.

Cadman, W. H., Misback, L., & Brown, D. V. An assessment of roundtable psychotherapy. *Psychological Monographs,* 1954, *68* (13), 1–49.

Camus, A. The wager of our generation (1957). Translated by J. O'-Brien. *Resistance, rebellion and death.* New York: Alfred A. Knopf, 1961.

Cartwright, D., & Zander, A. (Eds.). *Group dynamics: Research and theory.* New York: Harper & Row, 1960.

Cashdan, S. Sensitivity groups: Problems and promise. *Professional Psychology,* 1970, *1,* 217–224.

Casriel, D., & Deitch, D. New success in cure of narcotics addicts. *The Physician's Panorama,* October, 1966.

Castore, G. F. Number of verbal interrelationships as a determinant of group size. *Journal of Abnormal Social Psychology,* 1962, *64,* 456–457.

Castreel, J. C. The rise of interpersonal groups. In J. C. Castreel (Ed.), *The creative role of the interpersonal group in the church today.* New York: Associated Press, 1968.

Clark, D. H. Comment: Response to Lakin. *American Psychologist,* 1970, *25,* 880–882.

Claiborne, W. L. Monday night class: A caravan in search of America. *Washington Post,* December 24, 1970.

Coons, W. H. Interaction and insight in group psychotherapy. *Canadian Journal of Psychology,* 1957, *11,* 1–8.

Corsini, R. J., & Rosenberg, B. Mechanisms of group psychotherapy: Process and Dynamics. *Journal of Abnormal Social Psychology,* 1955, *51,* 406–411.

Corsini, R. J. Review of methods of group psychotherapy. *Comparative Group Studies,* 1970, *1,* 191–193.

Cowden, R. C., Zax, M., & Sproles, J. A. Group psychotherapy in conjunction with physical treatment. *Journal of Clinical Psychology,* 1956, *12,* 53–56.

Culbert, S. A. Innovative group experiences. Paper presented at Mid-Atlantic Group Psychotherapy Meeting, Washington, D.C., Fall, 1968.

Davis, F. How to read body language. *Glamour,* September, 1968.

DeSchill, S. *Introduction to psychoanalytic group therapy.* American Mental Health Foundation, Inc., New York, 1964.

Dubois, R. D., & Li, M.S. *The art of group conversation: A new break through in social communication.* New York: Associated Press, 1963.

Dymond, R. F. Personality and empathy. *Journal of Consulting Psychology,* 1950, *14,* 343–350.

Ehrlich, M. P. The role of body experience in therapy. *Psychoanalytic Review,* 1970, *57,* 181–195.

Eliot, T. S. *The hollow men. Poems* 1909–1925. London: Faber & Gwyer, 1926.

Exner, J. E. Therapist attendance as a variable in group psychotherapy. In G. E. Stollak, B. Guerney, & M. Rothberg (Eds.), *Research in Psychotherapy: Selected Readings.* Chicago: Rand-McNally, 1966.

Eyseneck, H. J. (Ed.) The effects of psychotherapy. *Handbook of abnormal psychology.* New York: Basic Books 1960. Pp. 697–725.

Ezriel, M. Notes on psychoanalytic group therapy: II. Interpretations and research. *Psychiatry,* 1952, *15,* 119–126.

Fairweather, G. W., & Simon, R. A. Relative effectiveness of psychotherapeutic programs: A multidimensional criteria comparison of four programs for three different patient groups. *Psychological Monographs,* 1960, *74,* (5, Whole No. 492).

Fairweather, G. W. et al. A further follow-up comparison of psycho-therapeutic programs. *Journal of Consulting Psychology,* 1963, *27* (3), 186.

Farber, L. H. *The ways of the will.* New York: Harper & Row, 1966.

Fast, J. *Body language.* New York: Evans, 1970.

Feifel, H. & Schwartz, A. D. Group psychotherapy with acutely disturbed psychotic patients. *Journal of Consulting Psychology,* 1953, *17,* 113–121.

Festinger, L. *A theory of cognitive dissonance.* Stanford, Calif.: Stanford University Press, 1957.

Fidler, J. W., & Waxenberg, S. E. A profile of group psychotherapy practice among A.G.P.A. members. *International Journal of Group Psychotherapy,* 1971, *21,* 34–43.

Fiedler, F. E. The leader's psychological and group effectiveness. In D. Cartwright & Zander (Eds.), *Group dynamics: Research and theory.* New York: Harper & Row, 1960. Pp. 586–606.

Fiedler, F. E. Leader's contribution to task performance in cohesive and uncohesive groups. *Journal of Abnormal Social Psychology,* 1963, *67,* 83–87.

Fluegel, J. C. *The psychology of clothes.* New York: International University Press, 1966.

Foulkes, S. H. & Anthony, E. *Group psychotherapy.* Baltimore: Penguin Books, 1957.

Frank, J. D. The dynamics of the psychotherapeutic relationship. *Psychiatry,* 1959, *22,* 17–39.

Freud, S. Freud's psychoanalytic method (1904). In P. Rieff (Ed.) *Freud: theory and technique.* New York, Collier Books, 1963. Pp. 55–61.

Freud, S. Lines of advance in psychoanalytic theory (1919). In H. Greenwald (Ed.), *Active psychotherapy.* New York: Atherton Press, 1967.

Garwood, D. S. The significance and dynamics of sensitivity training programs. *International Journal of Group Psychotherapy,* 1967, *17,* 457–472.

Gibb, J. R. & Gibb, L. Humanistic elements in group growth. In J. F. Bugental (Ed.), *Challenges of humanistic psychology.* New York: McGraw-Hill, 1967. Pp. 161–170.

Gibran, K. *The prophet.* New York: Alfred A. Knopf, 1923.

Giedt, F. H. Predicting suitability for group psychotherapy. *American Journal of Psychotherapy,* 1961, *15* (4), 582–591.

Ginnott, H. G. *Between parent and teenager.* New York: Macmillan, 1969.

Goffman, E. *The present action of self in everyday life.* New York: Doubleday, 1959.

Goldberg, C. Encounter group leadership. *Psychiatry and Social Science Review,* 1970, *4* (11), 2–8. (a)

Goldberg, C. *Encounter: Group sensitivity training experience.* New York: Science House, 1970. (b)

Goldberg, C. Group sensitivity training. *International Journal of Psychiatry,* 1970, *9,* 165–192. (c)

Goldberg, C. Reply to discussants. *International Journal of Psychiatry,* 1970, *9,* 226–232. (d)

Goldberg, C. An encounter with the sensitivity training movement. *Canada's Mental Health,* 1971, *19,* (5), 10–17.

Goldberg, C. A community is more than a psyche. *Canada's Mental Health,* 1972, (3), 15–21.

Goldberg, C. Group counselor or group therapist: Be prepared. *Psychotherapy and Social Science Review,* 1972, *6* (8), 24–27.

Goldstein, A. D. & Shipman, W. G. Patient expectancies, symptom reduction, and aspects of the initial psychotherapeutic interview. *Journal of Clinical Psychology,* 1961, *17,* 129–133.

Goldstein, A. D., Heller, K. & Sechrest, L. *Psychotherapy and the psychology of behavior change.* New York: John Wiley, 1966.

Greening, T. C Sensitivity training: Cult or contribution? *Personnel,* 1964, *41,* 18–25.

Greening, T. C. The transparent self. Mimeographed. Los Angeles: UCLA Extension Course.

Gunther, B. Sensory awaking and relaxation. In H. A. Otto & J. Mann (Eds.), *Ways of growth.* New York: Viking Press, 1968. Pp. 60–68.

Haigh, G.V. Psychotherapy as interpersonal encounter. In J. F. Bugental (Ed.), *Challenges of humanistic psychology,* New York: McGraw-Hill, 1967.

Haigh, G.V. The residential basic encounter group. In H.A. Otto & J. Mann (Eds.), *Ways of growth,* New York: Viking Press, 1968. Pp. 86–100.

Hall, E.T. The anthropology of manners. *Scientific American,* 1955, *192,* 84–90.

Halpern, H. M. Some factors in empathy. *Journal of Consulting Psychology,* 1955, *19,* 449–452.

Hare, A. P. *Handbook of small group research.* New York: Free Press, 1962.

Hare, A. P., Borgotta, E. F., & Bales, R. F. *Small groups: Studies in social interaction.* New York: Alfred A. Knopf, 1955.

Harper, R. A. *Psychoanalysis and psychotherapy: 36 systems.* Englewood Cliffs, N.J.: Prentice-Hall, 1959.

Hartley, E. E., & Hartley, R.E. *Fundamentals of social psychology,* New York: Alfred A. Knopf, 1955.

Haythorn, W., Couch, A., Langham, P., & Carter, L. The effects of varying combinations of authoritarian and equalitarian leaders and followers. *Journal of Abnormal and Social Psychology,* 1956, *53:* 210–129.

Heckel, R.V., & Salzberg, H.C. Predicting verbal behavior change in group therapy using a screening scale. *Psychological Reports,* 1967, *20,* 403–406.

Heider, F. *The psychology of interpersonal relations.* New York: John Wiley, 1967.

Heincke, C., & Bales, R.F. Developmental trends in the structure of small groups. *Sociometry.* 1953, *16,* 7–39.

Homans, G. *The human group.* New York: Harcourt, Brace & World, 1950.

Houriet, R. Life and death of a commune called Oz. *New York Times,* February 16, 1969, (Sunday Magazine Section).

Hurvitz, N. Similarities and differences between peer self-help psychotherapy groups and professional psychotherapy. Paper presented at the meeting of the American Psychological Association, San Francisco, September, 1968.

Imber, S.D., Frank, J.D., Nash, E. H., Stone, A.R., & Gliedman, L.H. Improvement and amount of therapeutic contact: An alternative to the use of no-treatment controls in psychotherapy. *Journal of Consulting Psychology,* 1957, *21* (4), 309–315.

Jacobs, R. C., & Campbell, D.T. The perpetuation of an arbitrary tradition through several generations of a laboratory microculture. *Journal of Abnormal Social Behavior,* 1961, *62,* 649–658.

Jennings, H. H. *Leadership and isolation.* New York: Longmans, Green, 1943.

Johnson, K. E. Personal religious growth through small group participation: A psychological study of personality changes and shifts in religious attitudes which result from participation in a spiritual growth group. *Dissertation Abstracts,* 1964, *25* (1).

Jones, F.D., & Peters, H. H. An experimental evaluation of group psychotherapy. *Journal of Abnormal Social Psychology,* 1953, *47,* 345–353.

Jourard, S. M. I–Thou relationships versus manipulation in counseling and psychotherapy. *Journal of Individual Psychology,* 1959, *15,* 174–179.

Jourard, S. M. *The transparent self.* Princeton, N. J.: Nostrand, 1964.

Kanter, R. M. Commitment and social organization: A study of commitment mechanisms in utopian communities. *American Sociological Review,* 1968, *33,* 499–517.

Kanter, R. M. Communes, *Psychology Today,* 1970, *4* (2), 53–57; 78.

Keen, S. Sing the body electric. *Psychology Today,* 1970, *4* (5).

Kelly, G. A. A theory of personality: *The psychology of personal constructs.* New York: Norton, 1963.

Klapman, J. W. *Group psychotherapy: Theory and practice.* New York: Grune & Stratton, 1946.

Kretch, D., Crutchfield, R., & Ballachey, E. *Individual in society: A textbook of social psychology.* New York: McGraw-Hill, 1962.

Leavitt, E.E. The undemonstrated effectiveness of therapeutic processes with children. In B. G. Berenson & R. R. Carkhuff (Eds.), *Sources of gain in counseling and psychotherapy.* New York: Holt, Rinehart, and Winston, 1967. Pp. 33–45.

Lewin, K. *Field theory in social science: Selected theoretical papers.* Cartwright, D. (Ed.), New York: Harper & Row, 1951.

Lippitt, R. Dimensions of the consultant's job. *Journal of Social Issues,* 1959, *15,* 5–12.

Lorr, M. Client perception of therapists: A study of the therapeutic relationship. *Journal of Consulting Psychology,* 1965, *29,* 146.

Lorr, M. Dimensions of interaction in group therapy. *Multivariate Behavioral Research,* 1966, *1,* 67–73.

Luria, Z. A semantic analysis of a normal and neurotic therapy group. *Journal of Abnormal Social Psychology,* 1959, *58,* 216–220.

Mahrer, A. R. Some known effects of psychotherapy and a reinterpretation. *Psychotherapy: Theory, Research and Practice,* 1970, *7,* 186–191.

Mann, J. Group therapy with adults. *American Journal of Orthopsychiatry,* 1953, *23,* 332–337.

Mann, J. Evaluation of group therapy. In J. L. Moreno (Ed.), *International handbook of group psychotherapy.* New York: Philosophical Library, 1966.

May, R. The emergence of existential psychology. In R. May (Ed.), *Existential psychology.* New York: Random House, 1961. Pp. 11–51.

McDavid, J. W. Immediate effects of group therapy upon response to social reinforcement among juvenile delinquents. *Journal of Consulting Psychology,* 1964, *28* (5), 409–412.

McFarland, R. L., Nelson, C. L., & Rossi, A. M. Prediction of participation in group psychotherapy from measures of intelligence and verbal behavior. *Psychology Reports,* 1962, *11,* 291–298.

Meltzoff, J., & Kornreich, M. *Research in psychotherapy,* New York: Atherton Press, 1970.

Michener, J. *The fires of spring.* New York: Random House, 1949.

Middleman, R. *The nonverbal method in working with groups.* New York: Association Press, 1968.

Minuchin, S. et al. *Families of the slums: An exploration of their structure and treatment.* New York: Basic Books, 1967.

Moerman, C. Psychotherapy credo: Motion precedes word. *Washington Evening Star,* December 7, 1968.

Moore, O. K. Technology and behavior. *Proceedings of the 1964 Invitational Conference on Testing Problems.* Princeton, N. J.: Educational Testing Service, 1965, 62–64.

Moreno, J. L. *Who shall survive?:* Baltimore: *Journal of Nervous and Mental Diseases,* 1953.

Mullan, H., & Rosenbaum, M. *Group psychotherapy: Theory and practice.* New York: Free Press, 1962.

Murphy, M. Esalen where it's at. *Psychology Today,* 1967, *1* (7), 35–39.

Novick, J. I. Comparison between short-term group and individual psychotherapy in effecting change in nondesirable behavior in children. *International Journal of Group Psychotherapy,* 1965, *15* (3), 336–373.

Parker, S. Role therapy and the treatment of the anti-social acting-out disorders. *British Journal of Delinquency,* 1957, *7,* 285–300.

Parloff, M. B. Advances in analytic group psychotherapy. In J. Marmor (Ed.), *Frontiers of psychoanalysis.* New York: Basic Books, 1967. Pp. 492–531.

Parloff, M. B. Group therapy and the small-group field: An encounter. *International Journal of Group Psychotherapy,* 1970, *3,* 267–304. (a)

Parloff, M.B. Sheltered workshops for the alienated. *International Journal of Psychiatry,* 1970, *9,* 197–204. (b)

Parsons, T. General theory in sociology. In R. K. Merton, L. Broom, & L. S. Cottrell (Eds.), *Sociology Today,* New York: Basic Books, 1959.

Polsky, H. W., Claster, D. S., & Goldberg, C. *Dynamics of Residential Treatment.* Chapel Hill, N.C.: North Carolina Univ. Press, 1968.

Polsky, H. W., Claster, D. S., & Goldberg, C. *Social system perspectives in residential institutions.* East Lansing, Mich.: Michigan State Univ. Press, 1970.

Powdermaker, F. B., & Frank, J. D. *Group psychotherapy: Studies in methodology of research and therapy.* Cambridge, Mass.: Harvard Univ. Press, 1963.

Powell, J. W. *Education for maturity: An empirical essay on adult group study.* New York: Hermitage House, 1949.

Reibel, D.B. Letter to the editor. *New York Times,* March 9, 1969.

Reik, T. *Listening with the third ear.* New York: Pyramid Edition, 1964.

Reisper, M., & Waldman, M. Group therapy in a work adjustment center. *Journal of Jewish Community Service,* 1961, *38,* 167–170.

Rioch, M. J. et al. National Institute of Mental Health pilot study in training mental health counselors. *American Journal of Orthopsychiatry,* 1963, *33,* 678–689.

Rogers, C. The attitude and orientation of the counselor. *Journal of Consulting Psychology, 1949, 13,* 82–94.

Rogers, C. *Becoming a person.* Boston: Houghton Mifflin, 1961.

Rogers, C. A conversation with Carl Rogers. *Psychology Today,* 1967, *1* (7), 18–21; 62–66.

Rogers, C. Interpersonal relationships: Year 2000. *Journal of Applied Behavioral Science,* 1968, *4,* 265–280.

Rosenbaum, M. Group psychotherapy and psychodrama. In B. B. Wolman (Ed.), *Handbook of clinical psychology.* New York: McGraw-Hill, 1965. Pp. 1254–1274.

Rosenbaum, M., & Hartley, E. A summary of current practices of ninety-two group psychotherapists. *International Journal of Group Psychotherapy,* 1962, *12,* 194–198.

Ruitenbeck, H. M. *Group therapy today: Styles, methods and techniques.* New York: Atherton Press, 1969.

Sacks, J. M., & Berger, S. Group therapy techniques with hospitalized chronic schizophrenic patients. *Journal of Consulting Psychology,* 1954, *18,* 297–307.

Samuels, A. Use of group balance as a therapeutic technique. *Archives of General Psychiatry,* 1964, *2,* 411–420.

Schofield, W. *Psychotherapy, the purchase of friendship.* Englewood Cliffs, N. J.: Prentice-Hall, 1964.

Schorer, C. E., Lowinger, P., Sullivan, T., & Hartlaub, G. H. Improvement without treatment. *Diseases of the Nervous System,* 1968, *29,* 100–104.

Schwartz, E. K. The trend to grouping. *International Journal of Psychiatry,* 1970, *9,* 205–218.

Schutz, W. C. *Joy.* New York: Grove Press, 1967.

Sechrest, L. B., & Barger, B. Verbal participation and perceived benefit from group psychotherapy. *International Journal of Group Psychotherapy,* 1961, *11,* 49–59.

Semon, R.G., & Goldstein, W. The effectiveness of group psychotherapy with chronic schizophrenics and an evaluation of different therapeutic methods. *Journal of Consulting Psychology,* 1957, *21,* 317–322.

Senden, M.V. Raum-und Gestalt au fassung bei operierten Blindgeborenen vor und nach der operation. Leipzig: Barth. Cited by W. N. Dember, *Psychology of Perception.* New York: Holt, Rinehart, and Winston, 1961.

Shakespeare, W. *As you like it.* II, 7.

Sharoff, R. L. Character problems and their relationship to drug abuse. *American Journal of Psychoanalysis,* 1969, *29,* 186–193.

Sherif, M., & Sherif, C. W. *An outline of social psychology.* New York: Harper and Brothers, 1948.

Shostrom, E. Group therapy: Let the buyer beware. *Psychology Today,* 1969, *2* (12), 36–40.

Slater, P. E. Cultures in collision. *Psychology Today,* 1970, *4* (2), 31–32; 66–68.

Slavson, S. R. Eclecticism versus sectarianism in group psychotherapy. *International Journal of Group Psychology,* 1970, *20,* 3–13.

Smith, R. J. A closer look at encounter therapies. *International Journal of Group Psychotherapy,* 1970, *20,* 192–209.

Snyder, R., & Sechrest, L. An experimental study of directive group therapy with defective delinquents. *American Journal of Mental Deficiency,* 1959, *64,* 117–123.

Spotnitz, H. *The couch and the circle.* New York: Alfred A. Knopf, 1961.

Sprott, W.J. *Human groups.* Baltimore: Penguin Books, 1958.

Stoller, F. H. The long weekend. *Psychology Today,* 1967, *1* (7), 23–33.

Stone, A. A. The quest of the counter culture. *International Journal of Psychiatry,* 1970, *9,* 219–226.

Storr, A. Review of C. Rycropf, *How human beings respond to the dangers of anxiety and neurosis. Washington Post* (Book World), March 29, 1970.

Strunk, O. Training of emphatic abilities: A note. *Journal of Pastoral Care,* 1957, *11,* 222–225.

Szasz, T. *The ethics of psychoanalysis: The therapy and method of autonomous psychotherapy.* New York: Dell, 1965.

Talland, G. A., & Clark, D. H. Evaluation of topics in therapy group discussion. *Journal of Clincial Psychology,* 1954, *10,* 131–137.

Teahan, J. E. Effects of group psychotherapy on academic low achievers. *International Journal of Group Psychotherapy,* 1966, *16* (1), 78–85.

Thelen, H. A. *Dynamics of groups at work.* Chicago: Univ. of Chicago Press, 1954.

Thomas, E. J., & Fink, C. F. Effects of group size. *Psychological Bulletin,* 1963, *60,* 371–384.

Thomas, H. F. An existential attitude in working with individuals and groups. In J. F. Bugental (Ed.), *Challenges of humanistic psychology.* New York: McGraw-Hill, 1967. Pp. 227–232.

Time, September 19, 1969.

Time, December 28, 1970.

Truax, C. B. Antecedents to outcome in group counseling with institutionalized juvenile delinquents: Effects of therapeutic conditions, patient self-exploration, alternate sessions and vicarious therapy pretaining. Vol. 2, No. 14, Discussion paper, Arkansas Rehabilitation Research and Training Center, #264, University of Arkansas.

Truax, C. B. The process of group psychotherapy: Relationships between hypothesized therapeutic conditions and intrapersonal exploration. *Psychological Monographs,* 1961, *75* (7), 1–35.

Truax, C. B. Counseling and psychotherapy: Process and outcome. Unpublished final report, V.R.A. Research and Demonstration Grant, No. 906-p, 1966.

Truax, C. B., & Carkhuff, R. R. For better or worse: The process of psychotherapeutic personality change. In *Recent advances in the study of behavior change.* Montreal: McGill Univ. Press, 1964. Pp. 118–163.

Truax, C. B., & Carkhuff, R. R. New directions in clinical research. In B. G. Berenson and R. R. Carkhuff, (Eds.), *Sources of gain in counseling and psychotherapy.* New York: Holt, Rinehart, and Winston, 1967. Pp. 358–391.

Truax, C. B., Shapiro, J. G., & Wargo, D. G. Effects of alternate sessions and vicarious therapy pretraining on group psychotherapy. *International Journal of Group Psychotherapy,* 1968, *18,* 186–198.

Truax, C. B., Schuldt, W. J., & Wargo, D. G. Self-ideal concept congruence and improvement in group psychotherapy. *Journal of Consulting and Clinical Psychology,* 1968, *32,* 47–53.

Tucker, J. E. Group psychotherapy with chronic psychotic soiling patients. *Journal of Consulting Psychology,* 1956, *20* (6), 430.

Walton, H. (Ed.) *Small group psychotherapy.* Baltimore: Penquin

Books, 1971.

Warkentin, J. Intensity in group encounter. In A. Burton (Ed.), *Encounter, the theory and practice of encounter groups.* San Francisco: Jossey-Bass, 1969. Pp. 162–170.

Washington Post, Statement contained in William Rasberry's column, 1970.

Weschler, I. R., & Reisel, J. Inside a sensitivity training group. Monograph Series: *Los Angeles Institute of Industrial Relations,* 1960, No. 4.

Whyte, W. F. *Street corner society.* Chicago: Univ. of Chicago Press, 1943.

Wilcox, G. T., & Guthrie, G. M. Changes in adjustment of institutionalized female defectives following group psychotherapy. *Journal of Clinical Psychology,* 1957, *13,* 9–13.

Williams, M., McGee, T. F., Kittleson, S., & Halperin, L. An evaluation of intensive group living programs with schizophrenic patients. *Psychological Monographs,* 1962, *76* (24, Whole No. 543).

Wilson, D. L., Wilson, M. E., Sakata, R., & Frunkin, R. M. Effects of short–term group interaction on social adjustment in a group of mentally retarded clients. *Psychological Reports,* 1967, *21,* 7–16.

Wolfe, A., & Schwartz, E. K. *Psychoanalysis in groups.* New York: Grune & Stratton, 1962.

Wurmser, L. A new synopsis of problems of drug abuse. Mimeographed. Baltimore: Johns Hopkins Hospital, 1970.

Yablonsky, L. *Synanon: The tunnel back.* Baltimore: Penguin Books, 1965.

Yalom, I. D. A study of group therapy drop-outs. *Archives of General Psychiatry,* 1966, *14,* 393–414.

Yalom, I. D. *The theory and practice of group psychotherapy.* New York: Basic Books, 1970.

Yalom, I. D., & Rand, K. Compatibility and cohesiveness in therapy groups. *Archives of General Psychiatry,* 1966, *13,* 267–276.

Yalom, I. D. et al. Prediction of success in group therapy. *Archives of General Psychiatry,* 1967, *17,* 159–168. (a)

Yalom, I. D. et al. Preparation of patients for group therapy. *Archives of General Psychiatry,* 1967, 17, 416–427. (b)

Yalom, I. D. et al. Encounter groups and psychiatry. Task Force Report. American Psychiatric Association, Washington, D. C., 1970.

Zimet, C. N., & Fine, H. J. Personality changes with a group therapeutic experience in human relations seminar. *Journal of Abnormal Social Psychology,* 1955, *51,* 68–73.

INDEXES

NAME INDEX

A

Abrahams, J., 68, 94
Adorno, T.W., 222
Angyal, A., 28–29
Anker, J.M., 222
Aristotle, 25
Attneave, F., 118

B

Bach, G.R., 86–87
Baehr, G.O., 225–26
Bales, R.F., 70, 106, 109
Barron, F., 225
Bassin, A., 175, 176, 177
Bednar, R.L., 209, 220, 221, 222, 223, 225, 227, 228
Bergin, A.E., 211, 221
Berne, E., 62
Berzon, B., 228
Bion, W.R., 64, 135–36
Blake, R.R., 117, 124
Boe, E.E., 222
Bonner, H., 112
Bookbinder, L., 211, 214
Bradford, L.P., 179
Burrow, T., 64–65
Burton, A., 6, 140

C

Cadman, W.H., 228

Camus, A., 63–64
Cartwright, D., 102–3, 104, 106, 112, 113, 114
Cashdan, S., 6
Casriel, D., 163, 164, 175
Casteel, J.C., 199
Castore, G.F., 223
Chace, M., 193–94
Charcot, J., ix
Clairborne, W., 205, 207
Clark, D.H., 21
Coons, W.H., 222, 226
Corsini, R.J., 12–13, 226
Cowden, R.C., 222
Culbert, S.A., 20

D

Davis, F., 190
DeSchill, S., 89
Dubois, R.D., 155
Durkheim, E., 92
Dymond, R.F., 83

E

Ehrlich, M.P., 189
Eliot, T.S., 151
Ellis, A., 20
Exner, J.E., 228
Eysenek, H.S., 2
Ezriel, H., 64

F

Fairweather, G.W., 220, 221, 224, 225, 226
Farber, L.H., 57
Farson, R., 202
Fast, J., 180, 184
Feifel, H., 222
Festinger, L., 173
Fidler, J.W., 223
Fiedler, F.E., 112, 144
Flugel, J.C., 186
Foulkes, S.H., 81, 83, 126, 210
Frank, J.D., 227, 228
·Freud, S., ix, xii, 58, 59, 63, 190
Fromm–Reichmann, F., 189

G

Garwood, D.S., 15
Gibb, J.R., 144
Gibran, K., 101
Giedt, F.H., 224
Ginnott, H.G., 166
Goffman, E., 126
Goldberg, C., x, 6, 8, 10, 52, 76, 77, 90–91, 106, 122, 123, 127, 135, 191, 211
Goldstein, A.D., 220, 223, 227, 228
Greening, T.C., 27, 51, 53, 54, 97, 123, 139, 144
Gunther, B., 19

H

Haigh, G.V., 25, 143
Hall, E.T., 184–85
Halpern, H.M., 83
Hare, A.P., 111, 126
Harper, R.A., 34
Hartley, E.L., 104, 105
Haythorn, W., 112

Heckel, R.V., 224
Heider, F., 118
Heincke, C., 113
Heraclitus, 25
Homans, G., 106
Houriet, R., 204, 205, 206, 207, 208
Hurvitz, N., 74

I

Imber, S.D., 225

J

Jacobs, R.C., 227
Jennings, H.H., 105
Johnson, K.E., 222
Jones, F.D., 222
Jourard, S.M., 49, 51, 83

K

Kanter, R.M., 203, 204, 207, 208
Keen, S., 19
Kelly, G.A., 34
Klapman, J.W., 94
Kretch, D., 33

L

Laing, R.D., 202
La Rochefoucauld, 28
Leavitt, E.E., 2
Lewin, K., 147, 176
Lippitt, R., 172
Lorr, M., 226, 227
Luria, Z., 222

M

Mahrer, A.R., 83
Mann, James, 125, 148

Mann, John, 220
Marsh, L.C., 94
Maslow, A., 46
May, R., ix, 61
McDavid, J.W., 222
McFarland, R.L., 224
Mead, G.H., 27
Meltzoff, J., 220, 221, 223, 226
Menninger, K., 4
Meyer, A., ix
Michner, J., 1
Middleman, R., 180
Minuchin, S., 152, 160
Moerman, C., 190, 193
Moore, O.K., 181
Moreno, J.L., 99
Mullan, H., 86
Murphy, M., 16

N

Novick, J.I., 225

P

Parker, S., 109
Parloff, M.B., 6, 10, 90, 91, 123, 225
Parsons, T., 106
Perls, F., ix, 12, 18, 20
Phillips, F., 166
Plato, 25
Polsky, H.W., 106
Powdermaker, F.B., 3, 88, 209, 224
Powell, J.W., 136

R

Rank, O., 57
Reibel, D.B., 200
Reich, W., 19, 189–90

Reik, T., 55, 139
Reisper, M., 222
Rioch, M.J., 21
Rogers, C., ix, 6, 9, 15, 21, 60–61, 139
Rosenbaum, M., 223
Ruitenbeck, H.M., 3

S

Sacks, J.M., 222
Samuels, A., 224
Santayana, G., 14
Sartre, J–P, 26–27
Schofield, W., 49
Schorer, E.C., 2
Schultz, W.C., ix, 12, 20, 195
Schwartz, E.K., 16–17, 121, 123
Sechrest, L.B., 227
Semon, R.G., 222, 226
Shakespeare, W., 179
Sharoff, R.L., 166, 176
Sherif, M., 103, 104
Shostrom, E., 21
Slater, P.E., 18–19
Slavson, S.R., 6
Smith, R.J., 6, 20
Snyder, R., 222
Spotnitz, H., 4
Sprott, W.J., 103
Stoller, F.H., 10
Stone, A.A., 17
Storr, A., 64
Strunk, O., 83
Sullivan, H.S., 40, 59
Szasz, T., 58–59, 62, 63

T

Talland, G.A., 227
Teahan, H.E., 222
Thelen, H.A., 126, 224–25

Thomas, E.J., 92
Thomas, H.F., 62, 221
Truax, C.B., 88, 219, 221, 227,
    228
Tucker, J.E., 222

V

Vahinger, H., 28
Von Senden, M., 32–33

W

Walton, H., 219
Warkentin, J., xii–xiii
Weschler, I.R., 15

Whyte, W.F., 111
Wilcox, G.T., 222
Williams, M., 222
Wilson, D.L., 222
Wolf, A., 7
Wurmser, L., 166, 167, 174, 177

Y

Yablonsky, L., 166, 170, 171, 176,
    178
Yalom, I., 11, 13, 88, 220, 224,
    226, 227, 228

Z

Zimet, C.N., 222

SUBJECT INDEX

A

Acting out, 43, 167, 174
Action training, 151–61
Actualization, 16, 31, 46, 50
Alienation, xi, 15, 28
Aloneness, 26
Anxiety, 58–59, 62, 63, 64, 86, 87, 151, 188
Assertion–structure theory, 34
Attitudes, core, 34, 39, 41
Autonomy, 29, 61
Awareness, 26, 32, 33, 50

B

Body armor, 19, 189
Body talk, 180

C

Case histories, 29, 30–32, 34–38, 38–40, 42–43, 44–45, 50–51, 52–54, 57–58, 60, 69–71, 77–79, 154
Choice, x, 21, 26, 27, 29, 33, 36, 38, 41, 42, 45, 50, 51, 58, 59, 60–61, 63
Cognitive dissonance, 37–38, 173
Commitment, 89, 146, 160
Common group concern, 154–57
Common group tensions, 133–35, 148–49, 156

Communes, 99, 199–208
Communication, 55, 63, 161
Community mental health, 1, 17, 76, 152
Confrontation, 55, 163–78
Consultant (consultation), 110–16, 120–36
Contemporary American education, 120
Contemporary American society, ix, xii, 1, 6, 200–201
Contract, therapeutic, 11, 84–85, 168–69
    administrative aspects of, 85
    psychological aspects of, 85
Counterculture, 139–40
Countertransference, 13
Counter–will, 57, 165–66
Crisis, 140, 152, 176

D

Deviant person, the, 73
"Difficult" patients, 1–2, 151–53
Disclosure, 14, 27, 32, 50, 58
Dominant person, 73
Drug addicts, group therapy with, 99, 163–78
Dyadic (individual) psychotherapy, 2, 5, 11, 88, 142, 154, 171–72, 225–26

E

Ego, 119, 160, 167, 190, 206–7
Empathy, therapeutic, 83
Encounter groups, 6, 12, 17
Equalitarian attitude, 13, 41
Existential–analytic group psy-
    chotherapy, xiii, 21, 22, 49–
    79, 98, 139–49
Existential postulates, ix, x, 1, 12,
    28–79, 123–24, 139–49, 151,
    159–60, 165–66, 221–23

F

Facilitative gestures in groups,
    60
Family, 94, 199–208
    consanguine, 99, 199–208
    communal, 199–208
    "re–enactment", 94
Fantasy, 32, 149
Feedback, 14, 15, 157
Fictional finalism, 28
First impressions, 185–186
Focal problem group, 98–99, 151–
    61
Freedom, psychological, 63

G

Genetic bias, 9, 14
Group composition, 46–47, 85–88,
    125–26
Group conversation, 156
Group dynamics, 174–76
Group hoppers, 10
Group performance, leadership
    and, 18, 97–98, 101–16
Group processes
    ephemeral, 128–132
    intentional, 124–27
    subtle, 133–37

Group size, 92–93, 125–26
Group therapy literature, xi, xii,
    211–12
Group transcripts, 131–32, 141–
    42, 142–43, 144–45
Groups, properties of
    duration, 127
    frequency, 127
    outside relationships, 127
    physical setting, 126

H

Healer, patient as, 3, 4, 13
Heteronomous choice, 28, 29, 30,
    31, 32
History of group therapy, 4–8
Homonomous choice, 28, 29, 30,
    32, 63
Human condition, 26–29
Human development movement,
    2, 16

I

Inexperienced practitioner, x, xi,
    5, 21, 81–82, 209–10, 211–12
Influence, therapeutic, 67–68
Integralists, 90–91
Intentionality, 41, 54, 57, 61
Interpersonal relations, ix, 15
Interpretation, 58, 60, 134–35,
    148
Intrapersonalists, 90–91
Isolated person, the, 73

K

Kinesics, 181–84, 187–88

L

Leaderless groups, 228

Leadership, 18, 97–98, 101–16,
    208
  situational, 105, 113–14
Level of analysis, conceptual, x,
    xii, 33–34, 41, 82–83, 97, 116,
    210, 221–23
Life script, 28, 62

M

Magical thinking, 171–72
Marathon group, 10
Marginal person, the, 73
Milling technique, 194–96
Movement (dance) therapy, 193–
    95

N

Narcissism, 167, 168
Natural groups, x, 68–75
Negotiation, 55, 89
New group therapies, xiii, 1–23
Nonverbal communication, 148–
    49, 156, 179–97
Norms, 111, 146, 147

O

Ontological prerequisite, x, 26,
    27, 33
Oversocialized person, the, 73

P

Participant–observer, therapist
    as, 117–19
Patient preparation, 88–90, 128–
    30
Peak experiences, 16
Personality, therapist's, xii, 21,
    83, 209–10

Personal strategies, 28, 34–47,
    62, 63, 74
Personal therapy, therapist's, 216
    –17
Power–field, 176–77
Problem–solving techniques, 151
    –61
Process group, 98, 117–37, 215–
    16
Professional responsibility, 11
Projective principle, 27
Psychic economy principle, 40–
    41, 190–91
Psychoanalysis, ix, xii, 9, 13, 59,
    65
Psychodrama, 47, 191–92
  double, 191
  protagonist of, 191
Psychodynamics, 213–14
Psychopathology, ix, 9, 14, 15, 16,
    17, 44, 52, 53, 55, 62, 64, 65,
    75–76, 95, 108–9, 152, 174–
    76
Psychotherapy phases, 51
  action, 53
  description, 51
  explanation, 51
  exploration, 53

R

Research in group therapy, 1, 21,
    49, 83, 219–29
  alternate sessions, 228–29
  economy–efficiency, 227–28
  effective varieties, 226
  group composition, 224
  group size, 223–24
  harmful aspects, 221
  individual versus group, 225–
    26
  leaderless sessions, 228–29

Research continued
   patients counterindicated, 221–
      22
   problems indicated, 221
   psychological functions af-
      fected, 222
   selection of patients, 222–23
   utility, 220–21
   vulnerable patients, 225
Resistance, 55–57, 147, 156–57,
   176
Resocialization, 168, 169, 169–70,
   176–78
Responsibility, 21, 26, 42–47, 61,
   62, 201–2
Role–modeling, 20, 58, 95, 147–
   48, 177–78
Role playing, 159
Roles, 12, 16, 41, 55, 68–71, 76–
   79, 109–10, 145–48
   asocial, therapist, 49
   "healer," patient as, 76–79
   "patient," patient as, 76–79
   "student," patient as, 76–79

S

Satisfaction, 40–41, 55, 64
Security, 40–41, 55, 64
Selection, patient, 46–47, 85–88,
   222–23
Self–help groups, 74, 143–44
Self–help process, 75–76, 76–79,
   153
Sensitivity training, 47, 119, 120
   –37
Service–in–kind program, 76
Sessions, group therapy, 145–48
Short–term psychotherapy, 153,
   154
Slavson activity group, 101

Social movements, 8
Social system theory, 98, 105–16
   adaptation, 107–16
   goal attainment, 107–16
   integration, 108–16
   pattern maintenance, 108–16
Standards for group therapist, 20,
   21
Subcultures, changing, 176–77
Supervision, 212–13, 214–16
Symptoms, 62, 63
Synanon, 99

T

Tavistock group, 101
Territoriality, 184–85
Therapeutic change process, 46–
   47, 65–66, 172–73
   environmental change, 46–47,
      65–66, 172–73
   self–change, 46–47, 65–66, 172
      –73
   trial–suggested change, 46–47,
      65–66, 172–73
Therapist–patient relationship,
   11, 12, 13, 14, 49–79, 139–49,
   165–66
Touch, physical, 18, 185
Traditional psychotherapy, 1–23
Training, group therapy, xi, 2, 5,
   21, 95, 207–17
Transactionalists, 90–91
Transference, 13, 139–40
Treatment plan, 84–85
Trust, fostering, 144–45, 148

U

Unmobilized person, the, 73

V

Values, 17, 18, 19, 27, 54–55, 55–
57, 69–70, 124, 146

W

Will, 165–66
Work group assumption (Bion),
135–136

Carl Goldberg, Ph.D., and **Merle Cantor Goldberg, M.S.W.,** a young husband-wife team of psychotherapists, have already established themselves as leading practitioners in their field.

Dr. Goldberg is director of the Laurel Comprehensive Community Mental Health Center in Laurel, Maryland. He also directs the Northern Prince George's County Mental Health Team and writes a weekly newspaper column on mental health for the Laurel *News Leader*. Besides his own private practice, he acts as a consultant in group sensitivity training, "hot lines" services, and the "free clinic" of Prince George's County.

Apart from her own private practice in individual, group, family, and couples psychotherapy, Mrs. Goldberg is an instructor in the Mental Health Associate Program at Montgomery College in Tacoma Park, Maryland, and a consultant to the Prince George's County Bureau of Mental Health. She trains professional group therapists and paraprofessional and nonprofessional workers in a variety of mental health areas.

Dr. Goldberg earned his bachelor's degree at the American International College, his master's at the University of Wyoming, and his doctorate in clinical psychology at Oklahoma University. He gained his Certificate in Analytic Group Psychotherapy at the Washington School of Psychiatry. His first book, *Encounter-Group Sensitivity Training Experience,* was a main selection of the Psychiatry and Social Science Book Club in 1971, and he has co-authored two other books in the field of mental health and psychotherapy.

Mrs. Goldberg, who has had special training in psychodrama, including work with its founder, Dr. J. L. Moreno, earned her B.A. in psychology at The University of Connecticut and her M.S.W. at the Maryland School of Social Work.